T0215723

Lecture Notes in Computer Science 14097

Founding Editors

Gerhard Goos
Juris Hartmanis

The series Lecture Notes in Computer Science (LNCS), including its subseries Lecture Notes in Artificial Intelligence (LNAI) and Lecture Notes in Bioinformatics (LNBI), has established itself as a medium for the publication of new developments in computer science and information technology research, teaching, and education.

LNCS enjoys close cooperation with the computer science R & D community, the series counts many renowned academics among its volume editors and paper authors, and collaborates with prestigious societies. Its mission is to serve this international community by providing an invaluable service, mainly focused on the publication of conference and workshop proceedings and postproceedings. LNCS commenced publication in 1973.

Budi Arief · Anna Monreale ·
Michael Sirivianos · Shujun Li
Editors

Security and Privacy in Social Networks and Big Data

9th International Symposium, SocialSec 2023
Canterbury, UK, August 14–16, 2023
Proceedings

 Springer

Editors
Budi Arief 🆔
University of Kent
Canterbury, UK

Anna Monreale 🆔
University of Pisa
Pisa, Italy

Michael Sirivianos 🆔
Cyprus University of Technology
Limassol, Cyprus

Shujun Li 🆔
University of Kent
Canterbury, UK

ISSN 0302-9743   ISSN 1611-3349 (electronic)
Lecture Notes in Computer Science
ISBN 978-981-99-5176-5   ISBN 978-981-99-5177-2 (eBook)
https://doi.org/10.1007/978-981-99-5177-2

This Springer imprint is published by the registered company Springer Nature Singapore Pte Ltd.
The registered company address is: 152 Beach Road, #21-01/04 Gateway East, Singapore 189721, Singapore

Preface

Social networks and big data have pervaded all aspects of our daily lives. With their unparalleled popularity, social networks have evolved from platforms for social communication and news dissemination into indispensable tools for professional networking, social recommendations, marketing, and online content distribution. Social networks, together with other activities, produce big data that is beyond the ability of commonly used computer software and hardware tools to capture, manage, and process within a tolerable time. It has been widely recognized that security and privacy are the critical challenges for social networks and big data applications due to their scale, complexity, and heterogeneity.

The 9th International Symposium on Security and Privacy in Social Networks and Big Data (SocialSec 2023) was held at the University of Kent, Canterbury, UK during August 14-16, 2023, co-located with the 17th International Conference on Network and System Security (NSS 2023). It followed the success of SocialSec 2015 in Hangzhou, China, SocialSec 2016 in Fiji, SocialSec 2017 in Melbourne, Australia, SocialSec 2018 in Santa Clara, CA, USA, SocialSec 2019 in Copenhagen, Denmark, SocialSec 2020 in Tianjin, China, SocialSec 2021 in Fuzhou, China, and SocialSec 2022 in Xi'an, China. The aim of the SocialSec conference series is to provide a leading-edge forum to foster interactions among researchers and developers within the security and privacy communities in social networks and big data.

The technical program of the conference included 14 research papers (10 full papers and 4 short papers) selected by the Technical Program Committee (TPC) from 26 submissions received in response to the call for papers, as well as 3 papers transferred from the co-located conference NSS 2023. The review process was organized and managed through EasyChair. All the papers were peer-reviewed by at least three reviewers (including TPC members and external reviewers). The submission process was anonymous and author names were not visible to the reviewers. Received reviews were also anonymized to other TPC members, as well as to the paper's authors. The reviewers were asked to declare any conflicts of interest for all submissions at the beginning of the process, and the EasyChair system was configured to ensure TPC members (including TPC chairs) could see neither the reviewer assignments nor the reviews of the papers for which they had a conflict of interest. For several papers, one TPC Co-Chair had a conflict of interest, and the discussion on each of such papers was held, and the decision was made, between the other two TPC Co-Chairs without a conflict of interest.

SocialSec 2023 and the co-located NSS 2023 shared three invited talks for both conferences' participants, given by Julia Hesse from IBM Research Zurich, Nishanth Sastry from University of Surrey, and Lorenzo Cavallaro from University College London.

The SocialSec 2023 TPC selected one paper to receive the Best Paper Award and another one to receive the Best Student Paper Award for the best paper first-authored by a student. Both awards included a certificate and a cash prize. The cash prizes were kindly sponsored by the University of Kent's Institute of Cyber Security for Society (iCSS).

The SocialSec 2023 TPC was co-chaired by Budi Arief, Anna Monreale, and Michael Sirivianos, who selected the TPC members and led their efforts in selecting the papers that appear in this volume. The organization of SocialSec 2023 and the co-located NSS 2023 was led by Budi Arief, Robert Deng, and Elena Ferrari as both conferences' joint General Co-Chairs. The conferences were made possible also due to the professional work of Yuntao Wang, Yulei Wu, and Zhe Xia as the Publicity Co-Chairs, Shujun Li as the Publication Chair, and Haiyue Yuan as the Web Chair.

As the TPC Co-Chairs of SocialSec 2023 and the Publication Chair of both SocialSec 2023 and NSS 2023, we would like to thank everyone who made this conference a success. First of all, we thank all the TPC members and external reviewers for their effort in reviewing and helping us select the papers for inclusion in the conference. We thank all the authors for submitting their manuscripts to the conference. We would also like to extend special thanks to members of the joint Organizing Committee for their work in making both SocialSec 2023 and NSS 2023 a successful event. Last but not least, we also thank all participants of SocialSec 2023 and NSS 2023 for their active participation during the three days of the conferences.

June 2023

Budi Arief
Anna Monreale
Michael Sirivianos
Shujun Li

Organization

General Chairs

Budi Arief   University of Kent, UK
Robert Deng   Singapore Management University, Singapore
Elena Ferrari   University of Insubria, Italy

Program Committee Chairs

Budi Arief   University of Kent, UK
Anna Monreale   University of Pisa, Italy
Michael Sirivianos   Cyprus University of Technology, Cyprus

Publicity Co-chairs

Yuntao Wang   Osaka University, Japan
Yulei Wu   University of Exeter, UK
Zhe Xia   Wuhan University of Technology, China

Publication Chair

Shujun Li   University of Kent, UK

Web Chair

Haiyue Yuan   University of Kent, UK

Technical Program Committee

Niyati Baliyan   National Institute of Technology Kurukshetra, India
Giuseppe Bianchi   University of Rome "Tor Vergata", Italy
Chiara Boldrini   IIT-CNR, Italy

Additional Reviewers

Athanasios Vasileios Grammatopoulos
Saloni Kwatra
Ying Li
Hebert Pérez-Rosés
Ioannis Stylianou

Contents

Information Abuse and Political Discourse

People Still Care About Facts: Twitter Users Engage More with Factual
Discourse than Misinformation 3
  Luiz Giovanini, Shlok Gilda, Mirela Silva, Fabrício Ceschin,
  Prakash Shrestha, Christopher Brant, Juliana Fernandes,
  Catia S. Silva, André Grégio, and Daniela Oliveira

Extracting Common Features of Fake News by Multi-Head-Attention 23
  Takayuki Ishimaru and Mamoru Mimura

Twitter Bots Influence on the Russo-Ukrainian War During the 2022
Italian General Elections 38
  Francesco Luigi De Faveri, Luca Cosuti, Pier Paolo Tricomi,
  and Mauro Conti

Did State-Sponsored Trolls Shape the 2016 US Presidential Election
Discourse? Quantifying Influence on Twitter 58
  Nikos Salamanos, Michael J. Jensen, Costas Iordanou,
  and Michael Sirivianos

Attacks

Data Reconstruction Attack Against Principal Component Analysis 79
  Saloni Kwatra and Vicenç Torra

The Impact of Synthetic Data on Membership Inference Attacks 93
  Md Sakib Nizam Khan and Sonja Buchegger

Time Is on My Side: Forward-Replay Attacks to TOTP Authentication 109
  Giuseppe Bianchi and Lorenzo Valeriani

Social Structure and Community

Cyber Security Researchers on Online Social Networks: From the Lens
of the UK's ACEs-CSR on Twitter 129
  Mohamad Imad Mahaini and Shujun Li

The Social and Technological Incentives for Cybercriminals to Engage
in Ransomware Activities 149
    Yichao Wang, Sophia Roscoe, Budi Arief, Lena Connolly,
    Hervé Borrion, and Sanaa Kaddoura

Security and Privacy Matters

Graph Analysis of Blockchain P2P Overlays and Their Security
Implications 167
    Aristodemos Paphitis, Nicolas Kourtellis, and Michael Sirivianos

Secure and Efficient Data Processing for Cloud Computing
with Fine-Grained Access Control 187
    Jingjing Wang, Hao Feng, Zheng Yu, Rongtao Liao, Shi Chen,
    and Ting Liang

Detection of Privacy-Harming Social Media Posts in Italian 203
    Federico Peiretti and Ruggero G. Pensa

Edge Local Differential Privacy for Dynamic Graphs 224
    Sudipta Paul, Julián Salas, and Vicenç Torra

Temporal Analysis of Privacy Enhancing Technology Traffic Using Deep
Learning 239
    Monika Kumari, Mohona Ghosh, and Niyati Baliyan

Author Index 253

Information Abuse and Political Discourse

People Still Care About Facts: Twitter Users Engage More with Factual Discourse than Misinformation

Luiz Giovanini[1], Shlok Gilda[1]([✉]), Mirela Silva[1], Fabrício Ceschin[2],
Prakash Shrestha[1], Christopher Brant[1], Juliana Fernandes[1], Catia S. Silva[1],
André Grégio[2], and Daniela Oliveira[1]

[1] University of Florida, Gainesville, FL, USA 32611
{lfrancogiovanini,shlokgilda,msilva1,prakash.shrestha,g8rboy15}@ufl.edu,
juliana@jou.ufl.edu, {catiaspsilva,daniela}@ece.ufl.edu
[2] Federal University of Paraná, Curitiba, Paraná, Brazil 81530-000
{fjoceschin,gregio}@inf.ufpr.br

Abstract. Misinformation entails disseminating falsehoods that lead to society's slow fracturing via decreased trust in democratic processes, institutions, and science. The public has grown aware of the role of social media as a superspreader of untrustworthy information, where even pandemics have not been immune. In this paper, we focus on COVID-19 misinformation and examine a subset of 2.1M tweets to understand misinformation as a function of engagement, tweet content (COVID-19- vs. non-COVID-19-related), and veracity (misleading or factual). Using correlation analysis, we show the most relevant feature subsets among over 126 features that most heavily correlate with misinformation or facts. We found that (i) factual tweets, regardless of whether COVID-related, were more engaging than misinformation tweets; and (ii) features that most heavily correlated with engagement varied depending on the veracity and content of the tweet.

Keywords: Engagement · Misinformation · Social Media

1 Introduction

Disinformation refers to false or deceptive content distributed via any communication medium (e.g., word-of-mouth, print, Internet, radio, broadcast) by an adversary who aims to hurt a target (usually a country, political party, or community) via the spread of propaganda and promotion of societal division, thus casting doubt in democratic processes, government institutions, and on science. Over the past few years, our society has grown wearily aware of the highly polarized schism that has developed beyond the context of mere political discourse. The perceived extremities of our thoughts and opinions are now intimately meshing with falsehoods and outright lies, calling into question the integrity of our

---

L. Giovanini and S. Gilda are co-first authors. They have equal contribution.
M. Silva and F. Ceschin are co-second authors. They have equal contribution.

government agencies', political representatives', and our own individual handling of public health crises, such as the COVID-19 pandemic [39].

*Mis*information, however, is closely related to disinformation and differs only in the lack of purposeful intent to harm, often coupled with the raw ignorance of the individual spreading such misleading facts. COVID-19-related misinformation primarily comes from domestic sources; we have seen politicians, pundits, and personalities pushing misleading narratives [6] that may prevent society from controlling the spread of the coronavirus, potentially increasing the number of deaths. With the advent of the COVID vaccines, misinformation has unequivocally been used to discredit its effectiveness, preventing efficient immunization and fueling further hyperpartisanship.

Engagement is a crucial dimension in disseminating falsehoods. Avram et al. [5] showed that higher social engagement results in less fact-checking and verification, especially for less credible content. This paper investigates the relationship between misinformation and user engagement in COVID-19-related tweets. We use the term *misinformation* to refer to tweets spreading deceptive content, even though some tweets may have been created with malice. Using a curated dataset of 2.1M tweets labeled as `fact` or `misinformation` for COVID-related and general topics, we aim to answer the following research questions:

① **RQ1:** Are COVID-19 misinformation tweets more engaging than COVID-19 factual tweets?
② **RQ2:** Are general topic misinformation tweets more engaging than general topics factual tweets?
③ **RQ3:** Which features are most correlated with engagement in COVID-19 vs. general topics misinformation tweets?
④ **RQ4:** Which features are most correlated with engagement in COVID-19 vs. general topics factual tweets?

We measured engagement in COVID-19-related tweets by combining the number of likes and retweets. After preprocessing the tweets, we analyzed our dataset with statistical and correlational methods. Our study found that: (i) factual tweets were more engaging than misinformation tweets, regardless of their topic; (ii) features correlated with engagement varied depending on the tweet's veracity and topic; yet (iii) syntactical features of informal speech and punctuation strongly correlated with general and COVID-related factual tweets, as well as COVID-related misinformation while (iv) user metadata strongly correlated with general topic misinformation but not COVID-19 misinformation; and (v) semantic features, such as sentiment and writing with clout, strongly correlated with factual COVID-related tweets but not misinformation. These findings suggest that addressing misinformation should be targeted toward specific issues rather than using a one-size-fits-all approach.

To our knowledge, prior work [8,18,24,31,34,37,43] has yet to study users' engagement related to factual and misinformation tweets relative to COVID- and general-related topics. This paper thus makes the following contributions:

1. We analyze Twitter discourse on COVID-19 and non-COVID-19 topics to discover whether misinformation tweets are more engaging than factual tweets.

2. We identify discriminating characteristics of a tweet and its author that can distinguish factual and misinformation tweets based on tweet engagement.
3. To support the broader research community, we offer guidance in acquiring the same datasets we employed, although we are not able to directly supply the dataset due to certain restrictions. Our dataset, derived from nine different sources, covers around 2.1M tweets on COVID-19 and various other topics. It encompasses a rich variety of features and labels, obtained through diverse analyses such as those focused on misinformation/factual content, sociolinguistic factors, moral aspects, and sentiment. Researchers eager to work with these datasets or replicate our study are encouraged to contact the authors[1].

Our paper is organized as follows. Section 2 reviews prior works on misinformation and public health and considers the added value of our work. Section 3 discusses our dataset, its curation process, and the preprocessing and feature extraction steps taken. Section 4 then analyses our cleaned datasets' results via statistical tests. Section 5 discusses the takeaways and limitations of our analyses and the future directions for this line of work. Section 6 concludes the paper.

2   Related Work

Intending to understand the nuances that correlate engagement to COVID-19 and other topics of misinformation in the Twittersphere, a few unique approaches have produced intriguing results. This section provides an overview of literature relevant to our work.

Various researchers have explored the presence, prevalence, and sentiment of misinformation on social media of COVID-19 discourse [1,8,18,24,34,37,43], user's susceptibility and psychological perceptions on this public health crisis [30,38], the predictors of fake news [4,19], and the role of bots [24,43] on spreading COVID-19 misinformation. For instance, Sharma et al. [34] examined Twitter data to identify misinformation tweets leveraging state-of-the-art fact-checking tools (e.g., Media Bias/Fact Check, NewsGuard, and Zimdars) along with topics, sentiments, and emerging trends in the COVID-19 Twitter discourse. Singh et al. [37] found that misinformation and myths on COVID-19 are discussed at a lower volume than other pandemic-specific themes on Twitter. They also concluded that information flow on Twitter shows a spatiotemporal relationship with infection rates. Jiang et al. [20] examined the usage of hashtags in 2.3M tweets in the United States and observed that the American public frames the pandemic as a core political issue. Cinelli et al. [8] went beyond Twitter and analyzed data from four other social media platforms: Instagram, YouTube, Reddit, and Gab, finding different volumes of misinformation on each platform.

Huang et al. [18] analyzed ~67.4M tweets and observed that news media and government officials' tweets are highly engaging and that most discussion

---

[1] In order to comply with Twitter's Terms of Service (https://developer.twitter.com/en/developer-terms/agreement-and-policy), we omitted the tweet's raw text, as well as any features that could potentially reveal the users' identity.

on misinformation originates from the United States. Unlike this work which explored the kind of users involved and the location of dissemination of highly engaging tweets, this present paper aims to identify the set of a tweet and user characteristics that can predict factual/misinformation tweets and engagement with factual/misinformation tweets.

Although studies on COVID-19 misinformation exist, few have focused on measuring users' engagement and discriminating features, as proposed in this paper. Al-Rakhami and Al-Amri [1] collected 409K COVID-related tweets and used entropy- and correlation-based ranking to distinguish between misinformation and factual information, but they did not examine engagement features. We curated a feature list with 126 features, including textual content, to understand which features contribute most to engagement. Our methodology differs from Al-Rakhami and Al-Amri's, who assumed that Twitter users with large followings are less likely to spread misinformation. However, recent studies [9,11] show that verified users and anti-vaxxers are responsible for a significant portion of misinformation; indeed, we found a positive correlation between followers and engagement with general topic misinformation.

Some studies have analyzed engagement metrics in the context of misinformation on social media in general (e.g., [36,41]). Vosoughi et al. [41] found that fake or false news tend to have higher engagement than verified ones on Twitter, contrasting our results. However, methodological differences between our works could explain this discrepancy. Our engagement analysis combined retweets and favorites, whereas Vosoughi et al. [41] measured diffusion relative to retweet count. Our dataset also contained a larger number of tweets from nine unique datasets, including non-COVID-related false and factual information. Additionally, we analyzed regular users' tweets and replies that did not contain URLs, while the authors specifically looked at fake news with verified true/false URLs. Lastly, we could not collect several tweets of our curated datasets using the Twitter API due to limitations (see Sec. 5.1). This could indicate that, in the three years since Vosoughi et al.'s [41] work, Twitter may have improved its ability to cull high-engagement misinformation tweets.

3   COVID Misinformation and Factual Datasets: Preprocessing and Feature Engineering

We curated data from multiple sources to compose four Twitter datasets used in our analysis for this paper: (1) COVID-19 misleading claims, (2) COVID-19 factual claims, (3) misleading claims on general topics, and (4) factual claims on general topics. We specifically combined different sources of data in each dataset to avoid biasing the results and to improve the generalizability of our findings. For example, our datasets of COVID-19 claims include discourse related to the spread of the virus, vaccine, etc. The two latter datasets were created to understand how user engagement with COVID-19 claims (misleading and factual) differs from engagement with other claims (e.g., politics, violence, terrorism). This section details our process for building the four datasets mentioned above and the steps taken for data preprocessing and feature extraction.

3.1 Dataset Selection

Several Twitter datasets can be found in the literature, with some designed explicitly for misinformation analysis. These datasets include ground truth labels of *true/factual* and *fake/misleading* for tweets, replies, and/or news articles included in the tweets via URLs. Ground truth labels are typically assigned manually through human annotators; however, automatic annotation strategies are sometimes employed to reach more labeled data. Below, we discuss publicly available Twitter datasets for misinformation analysis on different narratives (including COVID-19) and how we leveraged them to compose the datasets used in our analysis.

COVID-19 Tweets. We found five Twitter datasets potentially relevant for analyzing COVID-19 misinformation, which we combined to compose our datasets of COVID-19 *misleading* and *factual* claims.

Dataset 1. Shashi et al. [33] released a dataset[2] containing $1,736$ tweets mentioning Coronavirus-related news articles that have been fact-checked by over 92 professional fact-checking organizations and mentioned on Snopes and/or Poynter between January and July 2020. The tweets were classified into four categories based on the veracity of the claims: *false* ($N = 1,345$), *partially false* ($N = 315$), *true* ($N = 41$), and *other* ($N = 35$). We included only the tweets from the first two categories in our dataset of COVID-19 *misleading* claims, while the *true* tweets were included in our dataset of COVID-19 *factual* claims.

Dataset 2. Schroeder et al. [32] created a dataset[3] consisting of tweets linking COVID-19 with 5G conspiracy theories. They collected COVID-related tweets posted between January and May 2020 and filtered for those that mentioned 5G. A random sample of $3,000$ tweets was labeled manually as either *5G-corona conspiracy*, *other conspiracy*, or *non-conspiracy*, after which the authors automatically labeled the rest of the tweets based on the subgraphs extracted from the three groups. The resulting dataset contained ∼19K tweets promoting COVID-19 5G conspiracies, ∼38.7K tweets promoting other COVID-related conspiracies, and ∼157K tweets that did not promote any conspiracy. We included tweets from the first two groups in our COVID-19 *misleading* claims dataset and excluded those that did not promote conspiracies, as they contained both—factual and misleading claims.

Dataset 3. The Covid-19 Healthcare Misinformation Dataset (CoAID)[4] released by Cui and Lee [12] includes news articles and social media posts related to COVID-19 alongside ground truth labels of *fake claim* and *factual claim* manually assigned by human coders. We leveraged 484 *fake claim* tweets (e.g., "only older adults and young adults are at risk") and $8,092$ *factual claim* tweets (e.g.,

---

[2] https://github.com/Gautamshahi/Misinformation_COVID-19.
[3] https://datasets.simula.no/wico-graph/.
[4] https://github.com/cuilimeng/CoAID.

"5G mobile networks do not spread COVID-19") tweeted by the WHO official account.

Dataset 4. Paka et al. [27] published the COVID-19 Twitter fake news (CTF) dataset[5], consisting of a mixture of labeled and unlabeled tweets related to COVID-19. We focused only on the labeled part, comprising 45, 261 tweets, of which 18, 555 are labeled as *genuine* and 26, 706 as *fake*. However, the dataset was not entirely available, and the authors released a sample of 2, 000 *fake* and 2, 000 *genuine* tweets, which we included in our datasets of COVID-19 *misleading*, and *factual* claims, respectively.

Dataset 5. Muric et al. [26] released a dataset[6] of tweets related to anti-vaccine narratives, including falsehoods and conspiracies surrounding the COVID-19 vaccine. The dataset contains over 1.8 million tweets tweeted between October 2020 and April 2021, containing keywords indicating opposition to the COVID-19 vaccine. Additionally, the authors collected more than 135 million tweets from 70K accounts actively spreading anti-vaccine narratives, which may restrict the diversity of the data. To avoid this, we considered only the first part of their dataset in our study, which contains tweets posted by various users. We included such tweets in our COVID-19 *misleading* claims dataset.

General Topics Tweets. We combined four other sources of data to compose two diverse datasets of *misleading* and *factual* claims about general topics (e.g., politics, terrorist conflicts, entertainment, etc.).

Dataset 6. Mitra and Gilbert [25] released CREDBANK, a large-scale crowd-sourced dataset of approximately 60M tweets covering 96 days starting from October 2014. All tweets were related to 1, 049 real-world news events; 30 annotators from Amazon Mechanical Turk analyzed each tweet for credibility. We selected 18 events rated *certainly accurate* by all 30 annotators for a total of 1, 943, 827 tweets.

Dataset 7. The Russian Troll Tweets Kaggle dataset[7] contains 200K tweets from malicious accounts connected to Russia's Internet Research Agency (IRA) posted between July 2014 and September 2017. A team reconstructed this dataset at NBC News[8] after Twitter deleted data from almost 3K accounts believed to be connected with the IRA in response to an investigation of the House Intelligence Committee into how Russia may have influenced the 2016 U.S. election.

Dataset 8. Vo and Lee [40] released a dataset[9] of tweets that were fact-checked based on news articles from two popular fact-checking websites (Snopes and

---

[5] https://github.com/williamscott701/Cross-SEAN.
[6] https://github.com/gmuric/avax-tweets-dataset.
[7] https://www.kaggle.com/vikasg/russian-troll-tweets?select=tweets.csv.
[8] https://www.nbcnews.com/tech/social-media/now-available-more-200-000-deleted-russian-troll-tweets-n844731.
[9] https://github.com/nguyenvo09/LearningFromFactCheckers.

Politifact). The authors originally collected $247,436$ fact-checked tweets posted between May 2016 through 2018. After discarding certain tweets (non-English, removed by Twitter, etc.), their final dataset consisted of $73,203$ fact-checked tweets, where $59,208$ were labeled as *fake* and $13,995$ as *true*, which we included in our datasets of *misleading* and *factual* claims, respectively.

Dataset 9. Jiang et al. [21] released a dataset[10] of $2,327$ tweets from Twitter, labeled across a spectrum of fact-check ratings including *true, mostly true, half true, mostly false, false*, and *pants on fire*. We focused on purely misleading and factual claims and thus included only *true* ($N = 231$) in our *factual* claims dataset, and both *false* ($N = 1130$) and *pants on fire* ($N = 134$) tweets in our *misleading* claims dataset.

3.2   Data Collection & Stratified Random Sampling

First, we discarded repeated tweet IDs from the four composed datasets. We then used the Twitter API to collect these tweets along with metadata related to the tweets themselves (e.g., language, lists of hashtags, symbols, user mentions, and URLs included), the users/authors of the tweets (e.g., name, profile description, account date of creation, number of followers, number of friends), and the tweet engagement (e.g., number of retweets and number of likes). However, we were able to retrieve only a portion of tweets per each dataset. Many tweets were no longer available/accessible by the time of the data collection (especially those containing misleading claims), most likely because they had been deleted by either Twitter or the user. Moreover, we discarded non-English language tweets and tweets containing no text or very short texts. Upon collecting the entire dataset, we dropped $416,283$ entries with null values for the combined engagement metric—this likely was due to errors during poor parsing of the json strings after collecting the entire datasets; nonetheless, this step left us with $2,116,397$ total tweets (summarized in Table 1).

This data imbalance is not ideal for statistical analyses as it introduces biases, but it is, unfortunately, part of the misinformation phenomenon. COVID-related tweets are often misleading due to the rapidly evolving scientific research, leading to a rumor-prone environment [3]. To reduce the imbalance, we used stratified random sampling to obtain sample populations representing each dataset's engagement distribution. In other words, instead of randomly selecting data from each of the four datasets, we sampled subgroups, i.e., *strata*, of $n \approx 4,556$ from each dataset according to the distribution of combined engagement. This n was chosen as it is 50% of the smallest population size across our datasets (i.e., $N = 9,111$ for COVID-related factual tweets) and allowed us to maintain variability across all class sizes. We repeated this process 10 times, obtaining 10 stratified random samples of $17,982$ tweets each. Figure 1 compares the original datasets with one of the stratified random samples, demonstrating that we stayed true to the original distribution of engagement.

---

[10] https://shanjiang.me/resources/#misinformation.

Table 1. Descriptive statistics of our final four datasets based on the combined engagement metric.

	Factual		Misinformation	
	COVID-Related	*General Topics*	*COVID-Related*	*General Topics*
N	9,111	1,243,913	828,501	32,243
n_{strata}	4,814	4,448	4,533	4,147
μ	368.5	9,791.6	2,214.3	3,014.7
σ	7,157.9	73,305.6	10,051.9	28,727.4
Mean Rank	2407.5	2244.5	2267.0	2074.0

3.3 Data Preprocessing

Before feature extraction, the full text of the collected tweets was preprocessed by removing numbers (e.g., "1 million" or "12,345" become "million" and ","), emojis, hashtags (e.g., "#COVID"), mentions (e.g., "@WHO"), and URLs. Other typical NLP preprocessing steps, such as tokenization, removal of stop words, and lemmatization, were not performed, as both LIWC and sentiment analysis packages can work with raw text.

3.4 Feature Extraction

From the cleaned dataset, we extracted a total of 126 features per tweet, including features derived from the metadata (i.e., tweet- and user-related descriptors), addressing sociolinguistic (e.g., cognitive and structural components, such as formal and logical language) and moral frames (e.g., fairness or reciprocity), as well as sentiment characteristics of the tweet texts.

Tweet Metadata, User Metadata, and Engagement. We extracted the following features from the collected Twitter metadata:

- Six **tweet-related** features: # of likes, # of retweets, # of hashtags, # links/URLs, # of combined engagement (i.e., # retweets + # likes), and # of emojis in the tweet.
- Twelve **user-related** features: # of followers, # of friends, # of lists, # of favorited tweets, verified (binary), presence of profile image (binary), use of default profile image (binary) or default profile (binary), whether geolocation is enabled (binary), whether the user has an extended profile (binary) or background tile (binary), and # of tweets made by the user.

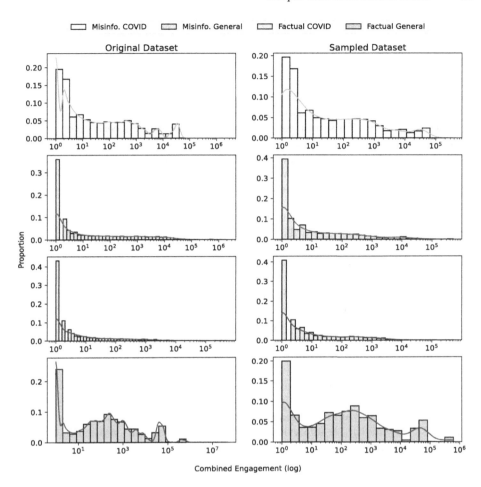

Fig. 1. Comparison of the distribution of combined engagement (log-normalized) versus the proportion of its occurrence for each dataset.

We combined likes and retweets to form an engagement metric, but it was left-skewed, so we log-normalized it using Aldous and Jansen's method [2]. The method suggests a 4-level scale to measure engagement on Twitter, where retweets are the highest level of engagement (level-4) and likes are level-2. Commenting (level-3) is more public than liking but less than retweeting (since retweeting is a deliberate effort to amplify the reach of the content through different networks), and viewing (level-1) is the most private. Our dataset lacked engagement metrics for levels 1 and 3, so we analyzed the likes and retweets combined as a single metric.

To capture sentiment and emotions in tweets, we implemented an emoji and emoticon counter, but we later decided to disregard emoticons due to a high occurrence of false positives. Many combinations of regular punctuations were incorrectly identified as emoticons, leading to misclassification. Therefore, we only counted for emojis.

Sociolinguistic Analysis. We performed a sociolinguistic analysis on the collected tweets using the Linguistic Inquiry and Word Count (LIWC) software (version 2015) [28]. This tool estimates the rate at which certain emotions, moods, and cognition (e.g., analytical thinking) are present in a text based on word counts (e.g., the words "nervous," "afraid," and "tense" counted as expressing anxiety). More specifically, we extracted 93 features related to emotional, cognitive, and structural components from the collected tweets, including:

- Four **language metrics**: total number of words, average number of words per sentence, number of words containing more than six letters, and number of words found in the LIWC dictionary.
- Eighty-five **dimensions**, including function words (e.g., pronouns, articles, prepositions), grammar characteristics (e.g., adjectives, comparatives, numbers), affect words (e.g., positive and negative emotions), social words (e.g., family, friends, male/female referents), cognitive process (e.g., insight, certainty), core needs (e.g., power, risk/prevention focus), time orientation (e.g., past/present/future focus), personal concerns (e.g., home, money, death), informal speech (e.g., swear words, netspeak), and punctuation (e.g., periods, commas, question marks). These features reflect the percentage of total words per dimension (e.g., "positive emotions" equal to 7.5 means that 7.5% of all words in the tweet were positive emotion words).
- Four **summary variables** expressed in a scale ranging from 0 (very low) to 100 (very high): (i) analytical thinking; (ii) clout; (iii) authenticity; (iv) emotional tone.

Moral Frames Analysis. We measured moral frames using the moral foundations dictionary [15] dictionary in LIWC. Based on moral foundations theory [17], the authors aggregated 295 words for each of five moral intuitions encompassing 11 total features, which encompass psychological preparations for reacting to issues about **harm/care, fairness/reciprocity, ingroup/loyalty, authority/respect**, and **purity/sanctity**.

Sentiment Analysis. For sentiment analysis, we used VADER [14], a rule-based NLP library available with NLTK [22]. Among the outputs generated by VADER, we used the *compound score*, a uni-dimensional normalized, weighted composite score. A compound score ≥ 0.05 denotes a positive sentiment, between -0.05 and 0.05 denotes a neutral sentiment, and ≤ -0.05 denotes a negative sentiment. We extracted three binary sentiment features for each collected tweet: positive, negative, and neutral.

3.5   Correlation Analysis

To investigate the correlation of engagement with COVID- and non-COVID-related misinformation and factual tweets (RQs 3 and 4), we used Pearson's correlation coefficient, r, to measure feature importance. However, as r only captures linear relationships, we employed another method to identify non-linear correlations. We used the Alternating Conditional Expectations (ACE) algorithm to find each feature's fixed point of Maximal Correlation (MC). The ACE algorithm transforms variables to maximize r for the dependent and independent variables, making it robust against noisy data and capable of detecting non-linear correlations more accurately than r [13]. Note that MC ranges from 0 to 1, indicating the polarity of the correlation. We used this method to supplement our analysis and provide a more comprehensive understanding of the relationships between engagement and tweets on COVID- and non-COVID-related misinformation and factual information.

Additionally, the Pearson correlation coefficient is biased such that the simple mean of r of all 10 samples would underestimate the true r. Therefore, performing a Fisher z-transformation correction of the rs allows us to reduce bias and more accurately estimate the population correlation [10]. In other words, we report the average Pearson's correlation coefficient, r_z, i.e., the inverse z-transform of the averaged z-values over all the 10 samples. Additionally, we rely on the Fisher method by the sum of logs to combine the p-values obtained for each sample into a single metric.

4   Results

This section details the statistical and correlation analyses performed on our curated dataset to answer each of our four research questions and their results. All statistical tests were performed based on a 1% significance level ($\alpha = .01$). Tables 2 and 3 summarize our results.

4.1   RQ1: Are COVID-19 Misinformation Tweets More Engaging Than COVID-19 Factual Tweets?

We investigated the difference in engagement between factual and misinformation tweets related to COVID-19. Firstly, we checked whether the combined engagement metric for factual and misinformation tweets followed a normal distribution using the Shapiro-Wilk ($p < .001$) and D'Agostino's K-squared ($p < .001$) tests. The results showed that the distribution was non-normal and heavily skewed towards zero for most tweets. Additionally, we found that the distribution was not homogeneous between the two groups ($W = 378.89$, $p < .001$), so we used non-parametric tests to analyze the log-normalized combined engagement metric for each group. The Two-Sample Kolmogorov-Smirnov test results indicated that the engagement distribution of COVID-19 factual tweets was significantly different from that of COVID-19 misinformation tweets ($KS = 0.21, p < .001$). These results were consistent across all stratified random samples, indicating that the strata adequately reflected the distribution of combined engagement.

Table 2. Summary results for statistical tests conducted on engagement metrics and bot/user account labels.

Data	Measure	Measurement Statistics	
Combined Engagement (raw)	Shapiro-Wilk	Factual COVID-Related	$W = 0.7875$***
		Misinformation General Topics	$W = 0.8946$***
		Factual General Topics	$W = 0.9374$***
		Misinformation General Topics	$W = 0.7969$***
Combined Engagement (log-norm)	Levene	Factual vs. Misinformation COVID-Related	$W = 378.89$***
		Factual vs. Misinformation General Topics	$W = 359.59$***
	Two-Sample Kolmogorov-Smirnov	Factual vs. Misinformation COVID-Related	$K_2 = 0.2133$***
		Factual vs. Misinformation General Topics	$K_2 = 0.3459$***
	Mann-Whitney U	Factual vs. Misinformation COVID-Related	$U = 7,662,279$***, $r = 0.35$
		Factual vs. Misinformation General Topics	$U = 5,725,193$***, $r = 0.31$

*** Significant at $p < .001$

A comparison of the mean distribution of factual and misinformation tweets was desirable, given the notable differences in the overall populations ($\mu_{COVID,factual} = 368.5$ and $\mu_{COVID,misinfo} = 2,214.3$. However, due to the non-normality and skew of these variables, we opted to conduct the Mann-Whitney U-test and compare the mean ranks of the two samples. For each strata, factual COVID-19 tweets ($n = 4,814$) had a larger average mean rank ($2,407.5$) than misinformation tweets ($n = 4,533, \mu_{rank} = 2,267.0$). Therefore, the combined engagement of the factual tweets was statistically and significantly higher than the misinformation tweets $U = 7,662,279$, $p < .001$), indicating that factual COVID-19 tweets tend to be more engaging than COVID-19 misinformation tweets. Given that $U_{max} = n_{strata,1} \times n_{strata,2} = 21,821,862$, we can convert the U-statistic to an effect size, $r = U/U_{max} = 0.35$. In simpler words, there is a medium probability that a combined engagement value from the factual tweets will be greater than misinformation tweets.

> COVID-19 factual tweets were statistically and significantly more engaging than misinformation tweets about COVID-19.

4.2   RQ2: Are General Topic Misinformation Tweets More Engaging Than General Topic Factual Tweets?

We repeated the analyses conducted for **RQ1**, finding that the combined engagement metrics also do not follow normal distribution based on the Shapiro-Wilk

($p < .001$) and D'Agostino's K-squared ($p < .001$) tests, and that the distribution of the data was not homogeneous for the two groups ($W = 359.59$, $p < .001$). The Two-Sample Kolmogorov-Smirnov test also showed that the distribution between factual and misinformation general topic tweets was significantly different ($KS = 0.35, p < .001$).

The Mann-Whitney U-test revealed that the average mean rank for combined engagement was higher for factual general topic tweets ($n = 4,448, \mu_{rank} = 2,244.5$) compared to misinformation tweets ($n = 4,147, \mu_{rank} = 2,074$). As a result, we concluded that factual general topic tweets have significantly higher combined engagement than misinformation tweets ($U = 5,745,193.0$, $p < .001$). The U-statistic was converted to an effect size of $r = 0.31$, suggesting a medium probability that combined engagement from factual general topic tweets will be higher than that of misinformation tweets.

> Factual tweets were statistically and significantly more engaging that misinformation tweets about general topics.

4.3 RQ3: Which Features Are Most Correlated with Engagement in COVID-19 Vs. General Topics Misinformation Tweets?

Our correlation analysis found that only a few of the extracted features were strongly correlated ($r_{MC,z} \geq 0.5$) with the log-normalized combined engagement metric. For COVID-related misinformation combined engagement, we observed a strong correlation with LIWC-based grammar features (i.e., use of informal speech, punctuation, impersonal pronouns) and word count, with correlation coefficients ranging from $[0.50, 0.75]$. On the other hand, for general topic misinformation, only three features showed a strong correlation, all related to user metadata: the number of followers ($r_{MC,z} = 0.73$), the number of public lists of which that a user is a member ($r_{MC,z} = 0.66$), and whether the user is verified ($r_{MC,z} = 0.53$).

> The top features related to engagement for COVID-19 and general topics misinformation were, respectively, the tweet's grammar (e.g., use of informal speech) and user metadata (e.g., verified user).

4.4 RQ4: Which Features Are Most Correlated with Engagement in COVID-19 Vs. General Topics Factual Tweets?

Compared to the other groups, factual COVID-related tweets showed several strong correlations. The highest correlation ($r_{MC,z} = 0.91$) was using third-person singular words, a feature not strongly correlated with any other group,

Table 3. Summary of correlation analysis between the log normalized combined engagement metric and all features. Only r_z values indicating a moderate correlation (> 0.5) and with a combined MC p-value $< .01$ are shown.

Feature Type	Feature	r_z	(MC) r_z
Factual: COVID-Related			
LIWC	Affective Processes	0.53	0.71
	All Punctuation	-0.05	0.58
	Assent (Informal Language)	0.65	0.74
	Clout	0.36	0.56
	Colon (Punctuation)	0.34	0.54
	Dictionary Words	0.13	0.56
	Past Focus	0.49	0.66
	Informal Speech	0.62	0.72
	Insight (Cognitive Processes)	0.32	0.68
	Male Referents (Social Words)	0.77	0.88
	Netspeak (Informal Language)	0.66	0.77
	Positive Emotion (Affect Words)	0.52	0.78
	Person Pronouns (Linguistic Dimensions)	0.31	0.56
	Question Marks (All Punctuation)	-0.31	0.53
	Reward (Drives)	0.33	0.67
	Sad (Affect Words)	0.48	0.65
	3rd Person Singular (Function Words)	0.81	0.91
	Words > 6 Letters	-0.26	0.59
	Social Words	0.41	0.63
	Time (Relativity)	0.21	0.51
Sentiment	VADER Compound	0.19	0.66
Factual: General Topics			
LIWC	Assent (Informal Speech)	0.36	0.68
	Colons (All Punctuation)	0.20	0.52
	Informal Speech	0.29	0.62
	Netspeak (Informal Speech)	0.32	0.63
	Prepositions (Function Words)	0.02	0.54
Misinformation: COVID-Related			
LIWC	Assent (Informal Speech)	0.26	0.75
	Colons (All Punctuation)	0.34	0.75
	Informal Speech	0.19	0.69
	Impersonal Pronouns	0.06	0.64
	Netspeak (Informal Speech)	0.26	0.73
	Quotation Marks (All Punctuation)	0.10	0.50
	Word Count	-0.10	0.51
Misinformation: General Topics			
User Metadata	Followers Count	0.28	0.73
	Listed Count	0.30	0.66
	User Verified	0.53	0.53

while the second-highest correlation ($r_{MC,z} = 0.88$) was related to male referents. Additionally, factual COVID tweets were strongly correlated with effective processes ($r_{MC,z} = 0.71$) and emotion, as measured by LIWC ($r_{MC,z,positive} = 0.78$ and $r_{MC,z,sad} = 0.65$) and VADER ($r_{MC,z} = 0.66$). Only one LIWC summary variable, Clout ($r_{MC,z} = 0.71$), indicated confidence and leadership in writing and appeared among any of the groups. In contrast, factual general topics tweets only strongly correlated with LIWC's grammar features, such as informal speech, punctuation, and prepositions, similar to the strongly correlated features for COVID-related misinformation.

The top features related to engagement for COVID-19 factual tweets pertained to grammar (e.g., use of netspeak), emotion (both positive and negative), and the writer's confidence, whereas general topic tweets pertained solely to grammar (e.g., use of colons or prepositions).

---

5   Discussion

In this paper, we set out to answer four research questions relating to COVID-19 and general topics tweets as a function of the combined engagement metric. This section summarizes the takeaways and limitations of our work and suggests possible future research directions.

First, it is essential to note that distinguishing between factual and misinformation tweets is challenging as research has shown that automatic detection of misinformation is a nuanced and open research problem in the machine learning field [44] and social media platforms are inherently rooted in big data that is unstructured and noisy [35]. Such problems exacerbate the difficulty of detecting misinformation. The digital revolution and the integration of social media into our daily lives have been leveraged as tools for the faster propagation of disinformation campaigns. Research has shown that humans are poor at detecting deception [16], and our ability to detect digital fake news is "bleak" [42]. Understanding how machines can detect highly engaging dis/misinformation will provide a first line of defense against deception in the online sphere. Government agencies and organizations can use this knowledge to convey critical public health information to the general populace. For example, with respect to the Italian Ministry of Health, Lovari [23] found that keeping the public constantly informed via dissemination of information in understandable forms (e.g., data and visuals) helps reduce the spread of misinformation.

Therefore, the primary purpose of this work was to point researchers toward potentially impactful metadata that could give inklings towards purposeful or unintentional false information. Importantly, we found that misinformation tweets about general topics strongly correlated with the users' metadata; these features all contained a positive polarity in terms of r_z, potentially indicating that influential users were responsible for generating engagement with general topics misinformation.

Assuming that real Twitter accounts are more likely to be verified and have several followers, we can infer that misinformation tweets by seemingly real and influential users can offer a perceived sense of credibility. However, this can be even more deceiving to the average user in the context of misinformation [44].

As such, the semantic content of the tweet itself (based on LIWC analysis) appears not to be relevant to engagement (except for factual COVID tweets). Instead, the *syntax* was highly correlated with engaging tweets for factual COVID tweets and factual and misinformation general topics. Interestingly, we found that tweet sentiment was not relevant to predict engagement, except in the context of truthful COVID-related tweets.

In stark contrast, we found that engagement with COVID-related factual tweets differed from engagement with other types of tweets. Engagement with factual tweets was highly correlated with sentiment and cognitive processing-related keywords, indicating that tweets appealing to pathos were more engaging. In contrast, fewer complex words (i.e., > 6 letters) and question marks were associated with high engagement (strong MC correlation—$r_{MC,z} = 0.59$ and 0.53, respectively), suggesting that clear and straightforward language drives engagement with misinformation. This highlights the importance of understanding and addressing different types of misinformation on a per-issue basis rather than lumping them together.

We also found that factual tweets were statistically more engaging than misinformation tweets, regardless of the tweet's context (general topics or COVID-19). To our knowledge, our study is the first to analyze engagement in COVID tweets relative to veracity and other topics. Surprisingly, we did not find that the # of ULRs in the tweet was a strongly correlated feature. We suspected that URLs could increase the veracity of the information presented in the tweet, thus helping distinguish factual information from misinformation and reinforcing false claims in misinformation tweets, increasing their engagement.

5.1   Limitations & Future Works

In light of the contributions made by our research, it is incumbent upon us to acknowledge the concomitant limitations of our study and delineate potential paths for future exploration. This section discusses these limitations and outlines promising trajectories for further research.

Dataset Imbalance and Representativeness. Our dataset was imbalanced, with factual general topics and COVID-related misinformation dominating over factual COVID-related and general misinformation tweets. We generated 10 stratified random samples to address this issue, but factual COVID tweets lacked variety and exhibited stronger correlations than the other groups. This limits the generalizability of our findings and could lead to overfitting in machine learning models. Future studies could generate larger synthetic datasets or adopt down-sampling strategies to overcome this.

Our meta-analysis of nine datasets included 2.1M tweets, but we could not collect some tweets removed by Twitter, potentially favoring high-engagement factual tweets. Future studies could conduct a time-series analysis of tweets to understand the relationship between engagement and truthfulness and identify factors contributing to tweet removal.

Although we demonstrated the impact of different meta features on engagement in tweets, future studies could take a more nuanced approach by comparing the impact of veracity and tweet context across different topics, such as COVID and measles vaccine hesitancy, or specific events and controversies associated with misinformation, such as the 2020 U.S. General Election.

Feature Engineering, Feature Selection, and Classification Models. Our research provides a foundation for future studies in machine learning, but there are still many other features to explore beyond the ones we analyzed. For example, studies have found that emojis can help determine Twitter sentiment, and automated feature extractors like Word Embedding, TF-IDF, Word2Vec, BERT, and GloVe could be used to predict misinformation and tweet engagement. Additionally, investigating how tweets are written may be a more straightforward approach than fact-checking every claim.

While previous works have studied the prevalence of COVID-19 misinformation on Twitter and characterized the role of bots in spreading misinformation, more research should examine how automatic adversaries spread misinformation. Investigating demographic attributes and their impact on engagement with falsehoods may also prove fruitful.

Two similar features were deemed negatively correlated with engagement for misinformation and factual COVID-related tweets: the tweet's length, as measured by word count, and the use of words > 6 words. Historically, we have seen the use of short texts, lots of images, a touch of sex, and a tendency towards sensationalism used as a recipe for propaganda success, leveraged by the KGB, Stasi, and CIA [29]. The presence of an image and the amount of text (and, therefore, information that a user must process) in a tweet might be leveraged by both disinformation campaigns and reputable sources alike to help users quickly digest information. Additionally, this suggests that users are likelier to engage with an image over words, especially considering that sociolinguistic and sentiment features were not of utmost importance in predicting engagement. While we did not measure for the presence of an image, few studies (e.g., [7]) have conducted exploratory research on visual misinformation videos, and we advise future work to consider this dimension in their work.

Another limitation of our study was our reliance on pairwise correlation analysis. Future work could benefit from utilizing multivariate analyses such as principal component analysis (PCA) to identify the most relevant features tailored to specific models. Additionally, examining the correlation between groups of features could help in the feature selection process.

6   Conclusion

This paper curated a dataset of 2.1M COVID-19- and non-COVID-related misinformation and factual tweets to investigate misinformation as a function of veracity, content, and engagement. Via the use of statistical and correlation analyses, we offer the following conclusions: (i) misinformation tweets were less engaging than factual tweets; (ii) features for general and COVID-related tweets varied in correlation to engagement based on veracity; for example, user metadata features (e.g., followers count) were most strongly associated with engagement for general misinformation, which COVID-related misinformation correlated most with grammar-related features present in the tweet's text. We propose several directions and suggestions for future works on misinformation in the online sphere. In particular, our insights on what features can aid with predicting high engagement can be leveraged for defense approaches against misinformation, such as increasing the engagement of factual tweets, especially those coming from verified government accounts and reputable organizations (e.g., WHO, NIH), thus contributing to factual public health information reaching the masses.

Acknowledgements. This work was supported by the National Science Foundation under Grant No. 2028734, by the University of Florida Seed Fund award P0175721, and by the Embry-Riddle Aeronautical University award 61632-01/PO# 262143. This material is based upon work supported by (while serving at) the National Science Foundation.

References

1. Al-Rakhami, M.S., Al-Amri, A.M.: Lies kill, facts save: detecting COVID-19 misinformation in Twitter. IEEE Access **8**, 155961–155970 (2020)
2. Aldous, K.K., An, J., Jansen, B.J.: View, like, comment, post: analyzing user engagement by topic at 4 levels across 5 social media platforms for 53 news organizations. Proc. Int. AAAI Conf. Web Soc. Med. **13**(01), 47–57 (2019)
3. Allport, G.W., Postman, L.: The psychology of rumor. J. Clin. Psychol. (1947)
4. Apuke, O.D., Omar, B.: Fake news and COVID-19: Modelling the predictors of fake news sharing among social media users. Telemat. Inform. 101475 (2020)
5. Avram, M., Micallef, N., Patil, S., Menczer, F.: Exposure to social engagement metrics increases vulnerability to misinformation. arXiv preprint arXiv:2005.04682 (2020)
6. Bell, B., Gallagher, F.: Who is spreading COVID-19 misinformation and why. https://abcnews.go.com/US/spreading-covid-19-misinformation/story?id=706159 95 (May 2020). Accessed 21 Nov 2020
7. Brennen, J.S., Simon, F.M., Nielsen, R.K.: Beyond (MIS) representation: Visuals in COVID-19 misinformation. Int. J. Press/Politics (2020)
8. Cinelli, M., et al.: The COVID-19 social media infodemic. arXiv preprint arXiv:2003.05004 (2020)
9. Cohen, J.: Verified Twitter users shared an all-time-high amount of fake news in 2020. https://www.pcmag.com/news/verified-twitter-users-shared-an-all-time-high-amount-of-fake-news-in-2020, February 2021. Accessed 4 Sept 2021

10. Corey, D.M., Dunlap, W.P., Burke, M.J.: Averaging correlations: expected values and bias in combined Pearson RS and Fisher's Z transformations. J. Gener. Psychol. **125**(3), 245–261 (1998)
11. for Countering Digital Hate, C.: The disinformation dozen: why platforms must act on twelve leading online anti-vaxxers (2021). https://counterhate.com/
12. Cui, L., Lee, D.: COAID: COVID-19 healthcare misinformation dataset (2020)
13. Deebani, W., Kachouie, N.N.: Ensemble Correlation Coefficient. In: International Symposium on Artificial Intelligence and Mathematics (2018)
14. Gilbert, C., Hutto, E.: Vader: A parsimonious rule-based model for sentiment analysis of social media text. In: Eighth International Conference on Weblogs and Social Media (ICWSM-2014), vol. 81 (2014)
15. Graham, J., Haidt, J., Nosek, B.A.: Liberals and conservatives rely on different sets of moral foundations. J. Pers. Soc. Psychol. **96**(5), 1029–1046 (2009)
16. Granhag, P.A., Andersson, L.O., Strömwall, L.A., Hartwig, M.: Imprisoned knowledge: criminals' beliefs about deception. Leg. Criminol. Psychol. **9**(1), 103–119 (2004)
17. Haidt, J., Graham, J.: When morality opposes justice: conservatives have moral intuitions that liberals may not recognize. Soc. Justice Res. **20**(1), 98–116 (2007)
18. Huang, B., Carley, K.M.: Disinformation and misinformation on twitter during the novel coronavirus outbreak. arXiv preprint arXiv:2006.04278 (2020)
19. Islam, A.N., Laato, S., Talukder, S., Sutinen, E.: Misinformation sharing and social media fatigue during COVID-19: an affordance and cognitive load perspective. Technol. Forecast. Soc. Change **159** (2020)
20. Jiang, J., Chen, E., Yan, S., Lerman, K., Ferrara, E.: Political polarization drives online conversations about COVID-19 in the united states. Human Behavi. Emerg. Technol. **2**(3), 200–211 (2020)
21. Jiang, S., Wilson, C.: Linguistic signals under misinformation and fact-checking: evidence from user comments on social media. Proc. ACM Hum. Comput. Interact. **2**(CSCW), 1–23 (2018)
22. Loper, E., Bird, S.: NLTK: The natural language toolkit. arXiv preprint cs/0205028 (2002)
23. Lovari, A.: Spreading (dis) trust: COVID-19 misinformation and government intervention in Italy. Media Commun. **8**(2), 458–461 (2020)
24. Memon, S.A., Carley, K.M.: Characterizing COVID-19 misinformation communities using a novel twitter dataset. arXiv preprint arXiv:2008.00791 (2020)
25. Mitra, T., Gilbert, E.: CredBank: a large-scale social media corpus with associated credibility annotations. In: Ninth International AAAI Conference on Web and Social Media (2015)
26. Muric, G., Wu, Y., Ferrara, E.: COVID-19 vaccine hesitancy on social media: building a public twitter data set of antivaccine content, vaccine misinformation, and conspiracies. JMIR Public Health Surveill. **7**(11), e30642 (2021)
27. Paka, W.S., Bansal, R., Kaushik, A., Sengupta, S., Chakraborty, T.: Cross-sean: A cross-stitch semi-supervised neural attention model for COVID-19 fake news detection. Appl. Soft Comput. **107** (2021)
28. Pennebaker, J.W., Boyd, R.L., Jordan, K., Blackburn, K.: The development and psychometric properties of liwc2015. Technical report (2015)
29. Rid, T.: Active measures: The secret history of disinformation and political warfare. Farrar, Straus and Giroux (2020)
30. Roozenbeek, J., et al.: Susceptibility to misinformation about COVID-19 around the world. R. Soc. Open Sci. **7**(10) (2020)

31. Schild, L., Ling, C., Blackburn, J., Stringhini, G., Zhang, Y., Zannettou, S.: "go eat a bat, chang!": an early look on the emergence of Sinophobic behavior on web communities in the face of COVID-19. arXiv preprint arXiv:2004.04046 (2020)
32. Schroeder, D.T., Pogorelov, K., Schaal, F., Filkukova, P., Langguth, J.: Wico graph: a labeled dataset of twitter subgraphs based on conspiracy theory and 5g-corona misinformation tweets. In: ICAART 2021 : 13th International Conference on Agents and Artificial Intelligence. OSF Preprints (2021)
33. Shahi, G.K., Dirkson, A., Majchrzak, T.A.: An exploratory study of COVID-19 misinformation on twitter. Online Soc. Netw. Med. **22** (2021)
34. Sharma, K., Seo, S., Meng, C., Rambhatla, S., Liu, Y.: COVID-19 on social media: analyzing misinformation in twitter conversations. arXiv preprint arXiv:2003.12309 (2020)
35. Shu, K., Sliva, A., Wang, S., Tang, J., Liu, H.: Fake news detection on social media: a data mining perspective. SIGKDD Explor. Newsl. **19**(1), 22–36 (2017)
36. Silva, M., Giovanini, L., Fernandes, J., Oliveira, D., Silva, C.S.: What makes disinformation ads engaging? A case study of Facebook ads from the Russian active measures campaign. J. Interact. Advert. 1–20 (2023)
37. Singh, L., et al.: A first look at COVID-19 information and misinformation sharing on twitter. arXiv preprint arXiv:2003.13907 (2020)
38. Swami, V., Barron, D.: Analytic thinking, rejection of coronavirus (COVID-19) conspiracy theories, and compliance with mandated social-distancing: Direct and indirect relationships in a nationally representative sample of adults in the united kingdom. OSF Preprints (2020)
39. Tagliabue, F., Galassi, L., Mariani, P.: The "pandemic" of disinformation in covid-19. SN Compr. Clin. Med. **2**, 1287–1289 (2020)
40. Vo, N., Lee, K.: Learning from fact-checkers: analysis and generation of fact-checking language. In: The 42nd International ACM SIGIR Conference on Research and Development in Information Retrieval (2019)
41. Vosoughi, S., Roy, D., Aral, S.: The spread of true and false news online. Science **359**(6380), 1146–1151 (2018)
42. Wineburg, S., McGrew, S., Breakstone, J., Ortega, T.: Evaluating information: the cornerstone of civic online reasoning. Stanford Digital Repository. Accessed 8 Jan 2018 (2016)
43. Yang, K.C., Torres-Lugo, C., Menczer, F.: Prevalence of low-credibility information on twitter during the COVID-19 outbreak. arXiv preprint arXiv:2004.14484 (2020)
44. Zhou, X., Zafarani, R.: A survey of fake news: fundamental theories, detection methods, and opportunities. ACM Comput. Surv. **53**(5), 1–40 (2020)

Extracting Common Features of Fake News by Multi-Head-Attention

Takayuki Ishimaru$^{(\boxtimes)}$ and Mamoru Mimura[ID]

National Defense Academy of Japan, Yokosuka, Kanagawa 239-8686, Japan
{em61057,mim}@nda.ac.jp

Abstract. Several methods for detecting fake news using machine learning have been proposed. Previous studies have only focused on a limited dataset, and few researchers have proposed versatile models that can be applied to various fields. In this study, we focus on common features of multiple datasets. The three datasets consisted of 27442 real news and 28359 fake news. Feature extraction is based on attention weights in the BERT (Bidirectional Encoder Representations from Transformers) model. Comparing the top words in each dataset to each other, only 15 words 14%) of the total are common. To evaluate the generality, each dataset was classified using models trained on the other dataset. As a result, detection accuracy was found to be greatly reduced and almost impossible to classify. This indicates that the detection model using the fine-tuning model of BERT is dependent on features of the training data. We also observed that the proportion of words commonly focused on classifying fake news was small. The high number of sub-words at the top of the aggregate results did not allow for adequate analysis of word characteristics. In the future, we have to improve the accuracy of the detection model and modify the feature extraction method to improve the versatility of the fake news detector.

Keywords: fake news · BERT · NLP

1 Introduction

During the 2016 US presidential election, the term "fake news" began to attract attention as various false information spread on social media on a large scale [13]. COVID-19, which occurred in 2019, has also had a major impact on society as untrue information spreads on social media.

In order to reduce the impact of fake news on society, methods to detect fake news using machine learning models have been studied. In previous studies, models using natural language processing technology and deep learning have been proposed [6,11,15]. Many of these studies examine fake news related to specific genres [14,20]. Examples include politics, gossip, and the novel coronavirus disease. In previous research, many models with high accuracy have been proposed [4,9]. Most of those studies split a specific dataset into training and test data for evaluation. In addition, related studies exist that test detection

© The Author(s), under exclusive license to Springer Nature Singapore Pte Ltd. 2023
B. Arief et al. (Eds.): SocialSec 2023, LNCS 14097, pp. 23–37, 2023.
https://doi.org/10.1007/978-981-99-5177-2_2

accuracy by creating datasets that combine data such as politics, health, sports and entertainment [11], However, few detection models have been proposed to evaluate generality.

There are many types of information in modern society, a detection model that can handle more types is required. For example, implementing a detection model on SNS and considering a mechanism to warn viewers that possible fake news, it should work regardless of category. In that case, a model that increases false positives in categories not used for training is not practical. In addition, as a feature analysis of fake news datasets, studies that visualize frequent words using word clouds have been reported [6,9]. A word cloud is a mechanism that displays and visualizes words that appear frequently in a specified text. However, words with high frequency are not the only words that influence machine learning models. The words that machine learning models look for when classifying are not determined by simple frequency of occurrence. They are determined by reading the context.

In addition, no studies have been reported to evaluate which words in fake news the machine learning model focused on for classification. Therefore, in this study, we use the BERT model to analyze the common words of interest in classifying fake news using machine learning. BERT is one of the natural language processing models, and a model that has been pre-trained using a large amount of data has been published [8]. As the model is pre-trained, highly accurate classification results can be obtained even with small amounts of data. BERT uses a deep learning model called Transformer. Multi-Head-Attention included in Transformer is a mechanism that weights one sentence from multiple angles, and can obtain weights with higher accuracy than conventional attention models [12].

Therefore, in this study, we quantified the weight of Multi-Head-Attention of BERT and analyzed words with large weight. As far as the authors know, this is the first attempt to analyze the weights of Multi-Head-Attention for fake news detection models. We also evaluated that the fake news detection model depends on the features of the training data. The contributions of this paper are as follows.

1. We quantified the weight of Multi-Head-Attention of BERT and analyzed what kind of words are attracting attention.
2. As a result of arranging and comparing the top 40 words for each data set, 15 words, or 14%, of the total 120 words are duplicated between data sets. We confirmed that the percentage of words that received attention was small.
3. Accuracy is less than 0.5 in classifying other datasets with a trained model that had an accuracy of 0.99.
4. We evaluated that the fake news detection model depends on the features of the training data by combining three datasets with different features.

2   Related Work

Due to the spread of social media, information of unknown truth is easily spread. However, evaluating their authenticity is very difficult. Therefore, various methods such as natural language processing technology and machine learning have been proposed to detect fake news.

Ahmed et al. proposed an online fake news detection model using a linear SVM classifier [4]. This study used a representative dataset for fake news classification, called ISOT FAKENEWS, with an accuracy of 0.92. Sastrawan et al. also proposed a CNN-RNN based deep learning detection model. The accuracy of this method on the ISOT FAKENEWS dataset was 0.99 [17]. Samadi et al. proposed an embedding layer consisting of pre-trained models of BERT, RoBERTa, GPT2, and Funnel Transformer, followed by a model that connects CNN. Accuracy of this method on the ISOT FAKENEWS dataset was over 0.99 [16]. Kaliyar et al. proposed a detection model called FakeBERT, which combines BERT and CNN. Accuracy is 0.99 in the classification of datasets related to the US presidential election [10]. Rai et al. proposed a model in which the output of BERT is connected with LSTM. A data set called FakeNewsNet was classified, and a higher Accuracy value than the previous research on the same data set was reported [15].

These studies divided the target dataset into training data and test data, conducted experiments, and proposed models with high accuracy. They showed that the fake news detection model using machine learning is effective for a specific dataset. As for the analysis of the features of datasets, many studies extract frequently occurring words, and most studies focus on detection accuracy. However, the result of extracting the features of fake news can be reflected in the training data, it may lead to the improvement of versatility. Therefore, in this research, in order to investigate important words in fake news detection using machine learning, we quantify the weight of Multi-Head-Attention and aggregate the words that are attracting attention in classifying fake news. We also classify datasets with three different features. Evaluation whether the training model of each dataset is effective for classification of another dataset, and examine the dependence of the fake news detector on the training data.

3   Related Techniques

This section describes the BERT model, fine-tuning, and Multi-Head-Attention of the natural language processing technology used in this research.

3.1   BERT Model

BERT (Bidirectional Encoder Representations from Transformers) is an advanced pre-trained natural language processing model. Designed to remove one-way constraints using a Masked Language Model (MLM) and pre-train deep two-way representations from unlabelled text. Devlin et al. obtained high results in each task of GLUE (General Language Understanding Evaluation), a standard benchmark for natural language processing in the English-speaking world [8]. In addition, Devlin et al. proposed two types of BERT models, $BERT_{BASE}$ and $BERT_{LARGE}$, and Table 1 shows the details of the parameters. In this study, experiments are performed using the $BERT_{BASE}$ model used in previous studies [10, 15].

Table 1. Parameter of BERT model

Parameter name	$BERT_{BASE}$	$BERT_{LARGE}$
Layer num	12	24
Hidden layer	768	1024
Attention Heads	12	16
Parameter num	110M	340M

3.2   Fine-Tuning

BERT has two steps: pre-training and fine-tuning [8]. In pre-training, learning is performed using a large amount of unlabeled data. In fine-tuning, a classification model corresponding to specific data is created by giving the type of labeled data to be learned to the parameters of the pretrained model. By using the parameters of a pre-trained model as initial values, a highly accurate classification model can be obtained even with relatively small amounts of training data. The pre-trained model of BERT created by Devlin et al. has been published [7]. Figure 1 shows the fine-tuning mechanism for the binary classification task, where E is the input embedding, Trm is the transformer, and T is the contextual representation of the token. In this research, fine-tuning is performed using a pretrained model of BERT called $bert - base - uncased$.

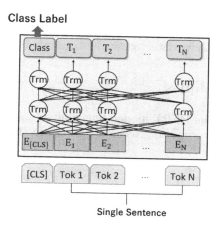

Fig. 1. Fine-tuning model of Devlin et al. multi-class classification task [8]

3.3   Multi-Head-Attention

The BERT model uses a deep learning model called Transformer, which was announced by Vaswani et al. in 2017 [19]. The Transformer is based on the encoder-decoder model shown in Fig. 2, in which Self-Attention is incorporated.

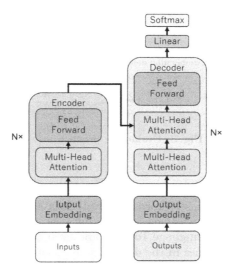

Fig. 2. Transformer model of Vaswani et al. [19]

Self-Attention is a model proposed in Lin et al. research. That mechanism can quantify the weight of the embedded word in embedding vectorized sentences in the hidden layer [12]. Multi-Head-Attention is a mechanism to obtain the final output by repeating Self-Attention for the set number of layers and multiplying the obtained outputs. In this research, we quantify the weight vector of Multi-Head-Attention by normalizing it, and aggregate the words that are noticed during classification.

4   Evaluation Method

4.1   Overview

Figure 3 shows the evaluation procedure. Evaluation is divided into three phases: training phase, detection accuracy comparison phase, and combination detection phase. Evaluation uses three datasets with different categories. Data pre-processing each datasets and split it into training and test data. We create a trained model in the training phase. In the detection accuracy comparison phase, we compare the detection accuracy with previous studies. At that time, the weight of Multi-Head-Attention is quantified. Finally, in the combination detection phase, we confirm the detection accuracy for test data of different categories. The details of each procedure are explained below.

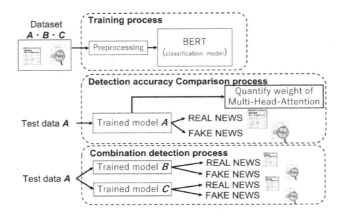

Fig. 3. Evaluation procedure

4.2 Data Pre-processing

In the data pre-processing, stopwords removal, data cleansing, tokenizing, and data set partitioning are performed for each data set. Stopwords were installed from the NLTK (Natural Language Toolkit) library and deleted from the text [5]. In data cleansing, blank lines in the dataset were deleted, and items other than REAL or FAKE labels and text were deleted. In addition, comment-outs, URLs, and special symbols that have no meaning in the text were deleted using regular expressions. Word segmentation was performed using Wordpiece-Tokenizer, a tokenization algorithm for BERT published in Huggingface [1]. The dataset was randomly split into training and test data in a ratio of 8:2.

4.3 Detection Accuracy Comparison Phase

Using a BERT fine-tuning model as a classifier, we create a trained model and compare detection accuracy. The BERT fine-tuning model is based on the published basic model shown in the Fig. 4 with the Linear module added.

Mini-batch learning is performed by setting hyper parameters such as the number of epochs and batch size. Each hyper parameters are shown in Table 2.

Table 2. Hyper parameters

	ISOT	COVID-19	FA-KES
Batch size	128	64	16
Epochs	3	14	8
Max length	256	50	256
Optimizer	Adam		
Learning rate	0.00005		

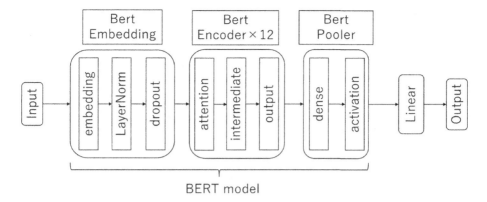

Fig. 4. Evaluation model

The optimizer and learning rate were selected from among the basic parameters given in the work of Devlin et al. [8]. For batch size, number of epochs, and data length, values with low validation loss were selected through preliminary experiments. Classification is performed using the same parameters as training, and its accuracy is compared with previous studies for each datasets.

During classification, the Multi-Head-Attention weights of each text are quantified and the top five words are extracted and aggregated for each confusion matrix.

4.4   Combination Detection Phase

We detect fake news using two different trained models in the detection accuracy comparison phase. These results are compared with the classification results of the detection accuracy comparison phase.

5   Evaluation Experiment

5.1   Dataset

In this study, we used three datasets of different genres. Table 3 shows the breakdown of the divided datasets.

Table 3. dataset

dataset name	training data		test data	
	REAL	FAKE	REAL	FAKE
ISOT FAKENEWS	17172	18709	4243	4772
COVID-19	4480	4080	1120	1020
FA-KES	338	315	89	63

ISOT FAKENEWS. This is a dataset of English fake news proposed by Ahmed et al. Real news was collected from Reuters.com and fake news from unreliable websites flagged by Politifact and Wikipedia [4]. The number of data is approximately 44,000. It contains information such as article titles, texts, and article publication dates, and is mostly global news and political news.

COVID-19. A dataset of fake news about COVID-19 proposed by Patwa et al. Collected from 10700 social media posts and articles such as Facebook, Twitter and Instagram [14]. Real news is collected from official accounts such as WHO (World Health Organization) and information sent from medical institutions such as CDC (Centers for Disease Control and Prevention). On the other hand, fake news is collected from information about the new coronavirus infectious disease that has been determined to be fake news by famous fact-checking sites such as PolitiFact, Snopes, and Boom live. There are 5600 real news and 5100 fake news.

FA-KES. A dataset of fake news related to the Syrian conflict proposed by Fatima et al., which consists of 804 news articles [2]. Article credibility is judged based on information obtained from VDC (Violations Documentation Center) of Syria.

5.2 Environment

Table 4 shows the environment used in the experiment, and Table 5 shows the main libraries used. WordPieceTokenizer and bert-base-uncased-vocab, which are used in BERT pre-training, were used as the tokenizer and vocabulary, respectively. Bert-base-uncased-vocab contains about 30000 words.

Table 4. Environment

CPU	Core i7-9700K 3.60 GHz
Memory	64 GB
GPU	NVIDIA GeForce RTX 2080 Ti
OS	Windows10 Home
Programing language	Python3.8.9

Table 5. Library

machine learning library	PyTorch 1.7.1 scikit-learn 1.0.2
Tokenizer	Wordpiece Tokenizer
Pre-train model	bert-base-uncaced
Vocab	bert-base-uncased-vocab

5.3   Experiment Content

Experimental Conditions. For each dataset, we extracted training data and test data by label of FAKE and REAL, and combined them to create training data. test data was also created by the same process, and the same process was performed for each datasets. 20% of the training data was used as validation data.

Comparative Experiment. We compared the detection accuracy of fake news using a trained model of BERT with previous studies [3, 14, 16–18]. In some of the previous studies, the experimental conditions and hyperparameters were not publicly available and could not be matched. In addition, in order to investigate the words attracting attention in fake news classification, we quantified the weight of Multi-Head-Attention in each dataset. Numericalization of weights was performed by the following method.

1. Weights were quantified for each text.
2. The weight of Self-Attention given to each word was extracted 12 times, and the weight of Multi-Head-Attention was calculated by averaging the weight of each word.
3. Only words with a standardized weight value of 0 or more were targeted, and only the top 5 words with the highest weight were extracted, and aggregated by test data.
4. Special tokens such as "[SEP]" and "[UNK]" were excluded from the aggregation.

Furthermore, in order to confirm that the fake news detection model depends on the features of the training data, we evaluated 6 patterns by combining the 3 trained models and the test data. Since the data length differs depending on the dataset, it was set according to the data length of the test data.

5.4   Experimental Result

We confirm the results of comparison with previous studies in the fake news detection model, aggregate the weights of Multi-Head-Attention, and confirm the detection accuracy between different datasets. Figure 5, Fig. 6 and Fig. 7 show the results of comparison with previous studies for each datasets. The vertical axis of each graph is the classification model, and the horizontal axis is the value of each evaluation index. In this study, we focus on Accuracy and F1 to evaluate the accuracy of the detector. Regarding the results of ISOT FAKENEWS, the Accuracy of this study was 0.99 and the F1 was 0.99, which is a high result, confirming that the classification was done to the same extent as the previous study.

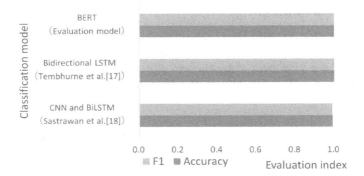

Fig. 5. Comparison with previous study of ISOT FAKENEWS

Regarding the results of COVID-19, the accuracy of this study was 0.91 and the F1 was 0.90, confirming a slightly lower accuracy than the previous study by Samadi et al.

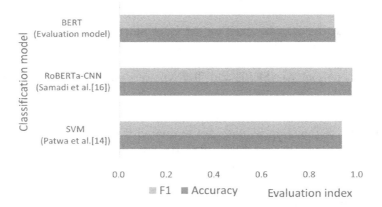

Fig. 6. Comparison with previous study of COVID-19

Regarding the results of FA-KES, Accuracy in this study was 0.52 and F1 was 0.40, confirming that classification is almost impossible. In the previous study by Fatima et al., accuracy was 0.74 and F1 was 0.78 even with the text-based detector, resulting in significantly inferior accuracy in this study.

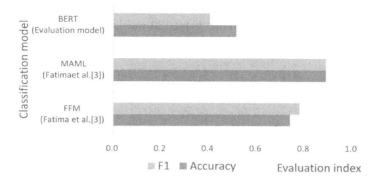

Fig. 7. Comparison with previous study of FA-KES

Figure 8 shows a comparison between the results of evaluation by combining the test data and the trained model and the evaluation results with the same data set. The vertical axis represents the combination of the test dataset and the trained model, and the horizontal axis represents the value of the evaluation index. In addition, the part surrounded by the frame shows the evaluation result with the same data set previously performed. The results of all six combination experiments showed that no combination improved both accuracy and F1 values compared to the same type of data set.

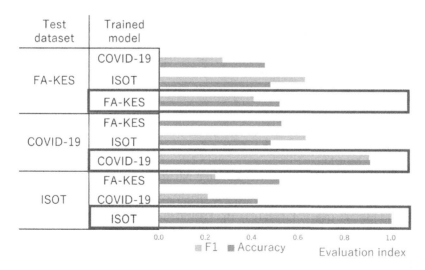

Fig. 8. Result of combining the test data and the trained model

The words that received attention in Multi-Head-Attention were tabulated for each dataset. The top 40 words aggregated from the text data classified as True Positive are shown in the Table 6. Background colors were applied to words that were duplicated in two or more datasets. As a result of tallying up to the top 40 words, 15 words, or 14%, of the total 120 words were duplicated between datasets.

Table 6. Top 40 words with the highest number of times Multi-Head-Attention weights in each datasets

RANK	ISOT	COVID19	FA-KES	RANK	ISOT	COVID19	FA-KES
1	**trump**	corona	##s	21	donald	##n	monday
2	**said**	##vid	al	22	watch	##p	##or
3	**would**	##virus	reported	23	states	fact	countryside
4	##s	19	##e	24	##ing	facebook	injured
5	hillary	**trump**	2011	25	##st	**said**	casualties
6	com	##e	damage	26	back	##t	according
7	time	**people**	conflict	27	bu	vaccine	##ad
8	##e	##19	**said**	28	obama	china	**says**
9	yo	lock	killing	29	**also**	b	**th**
10	##t	**says**	group	30	**twitter**	test	nu
11	sh	##de	**would**	31	candidate	italy	##r
12	**one**	president	##a	32	years	news	**twitter**
13	**says**	co	observatory	33	times	virus	attack
14	via	shows	government	34	aft	health	**ou**
15	like	claim	10	35	**w**	media	##t
16	**th**	##o	source	36	**ou**	testing	houses
17	**people**	##s	**people**	37	clinton	video	members
18	new	**w**	control	38	republican	##han	11
19	##ed	pan	statement	39	21st	patients	**one**
20	featured	india	**also**	40	press	##ing	2016

6   Discussion

6.1   Versatility of BERT Fine-Tuning Model

As a result of the experiment, it was confirmed that there are high-accuracy datasets and low-accuracy datasets in the BERT fine-tuning model. In particular, the results of FA-KES show an F1 of less than 0.5. This means that the BERT fine-tuning model is limited in the types of datasets that can be detected. For more difficult datasets, we consider it necessary to combine them with other machine learning models and pre-training with more data. In addition, as a result of combining the trained model and test data and evaluated, almost all combinations decreased detection accuracy. From the above, we believe that there is room for improvement regarding the versatility of the BERT fine-tuning model.

6.2   Commonalities of Fake News

A comparison of the top 40 words in each dataset showed that, with the exception of sub-words, only three words overlapped in the three datasets. Many other words were also confirmed to be in line with the characteristics of each dataset. This means that there are few common features in the words of interest for detecting. However, the detection accuracy was low in FA-KES. Therefore, if the detection accuracy is improved by pre-training and the weights of Multi-Head-Attention are aggregated, there is a possibility that words different from those in the present study will be focused on.

6.3   Study Ethics

All three datasets used in this study are publicly available. In addition, the library used to implement the BERT fine-tuning model is also available free of charge. Therefore, to construct an environment similar to this research is easy, and we think that the reproducibility of this research is high.

6.4   Study Limitations

In this study, in order to quantify the weight of Multi-Head-Attention, we conducted an experiment using a BERT fine-tuning model. However, there are data sets with low detection accuracy, and there is room for improvement such as combining with other machine learning models for detection accuracy. In addition, since we used the word list provided for the BERT model in this research, we were not able to aggregate using all the words included in the dataset. could not be confirmed. To perform pre-learning using the dataset used in the experiment and create vocabulary, it may be possible to extract features different from this study.

7   Conclusion

In this study, we focused on the weight of the Multi-Head-Attention of the BERT model, and aggregated what words were paid attention to detecting fake news. As a result, the data sets are different, the words to be focused on during detection are also different, indicating that there are few features common to fake news. By combining three datasets with different features, we show that fake news detection using fine-tuning model of BERT depends on the features of the training data. Since this is the first study to quantify and analyze the weight of Multi-Head-Attention in a fake news detection model, provided new knowledge regarding the improvement of text-based fake news detection models. A future issue is to improve the versatility of the detection model. We will create a pre-learning model for BERT, create a vocabulary for fake news, and combine it with other machine learning models to improve versatility. In addition, not only sentences but also senders of the information are important information for detecting fake news. By improving the detection accuracy in combination with other machine learning models so that information other than text can be processed, it may be possible to discover features of fake news detection that could not be confirmed this time.

References

1. Wordpiece tokenization - hugging face course. https://huggingface.co/course/chapter6/6?fw=pt
2. Abu Salem, F., Al Feel, R., Elbassuoni, S., Jaber, M., Farah, M.: Dataset for fake news and articles detection (2019). https://doi.org/10.5281/zenodo.2532642
3. Abu Salem, F.K., Al Feel, R., Elbassuoni, S., Ghannam, H., Jaber, M., Farah, M.: Meta-learning for fake news detection surrounding the syrian war. Patterns **2**(11), 100369 (2021). https://doi.org/10.1016/j.patter.2021.100369. https://www.sciencedirect.com/science/article/pii/S2666389921002312
4. Ahmed, H., Traore, I., Saad, S.: Detection of online fake news using N-gram analysis and machine learning techniques. In: Traore, I., Woungang, I., Awad, A. (eds.) ISDDC 2017. LNCS, vol. 10618, pp. 127–138. Springer, Cham (2017). https://doi.org/10.1007/978-3-319-69155-8_9
5. Bird, S., Klein, E., Loper, E.: Natural Language Processing with Python: Analyzing Text with the Natural Language Toolkit. O'Reilly Media Inc., Sebastopol (2009)
6. Chauhan, T., Palivela, H.: Optimization and improvement of fake news detection using deep learning approaches for societal benefit. Int. J. Inf. Manag. Data Insights **1**(2), 100051 (2021). https://doi.org/10.1016/j.jjimei.2021.100051. https://www.sciencedirect.com/science/article/pii/S2667096821000446
7. Devlin, J., Chang, M., Lee, K., Toutanova, K.: BERT: pre-training of deep bidirectional transformers for language understanding. CoRR abs/1810.04805 (2018). http://arxiv.org/abs/1810.04805
8. Devlin, J., Chang, M., Lee, K., Toutanova, K.: BERT: pre-training of deep bidirectional transformers for language understanding. In: Burstein, J., Doran, C., Solorio, T. (eds.) Proceedings of the 2019 Conference of the North American Chapter of the Association for Computational Linguistics: Human Language Technologies, NAACL-HLT 2019, Minneapolis, MN, USA, 2–7 June 2019, Volume 1 (Long and Short Papers), pp. 4171–4186. Association for Computational Linguistics (2019). https://doi.org/10.18653/v1/n19-1423
9. Hakak, S., Alazab, M., Khan, S., Gadekallu, T.R., Maddikunta, P.K.R., Khan, W.Z.: An ensemble machine learning approach through effective feature extraction to classify fake news. Future Gener. Comput. Syst. **117**, 47–58 (2021). https://doi.org/10.1016/j.future.2020.11.022. https://www.sciencedirect.com/science/article/pii/S0167739X20330466
10. Kaliyar, R.K., Goswami, A., Narang, P.: FakeBERT: fake news detection in social media with a BERT-based deep learning approach. Multimedia Tools Appl. **80**(8), 11765–11788 (2021). https://doi.org/10.1007/s11042-020-10183-2
11. Khan, J.Y., Khondaker, M.T.I., Afroz, S., Uddin, G., Iqbal, A.: A benchmark study of machine learning models for online fake news detection. Mach. Learn. Appl. **4**, 100032 (2021). https://doi.org/10.1016/j.mlwa.2021.100032. https://www.sciencedirect.com/science/article/pii/S266682702100013X
12. Lin, Z., Feng, M., dos Santos, C.N., Yu, M., Xiang, B., Zhou, B., Bengio, Y.: A structured self-attentive sentence embedding. CoRR abs/1703.03130 (2017). http://arxiv.org/abs/1703.03130

13. Ministry of Internal Affairs and Communications: Information and Communications in Japan WHITE PAPER 2019 | The Fake News Trend. https://www.soumu.go.jp/johotsusintokei/whitepaper/eng/WP2019/2019-index.html
14. Patwa, P., et al.: Overview of constraint 2021 shared tasks: detecting English Covid-19 fake news and Hindi hostile posts (2021)
15. Rai, N., Kumar, D., Kaushik, N., Raj, C., Ali, A.: Fake news classification using transformer based enhanced LSTM and BERT. Int. J. Cogn. Comput. Eng. **3**, 98–105 (2022). https://doi.org/10.1016/j.ijcce.2022.03.003. https://www.sciencedirect.com/science/article/pii/S2666307422000092
16. Samadi, M., Mousavian, M., Momtazi, S.: Deep contextualized text representation and learning for fake news detection (2021). https://doi.org/10.1016/j.ipm.2021.102723. https://www.sciencedirect.com/science/article/pii/S0306457321002077
17. Sastrawan, I.K., Bayupati, I., Arsa, D.M.S.: Detection of fake news using deep learning CNN-RNN based methods (2021). https://doi.org/10.1016/j.icte.2021.10.003. https://www.sciencedirect.com/science/article/pii/S2405959521001375
18. Tembhurne, J.V., Almin, M.M., Diwan, T.: MC-DNN: fake news detection using multi-channel deep neural networks. Int. J. Semant. Web Inf. Syst. **18**(1), 1–20 (2022). https://doi.org/10.4018/IJSWIS.295553
19. Vaswani, A., et al.: Attention is all you need. In: Guyon, I., et al. (eds.) Advances in Neural Information Processing Systems, vol. 30. Curran Associates, Inc. (2017)
20. Wani, A., Joshi, I., Khandve, S., Wagh, V., Joshi, R.: Evaluating deep learning approaches for Covid19 fake news detection. In: Chakraborty, T., Shu, K., Bernard, H.R., Liu, H., Akhtar, M.S. (eds.) CONSTRAINT 2021. CCIS, vol. 1402, pp. 153–163. Springer, Cham (2021). https://doi.org/10.1007/978-3-030-73696-5_15

Twitter Bots Influence on the Russo-Ukrainian War During the 2022 Italian General Elections

Francesco Luigi De Faveri[1] , Luca Cosuti[1] , Pier Paolo Tricomi[1,2](✉) ,
and Mauro Conti[1,2]

[1] University of Padua, Padua, Italy
{francescoluigi.defaveri,luca.cosuti}@studenti.unipd.it,
{tricomi,conti}@math.unipd.it
[2] Chisito S.r.l, Padua, Italy

Abstract. In February 2022, Russia launched a full-scale invasion of Ukraine. This event had global repercussions, especially on the political decisions of European countries. As expected, the role of Italy in the conflict became a major campaign issue for the Italian General Election held on 25 September 2022. Politicians frequently use Twitter to communicate during political campaigns, but bots often interfere and attempt to manipulate elections. Hence, understanding whether bots influenced public opinion regarding the conflict and, therefore, the elections is essential.

In this work, we investigate how Italian politics responded to the Russo-Ukrainian conflict on Twitter and whether bots manipulated public opinion before the 2022 general election. We first analyze 39,611 tweet of six major political Italian parties to understand how they discussed the war during the period February-December 2022. Then, we focus on the 360,823 comments under the last month's posts before the elections, discovering around 12% of the commenters are bots. By examining their activities, it becomes clear they both distorted how war topics were treated and influenced real users during the last month before the elections.

Keywords: Russo-Ukrainian War · Italian Political Elections · Social Network Analysis · Bots Detection · Bots Influence · Twitter · Ukraine · Russia

1 Introduction

At the dawn of 24 February 2022, the president of the Russian Federation, Vladimir V. Putin, announced an imminent "Special Military Operation" in the oriental part of Ukraine. Soon thereafter, the global political leaders decided which side to support in the Russo-Ukrainian conflict. Along with most European countries, Italian politics sided with Ukraine by approving a law decree on 28 February 2022 [47]. The consequences of this decision were numerous. For

---

F. Faveri and L. Cosuti—Authors contributed equally.

B. Arief et al. (Eds.): SocialSec 2023, LNCS 14097, pp. 38–57, 2023.
https://doi.org/10.1007/978-981-99-5177-2_3

instance, Italy reported a massive increase (+138%) of cyber-attacks directed at critical infrastructures, apparently caused by hackers lined up with Russia [34]. Additionally, Italian public opinion soon divided over the modalities of supporting Ukraine, such as sending military aid or applying sanctions to Russia. Since international relations inevitably impact democratic domestic politics [23], the role of Italy in the Russo-Ukrainian conflict was a major campaign issue for the Italian (snap) general election on 25 September 2022.

People and politicians started expressing their concerns and opinions regarding the Russo-Ukrainian war on social media platforms like Facebook [11], Tik-Tok, Instagram, and Twitter. As largely demonstrated in the literature, opinions on social media are often manipulated by social bots [6,57,63] or colluding activities [18,55]. Clear evidence has been found, for instance, in Japan's 2014 general election [50] or USA presidential elections in 2016 [32] and 2020 [12]. Presumably, the last Italian general elections have not been exempted. Figure 1 illustrates a bot's provocative tweet in response to Matteo Salvini, a leader of Italian politics. Therefore, studying the impact of bots is fundamental for understanding the potential consequences they may have on social dynamics and online interactions. By investigating the role of bots in shaping the community, we can gain valuable insights into how they may have influenced the dissemination of information and the formation of opinions.

(a) Original tweet   (b) Translated version

Fig. 1. Bot response to an Italian politician expressing a strong-sided opinion regarding the conflict.

Contribution. In this work, we investigate how Italian politics responded to the Russo-Ukrainian conflict on Twitter and whether bots manipulated public opinion before the 2022 general elections. In particular, we collected 39,611 tweets made by members of the main 6 political parties that belong to a left-wing or right-wing coalition from the period February-December 2022. We first conduct a semantic and temporal analysis of how politicians discussed the war, showing that some parties showed a high level of interest in the conflict and were actively engaged in commenting on the issue while others remained relatively silent. Secondly, we analyze 360,823 comments made during the last month of the political campaigns, from 23 August 2022 to 23 September 2022, examining bots' activities and influences on genuine users. We detected bots using Botometer [64], a popular tool capable of evaluating the realness of an account using a Machine Learning-based classification method. Our results show that around

12% of the profiles commenting on political posts are bots. Particularly, we found that bots have manipulated topics related to the Russo-Ukrainian war, especially on the center-right coalition, and that they influenced real users, often driving o soliciting discussions related to the conflict. We summarize our contributions as follows:

- We collected a dataset of 39,611 tweets posted between 24 February 2022 and 31 December 2022, from the six major parties in Italy, and 360,823 comments from 105,603 unique users who replied during the last month of the 2022 Italian general elections. The dataset will be made publicly available for future research;
- We provide a detailed analysis of how the 6 major Italian parties expressed and sided concerning the Russo-Ukrainian war on Twitter from the beginning of the war to the end of 2022;
- We examine the bots' impact on Twitter and how they influenced real users regarding the Russo-Ukrainian war during the last month of the general elections.

Organization. Section 2 discusses related works, while Sect. 3 presents the dataset used in the experiments. In Sect. 4 and Sect. 5, we analyze politics in Italy during the conflict and the bots' influence on the elections, respectively. Section 6 makes further discussion and Sect. 7 concludes the paper.

2   Related Works

In this section, we focus on the state-of-the-art analysis of bot infiltration in delicate scenarios and opinion manipulation through Twitter. Antonakaki et al. [4] conducted a comprehensive literature review presenting different approaches and techniques used for Twitter research. The authors acknowledged that Twitter had become a valuable data source for researchers, offering data for many purposes, such as forecasting social, economic, or commercial indicators [5] as well as assessing and predicting political polarization [25,31]. For instance, Weber et al. [59], during the 2013 "Arab Spring" in Egypt, collected and analyzed a large dataset of tweets to categorize the users based on their political affiliation.

However, such information is often undermined by the presence of bots, i.e., automated accounts used to engage and behave mimicking human users, often controlled by a bot master. While there are some benevolent social media bots, many are used for dishonest and nefarious purposes [1,56]. The existence of bots on the Twitter platform has been firmly established through many academic investigations [2,13,14,26,35], and news articles [28,48]. Weng et al. [60] explained the differences between the opinion manipulations done by bots compared with those from real users, and Mazza et al. [38] investigated the difference between trolls, social bots, and humans on Twitter. Notably, these accounts can wield an exceptionally strong influence in delicate situations [3], such as stock trading [15], sensitive content diffusion [52], vaccination [10], or political elections manipulation. Regarding the latest, Pastor et al. [43] analyzed the presence and behavior of social bots on Twitter in the context of the November 2019 Spanish general election. They limited the analysis of the bots' interaction up to seven days before Election day using Social Feed Manager [24] to capture the tweets and analyze the bot. Fernquist et al. [19] presented a study on the influence of bots in the Swedish general election held in September 2018. Bessi and Ferrara [8] investigated how the presence of social media bots impacted the 2016 Presidential elections in America, and similar works were conducted on the latest one in 2020 [12,21]. For a comprehensive overview of bots, political elections, and social media, we refer to [20].

3   Dataset Creation

In this study, we collected our own Twitter dataset due to the unique nature of the analysis. We selected six parties to analyze according to the current political scenario in Italy. In particular, we considered:

- The coalition that preceded Mario Draghi's technical government (the so-called "giallo-rosso" government, who guided Italy from 5 September 2019 until 13 February 2021 [30,41]), made by the Democratic Party (Partito Democratico, PD), the Five Stars Movement (Movimento 5 Stelle, M5S)
- The Italian Green-Left party (Sinistra Italiana-Verdi, SiVe);
- The coalition that won the September 2022 elections, and is currently in power: Brothers of Italy (Fratelli d'Italia, FdI), League for Salvini Premier (Lega per Salvini Premier, Lega), and Forward Italy (Forza Italia, FI).

We then model each of the parties to be constructed as:

$$D_i = [P, L, p_1, \ldots, p_6]$$

where:

- D_i is the Dataset, $i = 1, \ldots, 6$, one for each party.
- P is the "Party account", e.g., @FratellidItalia.
- L is the "Leader account", e.g., @GiorgiaMeloni.
- $p_1, \ldots, p_6$ are six "major political figures" in that party, e.g., @DSantanche, @Ignazio_LaRussa, @FrancescoLollo1, @FidanzaCarlo, @fabiorampelli and @isabellarauti.

The final dataset has been constructed by collecting all the tweets from the party account, the leader account, and six other politicians in the party (following the structure defined above) that were posted from 24 February 2022 until 31 December 2022. To download the tweets, we queried the official Twitter API [16] to browse each profile's timeline and retrieve all the necessary tweets. After this initial collection of tweets, we focused on the posts published during the latest month of the political campaign in Italy, from 23 August 2022 until 23 September 2022. We considered all the content shared by the secretary of each party and every reply. An overview of the full dataset can be seen in Table 1. We indicate the party, the party leader, the selected profiles we fetched the information from, the cumulative number of followers of each party's profiles, and the overall number of posted tweets. For the last month of the political campaign, we considered all the content shared by the secretary of each party and every reply, as well as the number of unique commenters. These numbers represent only the tweets directly posted by the party members. During the collection, we excluded the retweets to reduce the number of repeated tweets between different accounts, to avoid redundancy, and to have a real and clear opinion from each profile.

Table 1. Complete overview of the dataset.

Party	Leader	Members	Total Followers	Posted Tweets	Replies to Secretary	Unique Users Replying
PD	Letta	Serracchiani, Orlando, Madia, Provenzano, Boldrini,Gentiloni	3.511M	4357	158747	35571
FdI	Meloni	La Russa, Santanchè, Lollobrigida, Fidanza, Rampelli, Rauti	2.471M	6610	60237	22670
M5S	Conte	Fico, Taverna, Appendino, Sibilia, Grillo, Maiorino	2.419M	3672	47886	14255
Lega	Salvini	Fontana, Arrigoni, Pillon, Rixi, Centinaio, Bongiorno	1.898M	15797	59317	20159
FI	Berlusconi	Tajani, Bernini, Gasparri, Fitto, Casellati, Ronzulli	804.2K	4172	29597	9962
SiVe	Fratoianni	Bonelli, Soumahoro, Alemanni, Evi, Marcon, Pellegrino	411K	5003	5038	2986

4   The Russo-Ukrainian War in Italian Politics

We start our analysis by understanding whether and how frequently the Italian parties mentioned the Russo-Ukranian conflict (Sect. 4.1). After that, we conduct a temporal analysis to determine when the conflict was primarily discussed, with a particular focus on election time (Sect. 4.2).

4.1   The Importance of Conflict for Italian Political Parties

Our objective in this section is to answer the question, "How did Italian politicians discuss the war?". After the creation of the datasets $D_1, \ldots, D_6$, we cleaned each tweet by (i) removing emojis with the tool clean-text [22], (ii) removing the links, and (iii) removing stop words [17]. Figure 2 shows the Word Clouds for each party.[1]

The first row contains the Word Clouds associated with the parties belonging to the center-left coalition: PD focuses mostly on "lavoro" ("job"), "destra" ("right-wing"), and "Ucraina" ("Ukraine"); M5S concentrates on their own public appearance, with words like "TV" and "intervista" ("interview"), and its leader "Giuseppe Conte". Finally, SiVe emphasizes their new coalition with the words "AlleanzaVerdiSinistra" ("Green Party-Italian Left Coalition") and "europaverde" ("Green Europe").

---

[1] We computed the word clouds using WordCloud Python Library [42].

(a) PD   (b) M5S   (c) SiVe

(d) FdI   (e) Lega   (f) FI

Fig. 2. Word Clouds for the tweets of parties captured.

On the other hand, the second row is made by the parties belonging to the center-right coalition: FdI, similarly to PD, concentrates on their opposing wing with words like "sinistra" ("left-wing") and "governo" ("government"); Lega is vastly influenced by its leader "Matteo Salvini" and his public appearances, indicated by words like "TV" and "Radio". FI rotates around its leader too, as the most commonly used words are "Presidente" ("President") and "Berlusconi". Since the word clouds only provide a high-level view of the most commonly used words, we refine our analysis by inspecting the topics addressed by the parties. Indeed, political parties usually shape their campaigns by supporting or emphasizing particular themes. Thus, we extracted the topic they mainly discussed, and analyzed whether the Russo-Ukrainian war played a prominent role. To extract the topics, we started by calculating the embeddings of our tweets using the pre-trained multilingual Sentence-Bert model [46] supporting Italian language[2]. The corresponding tweets' embeddings (i.e., vectors of 768 dimensions) were more similar when their content was semantically closer. By leveraging this feature, we could cluster the data to find topics. First, we used UMAP algorithm [40] to decrease the vectors dimension to 5, setting n_neighbors=15. Then, we applied the density-based HDBSCAN clustering algorithm [39] to define clusters of at least 15 points, using the Excess of Mass selection method and Euclidean distance as the similarity metric. Once the clusters were defined (i.e., collections of semantically similar tweets), we extracted their most important words to manually label the corresponding topic. We calculated words' importance by using class-based TF-IDF [27]. In this version of the algorithm, each document corresponds to a topic (or class), i.e., the aggregation of all the tweets belonging to that topic. We can then identify the most representative words of a topic by selecting its most frequent words that are less frequent in the other topics. Table 2 shows the most discussed topics for each party, along with the percentage

---

[2] We used the model `distilbert-multilingual-nli-stsb-quora-ranking`.

of tweets posted about them. For conciseness, we report only the top-7 topics for each party.

Table 2. Top-7 topics and the number of tweets for each party.

PD		M5S		SiVe		FdI		Lega		FI	
%	Topic	%	Topic	%	Topic	%	Topic	%	Topic	%	Topic
24.25	RU-UA War	16.42	Italy	80.10	Vote Left	24.57	Italy	26.90	Italy	88.97	Berlusconi
14.96	Salary	14.54	Energy	12.34	Do	16.28	Vote	17.45	Energy	5.10	RU-UA War
10.87	Truth	11.12	RU-UA War	3.04	RU-UA War	12.82	Meloni	10.84	RU-UA War	1.23	Agenda
10.16	Italy	10.35	Mafia	1.81	Education	10.27	Do	8.71	Immigrants	1.06	Pandemic
8.74	Europe	9.15	Salary	0.64	Military Exp	8.49	RU-UA War	7.15	Taxes	0.90	Italy
7.48	Vote	8.81	Agenda	0.48	Iran Women	8.34	Taxes	6.53	Rome	0.85	Foreign wars
6.85	Fascism	7.96	Courage	0.48	Climate	6.05	Energy	6.24	Vote	0.59	Europe

It immediately stands out that the Russo-Ukrainian conflict was a prominent topic for each party. Particularly, the topic placed in the first three positions for five out of six parties. PD mentioned the conflict the most, while FDI was the least. By inspecting the most important words for the topic, we find the words "sanctions" to appear frequently for PD, M5S, Lega, and FI, "weapons" for PD and SiVe, and "solidarity" for M5S and FDI. In any case, this topic appears to have a similar impact on other "internal" matters like taxes, migrants, or energy. Only SiVe and FI show a heavily unbalanced topic frequency. In both of these cases, however, the war played a prominent role. To conclude, all major Italian parties discussed and included the war in their campaigning.

4.2   Temporal Analysis of Russo-Ukrainian Discussions

We noted that each party included the Russo-Ukrainian war in their political campaigns. However, it is important to understand when the parties discussed it the most. We could expect, for instance, high frequencies at the beginning of the war or near the elections. In such a sense, a temporal analysis can help us understand which parties concentrated their whole campaigns on the war or only referred to it in crucial moments to express solidarity. To this aim, we created stack plots to inspect the temporal references to "Ukraine" and "Russia" during the year. Specifically, we computed the frequency of tweets related to Ukraine and Russia using a bag of words approach, i.e., by counting the number of occurrences of Ukraine/Russia-related words, such as "Ukrainian", "Zelensky" or "Russian", "Putin". The results are presented in Fig. 3. For clarity, we also reported four major events during the conflict, such as the three main phases described in [62] and [58].

All parties discussed the Russo-Ukrainian war mostly between the beginning and end of **phase 1**. Particularly, PD shows the most active involvement, which is in accordance with Table 2, while FI displays the highest number of tweets at

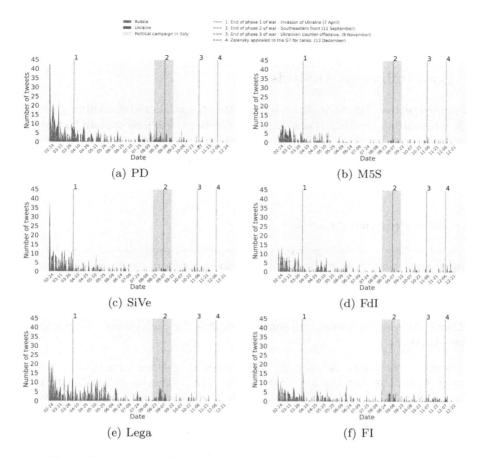

Fig. 3. Temporal trends for the war-related tweets, 15 days aggregation.

the end of **phase 1**. Over the year, all parties gradually decreased their discussion of the topic, except for PD, Lega, and FI, which devoted a significant portion of their campaign propaganda. Interestingly, while Russia and Ukraine-related words were balanced initially, these parties focused most on Russia-related words during the campaign, showing a condemnation attitude rather than solidarity, as confirmed by manual inspection. The remaining parties did not accentuate the topic during the campaign, except near the end of phase 2.

Following the election, which saw the center-right coalition led by FdI winning, there was a noticeable decline in the number of tweets related to the war from most political parties. In contrast, FdI and FI continued to post about the war, sometimes with increasing activity during **phase 3** and **phase 4**. In these cases, the focus seems to have switched to Ukraine rather than Russia, probably reflecting the evolution of the conflict. These considerations suggest that while the Russian-Ukrainian war may no longer be a trending topic among most political parties, it remained quite an important issue for FdI and FI, who continue supporting Ukraine in their political messages [53].

5   Bots Influence Analysis

In the previous section, we highlighted that the Russo-Ukrainian conflict played a major role during the 2022 Italian General Elections. We now explore how many bots participated in the political discussions (Sect. 5.1), whether bots manipulated or distorted the discussions of the Russo-Ukrainian conflict, (Sect. 5.2), and whether they influenced real users or simply followed the flow of the conversation (Sect. 5.3).

5.1   Bots Presence Analysis

To evaluate the bots' influence on elections, we retrieved all replies under the posts of each party's secretary during the last month of elections, between 23 August and 23 September 2022. To detect bots among the commenters, similar to previous works on Italian tweets [36,37], we employed Botometer [64], a widespread ML-based tool [33,51] that distinguishes between legitimate users and bots. Among the metrics, Botometer returns, for each checked account, the following scores:

- `overall raw score`: score in $[0, 1]$ determining whether an account is a bot;
- `cap`: (Complete Automation) Probability in $[0, 1]$ that an account with that score or greater is a bot. In other words, it expresses the prediction's confidence.

A classic approach to classify a bot takes the `overall raw score` and compares it to a fixed threshold (e.g., > 0.50 classified as a bot, ≤ 0.50 classified as human). Instead, for each user, we labeled as bot those with `overall raw score` $>$ `cap`, with `cap` > 0.80. By doing so, we adopted a dynamic and more accurate threshold than the classic approach, reducing the number of false positives. This method was confirmed by parsing several accounts manually, and among them, users with a high CAP (i.e., above 0.80) value were always classified as bots. Table 3 reports the number of unique accounts labeled as bots that replied under the party's secretary. On average, we found ∼12% of bots replying to each secretary, with Meloni showing the higher percentage of bots (15.08%) and Fratoianni the lowest (9.61%).

We further investigate the categories of bots interacting with Twitter profiles, according to Botometer classification. In particular, bots fall into the following categories:

- *Financial*: bots that post using cashtags;
- *Fake-follower*: bots purchased to increase follower counts;
- *Spammer*: accounts labeled as spambots from several datasets;
- *Self-declared*: known bots listed on botwiki.org;

Table 3. Percentages of bots and non-bots for each profile.

Profile	Unique Users	Bots (%)	Non-bots (%)
Letta	35,571	10.76	89.24
Conte	14,255	12.20	87.80
Fratoianni	2,986	9.61	90.39
Meloni	22,670	15.08	84.92
Salvini	20,159	11.12	88.88
Berlusconi	9,962	12.92	87.08

- *Astroturf*: accounts that primarily focus on influencing public opinion, often being part of a network;
- *Other*: miscellaneous bots.

Given that Botometer's response includes a percentage indicating the likelihood of an account belonging to each category, a bot was assigned to the category with the greatest likelihood. The final cumulative results for each politician are presented in Table 4.

Table 4. Categories of bots distribution replying to the tweets of the leaders.

Profile	Number of Bots	Financial (%)	Fake-followers (%)	Spammers (%)	Self-declared (%)	Astroturf (%)	Other (%)
Letta	3828	0.06	25.33	0.15	33.07	35.83	5.56
Conte	1739	0.08	33.87	0.08	31.27	32.04	2.67
Fratoianni	287	0.00	19.44	0.00	42.78	31.67	6.11
Meloni	3418	0.04	30.03	0.15	33.53	31.50	4.75
Salvini	2242	0.06	39.35	0.11	27.97	27.69	4.83
Berlusconi	1287	0.44	26.40	0.00	31.79	34.43	6.93

A significant proportion of counterfeit profiles engaged with political figures fall under the categories of "fake_followers" and "astroturf". This result confirms that most analyzed bots aim to influence or manipulate public opinion. Another notable percentage pertains to "self-declared" bots that, on the other hand, operate on the platform without any nefarious motives. In general, the bots distribution is consistent across all profiles.

We further investigate whether bots cooperate within the two coalitions we described in Sect. 3, namely, the Center-Right coalition (Berlusconi, Meloni, and Salvini) and the Center-Left coalition (Letta, Conte, and Fratoianni). Figure 4 shows the shared number of bots in the two coalitions. For the Center-Left coalition, many accounts identified as bots and commenting on multiple politicians are associated with Letta and Conte, the primary figures in the "giallo-rosso government" mentioned earlier. Additionally, the remaining shared bots are linked to Fratoianni and, once again, Letta, the leaders of the two largest parties comprising the Center-Left coalition in the most recent elections. On the other hand, in the Center-Right coalition, there is a significantly stronger affiliation between the three profiles, as confirmed by the interrelation between the three political parties. Several bot accounts are common to two profiles, with a select few being shared by all three, suggesting a much closer connection between the coalition's parties and their ideologies.

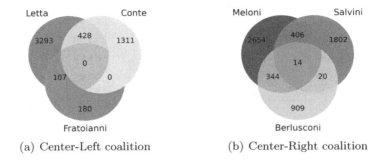

(a) Center-Left coalition   (b) Center-Right coalition

Fig. 4. Number of shared bots between profiles belonging to the same coalition. Colors are representative of the parties, according to the Italian press.

5.2   Bots Topics Distortion Analysis

We now investigate the lexical associations between the words employed by authentic and bot users during the last month of the Italian General Elections' political campaign. In this way, we can explore and understand how bots and humans communicated regarding the Russo-Ukrainian conflict, and whether bots distorted the vision of war-related topics. Inspired by the methodology introduced in Sartori et al. [49] and Tahmasbi et al. [54], we aim to discover associations between war-related words, e.g., how frequently they appear together in a tweet. For this purpose, we first trained a Word2Vec model [45] on our tweets to determine how words related to the Russian-Ukrainian war relate to each other. In this model, words with similar vectors are likelier to appear together in a tweet. Starting from the words "Russia", "Ukraine", and "War", we manually identified 10 frequent related words, selecting (i) institutional-related words, i.e., "USA", "EU", "NATO", "Europe", and "Italy"; (ii) war-related words, i.e., "weapons", "conflict", "invasion", "aggression'; (iii) "gas", as its price rose sharply due to the conflict. Subsequently, we calculated the incidence matrix $M \in \mathbb{R}^{3 \times 10}$ for each involved party, utilizing the trained Word2Vec model. The incidence matrix M can be mathematically formulated as in the Matrix 1.

$$M = \begin{pmatrix} m_{1,1} \ m_{1,2} \ \dots \ m_{1,9} \ m_{1,10} \\ m_{2,1} \ m_{2,2} \ \dots \ m_{2,9} \ m_{2,10} \\ m_{3,1} \ m_{3,2} \ \dots \ m_{3,9} \ m_{3,10} \end{pmatrix} \tag{1}$$

where $m_{ij} = \texttt{cosine\_similarity}(v_i, w_j)$, $i = 1, 2, 3$ and $j = 1, \dots, 10^3$. The words v_i are the selected words {"Russia", "Ukraine", "War"}, while the words

---

[3] The `cosine-similarity` was computed according to the formula in [61].

w_j are the selected words {"USA", "EU", "NATO", "Europe", "Italy", "weapons", "conflict", "invasion", "aggression", "gas"}. If the cosine similarity was negative, we truncated it to 0. This matrix M was computed for each party in two different scenarios:

- A *Complete* scenario, considering both replies from real and bot accounts;
- A *No Bots* scenario, considering only replies from real users.

We fed these matrices to the Gephi Software [7] to construct weighted undirected graphs, which we call "Spider Graphs" due to their shape, and we used Force-Atlas 2 [29] as Layout for the rendering. In our graphs, the nodes are the words, and the edges represent the cosine similarity. According to the incidence matrix, edges exist only between the three initial words ("Russia", "Ukraine", "War") and the 10 selected words. The node size reflects its degree (larger words have more connections), while the thickness of the edges reflects the similarity of the connected words (thicker edges connect more similar – or likely to appear together – words). Last, we applied the modularity algorithm [9] to build clusters of strictly connected words. We set the resolution parameter of the modularity algorithm to obtain three clusters: a red cluster with centroid "Russia", a green

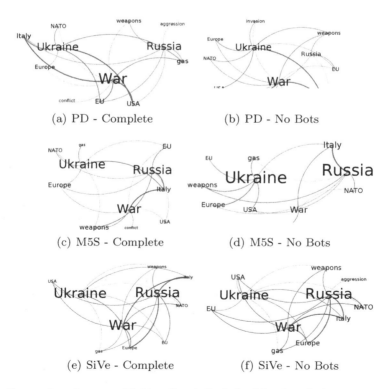

Fig. 5. Comparison between "Spider Graphs" of the Mixed and No-Bots Scenario in the Center-Left coalition.

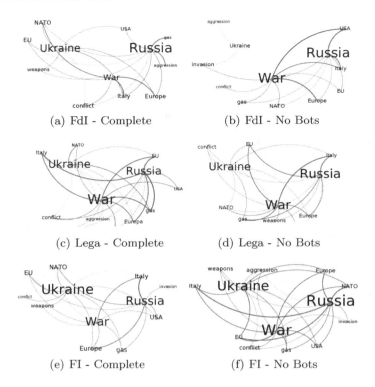

(a) FdI - Complete

(b) FdI - No Bots

(c) Lega - Complete

(d) Lega - No Bots

(e) FI - Complete

(f) FI - No Bots

Fig. 6. Comparison between "Spider Graphs" of the Complete and No Bots Scenario in the Center-Right coalition.

cluster with centroid "Ukraine", and a blue cluster with centroid "War". The remaining 10 words are then placed by the algorithm in the closest cluster, acquiring its color. Edges have the color of the cluster if they are connected to their centroid, or a mixed color if they are connected to the centroid of a different cluster. For instance, the edge between a word of the "War" (blue) cluster and "Russia" (red) will be purple (blue + red). Figure 5 and Fig. 6 present the spider graphs in the *Complete* and *No Bots* scenario of the Center-Left and Center-Right coalitions, respectively.

For the Center-Left coalition, the most significant change between the two scenarios concerns the M5S party. While the lexical similarity between "War" and "conflict" remains the same, there are no other words in the "War" cluster when considering the *No Bots* scenario. An important constant between the two M5S graphs is the strong link between the central node "Russia" and "Italy". The graphs of PD and SiVe seem to show several differences. In the graph Fig. 5(b) the word "gas" disappears and the cluster of "War" gains the word "Italy" from the "Ukraine" cluster. The word "weapons" is always clustered with "Russia" in all the graphs of PD and SiVe and the word "Italy" is always with Russia in M5S and SiVe. Moreover, the word "conflict" is present only in the graphs of PD and

M5S and it is absent from the ones of SiVe. The presence in the three clusters of institutional-related words, i.e. "NATO", "USA", "EU" and "Europe", seems not to have such relevant lexical importance for the parties except for "USA" and "War" in the PD scenarios.

For the Center-Right coalition, the primary observation concerns the intensified association between the central term "Russia" and words that frequently pertain to institutions, such as "Italy", "NATO", and "Europe". Another identifiable characteristic noted by the model is the substantial presence of words within the cluster associated with the term "War", whereby the most frequent ones include "gas", "invasion", and "conflict". Within this coalition, it appears that every "Russia" cluster encompasses a closely related term, such as "Italy" or "USA", with a strong connection. The strongest differences between the two scenarios appear around the "Ukraine" cluster. Indeed, for all three parties, the words within the cluster differ significantly between the *Complete* and *No Bots* scenarios. For instance, for FdI, the "Ukraine" cluster goes from "aggression" and "invasion" in the *No Bots* scenario to "NATO", "EU", and "weapons" in the *Complete* scenario. Significant differences between the scenarios also appear around the "Russia" cluster. Therefore, we notice how bots significantly impacted public opinion by going in the opposite direction of real users. Considering all the graphs, we can assert that the existence of bots appears to influence the outcomes of the clustering analysis, especially for the Center-Right coalition.

5.3 Bots Temporal Influence Analysis

To conclude our analysis, we deeply investigated the final month of the Italian elections, exploring the different discussions and perspectives surrounding the war that emerged under the leaders' posts. Our goal is to understand whether humans or bots discussed more the conflict, and which side influenced (or started) the debate. To this aim, we plot a two-scale graph for each party, considering the mean number of tweets concerning the war and the mean posting time (hour) for bots and real users. The results are shown in Fig. 7.

We computed the `harmonic_mean` with the Formula 2:

$$h_{\text{freq}} = 2 \times \frac{\text{Ukraine\_frequency} \times \text{Russia\_frequency}}{\text{Ukraine\_frequency} + \text{Russia\_frequency}} \tag{2}$$

as an indicator to visualize the number of tweets posted daily by both real users and bots during the last month of the political campaign. Ukraine and Russia posts included only strictly related words to the countries, e.g., "Ukraine", "Ukrainian", "Zelensky", and, "Russia", "Russian", "Putin".

This measure is bounded from above by the arithmetic mean, indicating its tendency to mitigate the influence of large outliers while accentuating the effect of small ones. This property allows for the evaluation of even the smallest frequencies to be computed, which may be otherwise masked by the influence of dominant outliers in the data. In this scenario, e.g., the results for a politician like Fratoianni, which has a smaller frequency of bots if compared to the other

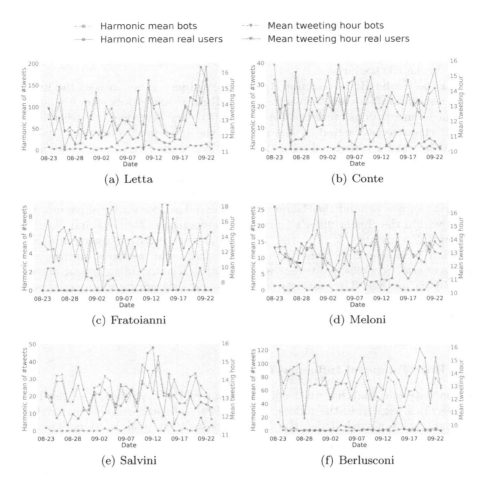

Fig. 7. Mean number of posts and mean posting time for war-related tweets in the last month of Italian elections. Data are reported for both real accounts and bots.

figures, are not suppressed, but his mean will clamp to 0. The other indicator we considered is the `mean_tweeting_hour`, which gives us the arithmetical average of posting time by both genuine and bot accounts.

We focus our attention on the blue spikes in the graphs, which indicate a quantitative increment in the number of tweets regarding the war. The majority of the spikes, either regarding the real or the fake users, concentrate on the period between 10 September and 24 September. The number of tweets posted by real users is always greater than bots' posts, which is in accordance with the percentage of bots found earlier (~12%). Looking at the `mean_tweeting_hour`, we can establish that on various occasions the bots posted tweets in a time before the spikes coming from the real users, on average. This trend is glaring for Conte, Meloni, Salvini, and Berlusconi, in which bots often started tweeting before the real users, hence influencing or driving the daily discussion.

6   Discussion

Our analyses found that Italian politics has actively considered the Russo-Ukrainian conflict in their campaigns, with parties taking on a greater role than others. Additionally, we found a fair number of bots to be active and influential during the last elections. The effect seems to be tied to the particular parties or coalitions, requiring further investigation. Indeed, we could not determine nor speculate on who was driving these bots or for what purpose. Anyhow, our findings demonstrate that external events can significantly impact local (national) ones, with unpredictable consequences. Social media platforms like Twitter are credited with democratizing discussions about politics and social issues, but as demonstrated in the literature, manipulation of information is an actual threat rather than a risk. Unfortunately, most studies addressing this issue focus on English-based data or countries, since state-of-the-art models are more reliable. However, analyzing non-English countries is of utmost interest nowadays, since every country has a significant impact on global political equilibrium.

As we found interferences in the political scenarios, bots or fake accounts might likely be involved in disinformation or other malicious activities in the country. With the rapid development of Artificial Intelligence, it could always become harder to detect these colluding entities. It is, therefore, necessary to conduct further studies to address the language-specific obstacles, as well as to identify who operates such bots to eventually detect their objectives and contrast them.

6.1   Limitations

As we mentioned earlier, our study was limited by the few models available to process the Italian language. However, we think our work can stimulate further research and improve NLP models for Italian, as well as other minor languages. An additional limitation relies on the use of the external tool Botometer for the detection of bots. As such, the reliability of our findings is contingent on the accuracy of this tool [44]. However, Botometer is widely recognized as a state-of-the-art bots detection mechanism, and we have taken a conservative approach in the detection phase to limit false positives. Indeed, the number of bots and their influence could be higher than our estimates, stressing the need for more research in the area.

7   Conclusion and Future Works

The purpose of this study was to investigate how Italian politics responded to the Russian-Ukrainian conflict on Twitter and understand the bots' influence and manipulations before the 2022 general elections in Italy. Our findings suggest that bots are a significant presence in political conversations on Twitter, with approximately 12% of commenters being identified as bots. We also analyzed the timing in which the bots posted concerning when the real users posted, and we can infer that in some cases, these accounts could have forced a certain direction in the topics discussed online. This highlights the potential impact of automated accounts on public opinion during political campaigns.

Our analysis can be improved in the future in several ways. For instance, we could consider the presence of comments in other languages. As our study focused solely on comments posted in the Italian language, taking into account comments in other idioms could offer a more comprehensive understanding of the discussion. In addition, users' attitudes and behaviors could be studied based on their location, in order to analyze potential regional differences in the discussion. Notably, identifying the geographical location of bots can provide more insight into *who* attempts to manipulate discussion and *why*.

References

1. Aiello, L.M., Deplano, M., Schifanella, R., Ruffo, G.: People are strange when you're a stranger: impact and influence of bots on social networks. In: International Conference on Web and Social Media (ICWSM), vol. 6, pp. 10–17 (2012)
2. Alothali, E., Zaki, N., Mohamed, E.A., Alashwal, H.: Detecting social bots on twitter: a literature review. In: 2018 International Conference on Innovations in Information Technology (IIT), pp. 175–180. IEEE (2018)
3. Alsmadi, I., O'Brien, M.J.: How many bots in Russian troll tweets? Inf. Process. Manag. **57**(6), 102303 (2020)
4. Antonakaki, D., Fragopoulou, P., Ioannidis, S.: A survey of twitter research: data model, graph structure, sentiment analysis and attacks. Expert Syst. Appl. **164**, 114006 (2021)
5. Arias, M., Arratia, A., Xuriguera, R.: Forecasting with twitter data. ACM Trans. Intell. Syst. Technol. **5**(1) (2014). https://doi.org/10.1145/2542182.2542190
6. Bardi, S., Conti, M., Pajola, L., Tricomi, P.P.: Social honeypot for humans: luring people through self-managed Instagram pages. In: Tibouchi, M., Wang, X. (eds.) ACNS 2023. LNCS, vol. 13905, pp. 309–336. Springer, Cham (2023). https://doi.org/10.1007/978-3-031-33488-7_12
7. Bastian, M., Heymann, S., Jacomy, M.: Gephi: an open source software for exploring and manipulating networks. In: International Conference on Web and Social Media (ICWSM), vol. 3, pp. 361–362 (2009)
8. Bessi, A., Ferrara, E.: Social bots distort the 2016 US presidential election online discussion. First Monday **21**(11–7) (2016)
9. Blondel, V.D., Guillaume, J.L., Lambiotte, R., Lefebvre, E.: Fast unfolding of communities in large networks. J. Stat. Mech. Theory Exp. **2008**(10), P10008 (2008)
10. Broniatowski, D.A., et al.: Weaponized health communication: Twitter bots and Russian trolls amplify the vaccine debate. Am. J. Public Health **108**(10), 1378–1384 (2018)
11. Caravaca, F., González-Cabañas, J., Cuevas, Á., Cuevas, R.: Estimating ideology and polarization in European countries using Facebook data. EPJ Data Sci. **11**(1), 56 (2022)

12. Chang, H.C.H., Chen, E., Zhang, M., Muric, G., Ferrara, E.: Social bots and social media manipulation in 2020: the year in review. arXiv preprint arXiv:2102.08436 (2021)
13. Chavoshi, N., Hamooni, H., Mueen, A.: Identifying correlated bots in Twitter. In: Spiro, E., Ahn, Y.-Y. (eds.) SocInfo 2016. LNCS, vol. 10047, pp. 14–21. Springer, Cham (2016). https://doi.org/10.1007/978-3-319-47874-6_2
14. Cresci, S.: A decade of social bot detection. Commun. ACM **63**(10), 72–83 (2020)
15. Cresci, S., Lillo, F., Regoli, D., Tardelli, S., Tesconi, M.: Cashtag piggybacking: uncovering spam and bot activity in stock microblogs on twitter. ACM Trans. Web (TWEB) **13**(2), 1–27 (2019)
16. Twitter's Developer: Twitter API platform. https://developer.twitter.com/en/docs
17. Diaz, G.: stopwords-it (2022). https://github.com/stopwords-iso/stopwords-it
18. Dutta, H.S., Chakraborty, T.: Blackmarket-driven collusion among retweeters-analysis, detection, and characterization. IEEE Trans. Inf. Forensics Secur. **15**, 1935–1944 (2019)
19. Fernquist, J., Kaati, L., Schroeder, R.: Political bots and the swedish general election. In: 2018 IEEE International Conference on Intelligence and Security Informatics (ISI), pp. 124–129. IEEE (2018)
20. Ferrara, E.: Bots, elections, and social media: a brief overview. In: Shu, K., Wang, S., Lee, D., Liu, H. (eds.) Disinformation, Misinformation, and Fake News in Social Media. LNSN, pp. 95–114. Springer, Cham (2020). https://doi.org/10.1007/978-3-030-42699-6_6
21. Ferrara, E., Chang, H., Chen, E., Muric, G., Patel, J.: Characterizing social media manipulation in the 2020 US presidential election. First Monday (2020)
22. Filter, J.: Clean-text (2022). https://github.com/jfilter/clean-text
23. Gaubatz, K.T.: Elections and War: The Electoral Incentive in the Democratic Politics of War and Peace. Stanford University Press, Redwood City (1999)
24. Social feed manager (2016). https://doi.org/10.5281/zenodo.3784836
25. Giakatos, D.P., Sermpezis, P., Vakali, A.: Pypoll: a python library automating mining of networks, discussions and polarization on twitter. arXiv preprint arXiv:2303.06478 (2023)
26. Gilani, Z., Farahbakhsh, R., Tyson, G., Wang, L., Crowcroft, J.: Of bots and humans (on twitter). In: Proceedings of the 2017 IEEE/ACM International Conference on Advances in Social Networks Analysis and Mining 2017, pp. 349–354 (2017)
27. Grootendorst, M.: Bertopic: neural topic modeling with a class-based TF-IDF procedure. arXiv preprint arXiv:2203.05794 (2022)
28. Insider, B.: Percentage of Bots on Twitter. https://www.businessinsider.com/twitter-bots-comprise-less-than-5-but-tweet-more-2022-9
29. Jacomy, M., Venturini, T., Heymann, S., Bastian, M.: Forceatlas2, a continuous graph layout algorithm for handy network visualization designed for the Gephi software. PLoS ONE **9**(6), e98679 (2014)
30. James Raynolds, B.: Italy pm conte vows more united italy as salvini leaves power. Italy PM Conte vows more united Italy as Salvini leaves power
31. Khan, A., et al.: Election prediction on twitter: a systematic mapping study. Complexity **2021**, 1–27 (2021)
32. Linvill, D.L., Boatwright, B.C., Grant, W.J., Warren, P.L.: "The Russians are hacking my brain!" investigating Russia's internet research agency twitter tactics during the 2016 united states presidential campaign. Comput. Hum. Behav. **99**, 292–300 (2019)

33. Lorenzo-Luaces, L., et al.: Sociodemographics and transdiagnostic mental health symptoms in social (studies of online cohorts for internalizing symptoms and language) I and II: cross-sectional survey and botometer analysis. JMIR Formative Res. **6**(10), e39324 (2022)
34. Ludovico, M.: Cybersecurity, 2022 annus horribilis: 13mila attacchi, +138%. Il Sole 24 Ore (2023)
35. Mannocci, L., Cresci, S., Monreale, A., Vakali, A., Tesconi, M.: Mulbot: unsupervised bot detection based on multivariate time series. arXiv preprint arXiv:2209.10361 (2022)
36. Martini, F., Samula, P., Keller, T.R., Klinger, U.: Bot, or not? Comparing three methods for detecting social bots in five political discourses. Big Data Soc. **8**(2), 20539517211033570 (2021)
37. Mattei, M., Caldarelli, G., Squartini, T., Saracco, F.: Italian twitter semantic network during the Covid-19 epidemic. EPJ Data Sci. **10**(1), 47 (2021)
38. Mazza, M., Avvenuti, M., Cresci, S., Tesconi, M.: Investigating the difference between trolls, social bots, and humans on twitter. Comput. Commun. **196**, 23–36 (2022)
39. McInnes, L., Healy, J., Astels, S.: HDBSCAN: hierarchical density based clustering. J. Open Source Softw. **2**(11), 205 (2017)
40. McInnes, L., Healy, J., Melville, J.: Umap: uniform manifold approximation and projection for dimension reduction. arXiv preprint arXiv:1802.03426 (2018)
41. Messia, H., Angela Dewan, C.: Italian prime minister giuseppe conte resigns, in calculated move amid coronavirus crisis (2021). https://edition.cnn.com/2021/01/26/europe/italy-giuseppe-conte-resignation-intl/index.html
42. Oesper, L., Merico, D., Isserlin, R., Bader, G.D.: Wordcloud: a cytoscape plugin to create a visual semantic summary of networks. Source Code Biol. Med. **6**(1), 7 (2011)
43. Pastor-Galindo, J., et al.: Spotting political social bots in twitter: a use case of the 2019 spanish general election. IEEE Trans. Netw. Serv. Manage. **17**(4), 2156–2170 (2020)
44. Rauchfleisch, A., Kaiser, J.: The false positive problem of automatic bot detection in social science research. PLoS ONE **15**(10), e0241045 (2020)
45. Rehurek, R., Sojka, P.: Gensim-python framework for vector space modelling. NLP Centre, Faculty of Informatics, Masaryk University, Brno, Czech Republic, vol. 3, no. 2 (2011)
46. Reimers, N., Gurevych, I.: Making monolingual sentence embeddings multilingual using knowledge distillation. In: Proceedings of the 2020 Conference on Empirical Methods in Natural Language Processing. Association for Computational Linguistics (2020). https://arxiv.org/abs/2004.09813
47. Gazzetta Ufficiale della Repubblica italiana: Decreto legge 28 febbraio 2022 (2022). https://www.gazzettaufficiale.it/eli/gu/2022/02/28/49/sg/pdf
48. Dubbin, R.: Percentage of Bots on the early stages of Twitter. https://www.newyorker.com/tech/annals-of-technology/the-rise-of-twitter-bots
49. Sartori, E., Pajola, L., Da San Martino, G., Conti, M.: The impact of Covid-19 on online discussions: the case study of the sanctioned suicide forum. In: Proceedings of the ACM Web Conference 2023, pp. 4060–4064 (2023)
50. Schäfer, F., Evert, S., Heinrich, P.: Japan's 2014 general election: political bots, right-wing internet activism, and prime minister Shinzō Abe's hidden nationalist agenda. Big Data **5**(4), 294–309 (2017)

51. Shevtsov, A., Tzagkarakis, C., Antonakaki, D., Ioannidis, S.: Identification of twitter bots based on an explainable machine learning framework: the US 2020 elections case study. In: International Conference on Web and Social Media (ICWSM), vol. 16, pp. 956–967 (2022)
52. Singh, M., Bansal, D., Sofat, S.: Behavioral analysis and classification of spammers distributing pornographic content in social media. Soc. Netw. Anal. Min. **6**(1), 1–18 (2016). https://doi.org/10.1007/s13278-016-0350-0
53. Stefanoni, F.: Un anno di guerra in ucraina, la risposta della politica italiana: le posizioni (e le evoluzioni) dei partiti. Corriere della Sera (2023)
54. Tahmasbi, F., et al.: "go eat a bat, chang!": On the emergence of sinophobic behavior on web communities in the face of Covid-19. In: Proceedings of the Web Conference 2021, pp. 1122–1133 (2021)
55. Tricomi, P.P., Tarahomi, S., Cattai, C., Martini, F., Conti, M.: Are we all in a tr
.man show? spotting instagram crowdturfing through self-training. arXiv preprint arXiv:2206.12904 (2022)
56. Varol, O.: Should we agree to disagree about twitter's bot problem? arXiv preprint arXiv:2209.10006 (2022)
57. Vasilkova, V., Legostaeva, N.: Social bots in political communication. RUDN J. Sociol. **19**(1), 121–133 (2019)
58. Institute for the Study of War: Ukraine conflict updates 2022 (2022). https://www.understandingwar.org/backgrounder/ukraine-conflict-updates-2022
59. Weber, I., Garimella, V.R.K., Batayneh, A.: Secular vs. islamist polarization in egypt on twitter. In: Proceedings of the 2013 IEEE/ACM International Conference on Advances in Social Networks Analysis and Mining, pp. 290–297 (2013)
60. Weng, Z., Lin, A.: Public opinion manipulation on social media: social network analysis of twitter bots during the Covid-19 pandemic. Int. J. Environ. Res. Public Health **19**(24), 16376 (2022)
61. Wikipedia: Cosine similarity (2023). https://en.wikipedia.org/wiki/Cosine_similarity
62. Wikipedia: Timeline of the 2022 Russian invasion of Ukraine (2023). https://en.wikipedia.org/wiki/Timeline_of_the_2022_Russian_invasion_of_Ukraine
63. Woolley, S.C.: Automating power: social bot interference in global politics. First Monday (2016)
64. Yang, K.C., Ferrara, E., Menczer, F.: Botometer 101: social bot practicum for computational social scientists. J. Comput. Soc. Sci. 1–18 (2022)

Did State-Sponsored Trolls Shape the 2016 US Presidential Election Discourse? Quantifying Influence on Twitter

Nikos Salamanos[1]([envelope]) [iD], Michael J. Jensen[2] [iD], Costas Iordanou[1] [iD],
and Michael Sirivianos[1] [iD]

[1] Department of Electrical Engineering, Computer Engineering and Informatics,
Cyprus University of Technology, Limassol 3036, Cyprus
{nik.salaman,michael.sirivianos}@cut.ac.cy,
costas.iordanou@eecei.cut.ac.cy
[2] Institute for Governance and Policy Analysis, University of Canberra,
Canberra 2601, Australia
Michael.Jensen@canberra.edu.au

Abstract. It is a widely accepted fact that state-sponsored Twitter accounts operated during the 2016 US presidential election, spreading millions of tweets with misinformation and inflammatory political content. Whether these social media campaigns of the so-called "troll" accounts were able to manipulate public opinion is still in question. Here, we quantify the influence of troll accounts on Twitter by analyzing 152.5 million tweets (by 9.9 million users) from that period. The data contain original tweets from 822 troll accounts identified as such by Twitter. We construct and analyze a very large interaction graph of 9.3 million nodes and 169.9 million edges using graph analysis techniques and a game-theoretic centrality measure. Then, we quantify the influence of all Twitter accounts on the overall information exchange as defined by the retweet cascades. We provide a global influence ranking of all Twitter accounts, and we find that one troll account appears in the top-100 and four in the top-1000. This, combined with other findings presented in this paper, constitute evidence that the driving force of virality and influence in the network came from regular users - users who have not been classified as trolls by Twitter. On the other hand, we find that, on average, troll accounts were tens of times more influential than regular users were. Moreover, 23% and 22% of regular accounts in the top-100 and top-1000, respectively, have now been suspended by Twitter. This raises questions about their authenticity and practices during the 2016 US presidential election.

Keywords: Disinformation · Information Diffusion · Twitter Trolls · Political Trolls

1 Introduction

The Russian efforts to manipulate the outcome of the 2016 US presidential election were unprecedented in terms of the size and scope of the operation. Millions of posts across multiple social media platforms gave rise to hundreds of millions of impressions targeting specific segments of the population in an effort to mobilize, suppress, or shift votes [11]. Trolls were particularly focused on the promotion of identity narratives [12], though that does not distinguish them from many other actors during the election [22]. The Special Counsel's report described this interference as "sweeping and systematic" [18, vol 1, 1]. Russian efforts focused on inflicting significant damage to the integrity of the communication spaces where Americans became informed and discussed their political choices during the election [15]. Therefore, the question of whether these disinformation campaigns had a significantly real impact on social media is of paramount importance [5,11,22].

In this paper, we address this question by measuring the influence of the so-called "troll" accounts together with the virality of information that they spread on Twitter during the period of 2016 US Presidential election. Let us note that a "troll" is any Twitter account that deliberately spreads disinformation, tries to inflict conflict, or causes extreme emotional reactions. A troll account could be human or operated automatically. An automated operated account is called a "bot" and is controlled by an algorithm that autonomously performs actions on Twitter. The term "bot" is not synonymous with "troll" as benign bots do operate and have a positive impact on users[1]. In fact, Twitter has set specific rules for acceptable automated behavior[2].

There are several obstacles to any empirical study on this subject: (i) the lack of complete and unbiased Twitter data – the Twitter API returns only a small sample of the users' daily activity; (ii) Tweets from deactivated profiles are not available; (iii) The followers and followees lists are not always accessible (i.e., the social graph is unknown). Having that in mind, we collected 152.5 million election-related tweets during the period of the 2016 US presidential election, using the Twitter API along with a set of track terms related to political content. The data contain original troll tweets from that period which later on were deleted by Twitter. Then, based on the ground-truth data released by Twitter regarding state-sponsored accounts linked to Russia, Iran, Venezuela, and Bangladesh states, we identified 822 trolls in our data. Finally, we constructed a very large *interaction-graph* of 9.3 million nodes/users and 169.9 million edges. Using graph analysis techniques and Shapley Value-based centrality, we analyze (i) the graph structure; (ii) the diffusion of potential political content as represented by the retweet cascades of tweets with at least one web or media URL embedded in the text.

Our approach is agnostic with respect to the actual political content of the tweets. The goal is to measure the impact of all users on the overall diffusion of information and consequently estimate the impact of ground-truth trolls. For the rest of the paper, we call *"regular"* the users that have not been classified as trolls by Twitter; they are just the rest of the population and might not always represent benign accounts.

---

[1] https://blog.mozilla.org/internetcitizen/2018/01/19/10-twitter-bots-actually-make-internet-better-place/.
[2] https://help.twitter.com/en/rules-and-policies/twitter-automation.

Research Questions (RQ): We address the following RQ:

RQ1: Who are the most influential trolls and regular users? Can we rank them in order of contribution (impact) to the overall information diffusion?

RQ2: Which are the viral retweet cascades initiated by regular users and specific troll accounts?

RQ3: What is the proximity of top-k influential regular users to bot accounts and how many of them have been suspended by Twitter later on?

Contributions: Our primary contributions are as follows:

C1: We construct one of the largest graphs representing the interactions between state-sponsored troll accounts and regular users on Twitter during the 2016 US Presidential election. This counts as an approximation of the original social graph.

C2: We introduce the notion of *flow graphs* – a natural representation of the information diffusion that takes place in the Twitter platform during the retweeting process. This formulation allows us to apply a Shapley Value-based centrality measure for a fair estimation of users' contribution to the information shared without imposing assumptions on the users' behavior. Moreover, we estimate the virality of retweet cascades by the *structural virality* along with the influence each user has on them by the *influence-degree*.

C3: We present strong evidence that troll activity was not the main cause of viral cascades of web and media URLs on Twitter. Our measurements show that the regular users were generally the most active and influential part of the population, and their activity was the driving force of the viral cascades. At the same time, we find that, on average, trolls were tens of times more influential than regular users – an indicator of the effectiveness of their strategies to attract attention. These findings further substantiate previously reported insights [26, 28,29]. Furthermore, more than 20% of the top-100 as well as the top-1000 regular users, have now been suspended by Twitter. This sets their authenticity in question, as well as their activity during that period.

Data Availability: Part of the dataset is available under proper restrictions for compliance with Twitter's ToS and the GDPR[3]. The ground truth data are provided by Twitter[4].

2   Related Work

In a seminal work on the general problem of disinformation on Twitter [26], the authors investigated the diffusion cascades of true and false rumors disseminated from 2006 to 2017 – approximately 126K rumor cascades spread by 3 million people. The main findings are (i) false news diffused faster and more broadly than true ones; (ii) human behavior contributes more to the spread of falsity than trolls. These findings are in line with our main result, that is, the regular users had the dominant role in the viral cascades. Moreover, part of our methodology for the construction of the retweet trees has been inspired by this work.

---

[3] https://doi.org/10.5281/zenodo.6526783.

[4] https://about.twitter.com/en/our-priorities/civic-integrity.

In [6], the authors analyzed 171 million tweets by 11 million users – collected five months prior to the 2016 US presidential election. They examined 30 million tweets that contained at least one web URL pointing to a news outlet website. 25% of the news was either fake or biased, representing the spreading of misinformation. Then, they investigated the flow of information by constructing retweet networks for each news category. Furthermore, they estimated the most influential users in the retweet networks using the Collective Influence (CI) algorithm [17]. One of their findings is that Trump supporters were the main group of users that spread fake news, although it was not the dominant one in the whole network. We note that in [6], the overall retweet graph is directly constructed by the data as they were provided by the Twitter API. In our study, we enrich the raw Twitter data by considering all the possible information paths, and at the same time, we provide an estimation of the retweet trees.

Grinberg et al. [10] investigates the extent to which Twitter users were exposed to fake news during the 2016 US presidential election. Their data consists of tweets from 16.4K Twitter accounts that were active during the 2016 US election season, along with their list of followers. They restrict their analysis to tweets containing a URL from a website outside Twitter. One of their main findings is that although a large part of the population had been exposed to fake news, only a small fraction (1%) was responsible for the diffusion of 80% of fake news. The authors introduce the notion of users' "exposures", i.e., tweets from a user to his followers. This approach is roughly in line with the *flow graphs* that we introduce in Sect. 4.2.

In [28,29], the authors analyzed the characteristics and strategies of 5.5K Russian and Iranian troll accounts on Twitter and Reddit. Using *Hawkes Processes*, they compute an overall statistical measure of influence that quantifies the effect these accounts had on social media platforms, such as Twitter, Reddit, 4chan, and Gab. One of their main results is that even though the troll accounts reach a considerably large number of Twitter users and effectively spread URLs on Twitter, their overall effect on the social platforms is not dominant. Our findings verify these results and support the fact that some trolls have above-average influence.

In [3,4], the authors examined the Russian disinformation campaigns on Twitter in 2016, based on 43M tweets shared by 5.7M users and 221 trolls. They focused on the characteristics of *spreaders*, namely the users that had been exposed to and shared content previously published by Russian trolls. They constructed the retweet graph by mapping retweet actions to edges. Then, they applied the label propagation algorithm to classify Twitter accounts as conservative or liberal. Finally, they used the *Botometer* [8] to determine whether spreaders and non-spreaders can be labeled as bots. We also apply this technique in order to examine whether the top-k influential users exhibit bot behavior.

In [14], a postmortem analysis is conducted on one million Twitter accounts, which although active during the 2016 US election period, later on, were suspended by Twitter. The authors focused on the community-level activities of the suspended accounts, and for that purpose, they clustered them into communities.

Then, they compared the characteristics of suspended account communities with the not suspended ones and found significant differences in their characteristics, especially in their posting behavior.

Finally, Bovet et al. [7] developed a method to infer the political opinion of Twitter users during the 2016 US presidential election. For that purpose, they constructed a directed social graph based on the users' actions (replies, mentions, retweets) between them – a similar graph formulation technique to ours in this paper. Then, they monitored the evolution of three structural graph properties, the Strongly Connected Giant Component, the Weakly Connected Giant Component, and the Corona.

3   Datasets

Ground-Truth Twitter Data: Twitter has released a large collection of state-sponsored trolls activities as part of Twitter's election integrity efforts (see footnote 4). This is ongoing work where the list of malicious accounts is constantly updated. We requested the unhashed version, which consists of 8,275 troll accounts information affiliated with Russia (3,838), Iran (2,861), Venezuela (1,565), and Bangladesh states (11), along with 25,076,853 tweets shared by them. In this study, we leverage only the troll IDs which served as ground-truth identifiers of the trolls in the tweets collection we presented next.

Our Twitter Dataset: Our analysis is based on 152,479,440 tweets from 9,939,698 users. We downloaded the data using the Twitter streaming (1%) and Tweepy[5] Python library, in the period before and up to the 2016 US presidential election – from September 21 to November 7, 2016 (47 days; we did not collect data on 02/10/2016). The tweets' track terms[6] were related to political content such as "hillary2016", "clinton2016", "trump2016" and "donaldtrump2016" – namely, a list of phrases used to determine which Tweets are delivered by the stream. In addition to the *tweet text*, *user screen name*, and *user ID*, we also collected metadata, including the *hashtags*, the URLs, and *mentions* that were included in the tweet text, as well as information on the *account creation*, *user timezone*, and *user location*. Based on the ground-truth Twitter data, we identified 35,489 tweets from 822 troll accounts.

Retweet Cascades: When a user retweets, usually, he/she agrees with the context of the original tweet (root-tweet) that has been retweeted. For this reason, the analysis of the retweet cascades – i.e., a series of retweets upon the same root-tweet – is important for the identification of the viral cascades as well as the influential users in them. We analyze only the retweet cascades where the root tweet-text contains at least one URL and has been retweeted by at least 100 distinct retweeters (excluding the root-user since he/she may have retweeted his/her own tweet). This process resulted in 46.4K retweet cascades consisting of 19.6M tweets (see Table 1). In a retweet cascade, it is not only the actual tweet

---

[5] https://www.tweepy.org/.

[6] https://developer.twitter.com/en/docs/tweets/filter-realtime/guides/basic-stream-parameters.html.

Table 1. Retweet cascades with minimum 100 unique retweeters

	Regular Users	Trolls
Total users	3,633,457	233
Root users	8,192	12
Root tweets	45,986	423
Retweeters	3,630,764	228
Total retweets	19,588,072	
Total URLs	43,989	

that has been diffused but mainly the information it contains. So, the web or media URLs (i.e., videos and photos) that are embedded in the tweets serve as "anchors" by which we connect distinct retweet cascades, considering that they are referring to the same information. For example, in Sect. 5.3 we analyze the cascades that refer to URLs that have been spread by trolls.

4 Methodology

4.1 The Social Network

We leverage the users' activity as is recorded in the data (152.5M tweets) to construct an approximation of the follower-graph – the social network, which is not publicly available to a large extent. Specifically:

Interaction-Graph: In short, we map users to nodes and interactions between users to directed edges. In Twitter, the interactions between users belong to three categories: (i) *replies*; (ii) *retweets* or *quotes* – a special form of retweet; (iii) *mentions*. We define the directed edge (i, j), from user i to user j, for every action of i on tweets of j. For example, if i had replied to a tweet of j. The direction of the edge implies that i is a *follower* of j, while the reverse direction represents the information flow from j to i. This process outputs a directed *multigraph*, where many edges may connect the same pair of users. It consists of 169,921,912 edges, 9,321,061 regular users, and 821 trolls. Even though the number of troll accounts is small, there are some indications that some troll accounts might have substantial activity, which is worth further investigation. For instance, we have 671K edges that point to 285 trolls. The total number of nodes is not equal to the total number of users who appear in the initial dataset because the isolated nodes have been discarded – i.e., users who, although tweeted, neither performed an action to other accounts nor received actions from others.

Follower-graph: Finally, we construct the follower-graph by discarding the duplicate edges and keeping only the earliest ones. It is a directed graph with 9.32M users/nodes and 84,1M edges, representing an approximation of the true follower-graph.

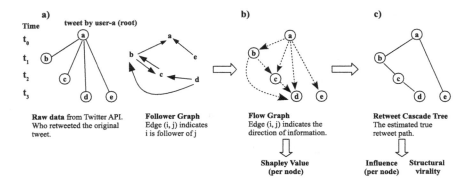

Fig. 1. Toy example of retweet analysis. (a) The raw data provided by Twitter API along with the follower-graph. (b) The flow graph shows the full information flow according to Twitter functionality and the follower-graph. The edges present the path of information that appears on the users' timeline prior to their retweets. For instance, user c has retweeted on date t_2. At the same time user b – whom user c follows – has retweeted on date $t_1 < t_2$. Note that a given retweet contains both the name of the user who retweeted and the name of the root user who posted the original tweet. Hence, we have an edge from the root to any retweeter because the users have retweeted the root tweet even if they did not follow the root user. (c) The time-inferred cascade tree is constructed from the flow graph by assuming (see Sect. 4.2) that each retweeter has been influenced by the friend who very recently retweeted the original tweet.

4.2   Retweet Cascade Tree and Flow Graph

Generally, the retweet data returned by the Twitter API have, by design, limited information regarding the true chain of retweet events. For a given retweet, the information provided is the retweeter ID as well as the root-user ID. Hence, in terms of influence, this corresponds to the case where all the retweeters have been influenced by the root-user. In Fig. 1a, we present an example of the raw data. This star-like cascade structure does not always depict the true chain of retweet events. For example, a user may have retweeted a friend's retweet and not the original one.

Retweet Cascade Tree: A widely used method for the reconstruction of the true retweet path is the time-inferred diffusion process [9,25,26]. It is based on the causality assumption that a given user, before retweeting, has been influenced by his "friend" who has recently retweeted the same original tweet. Moreover, since a user can retweet a tweet more than once, we assume that he has been influenced by another user on his first action only. Hence, the final retweet path (see Fig. 1c) is constructed by the raw data provided by Twitter in conjunction with the follower-graph (Fig. 1a). Thus, we have two rather extreme cases; one is the star tree that we take from Twitter API, where no real diffusion structure is present, and the other one is the cascade tree, where a specific hypothesis has been applied with respect to who was influenced by whom. The latter emphasizes the most recent friend, whereas the former is always the root user. In order to define an intermediate case, we introduce the notion of *flow graph*.

Flow Graph: We introduce the concept of *flow graph*, which presents the direction of all possible influence between the retweeters that may have taken place by the information-diffusion in the Twitter platform. Let us consider the toy example in Fig. 1. Before constructing the retweet cascade tree in Fig. 1c, we first have to identify all the time-inferred edges from the users that retweeted in time t to the users who will retweet in $t+1$. The edges direction indicates the information flow on the Twitter platform and is based on the fact that when a user retweets a given tweet, his action appears on his followers' timeline. For instance, when user b retweets the root tweet in t_1, he is transmitting this information to his followers c and d. Finally, we add an edge from the root user to any of the retweeters because, in any given retweet, the author's screen name is always visible. The construction of the flow graphs is based on the follower-graph, where the edges are time inferred. So, in a given time t_i, a given user i receives information from the users he had already started following at a certain time $t < t_i$.

The flow graph, together with the retweet tree, are the two graph structures we leverage to evaluate users' impact on the overall information exchange. Specifically, (a) Flow graph: we measure the contribution of the users to the overall diffusion of information by the Shapley Value-based centrality (see Sect. 4.3). (b) Retweet cascade tree: we measure the influence of every user in a given retweet tree by the influence-degree and the overall virality of the tree by the structural virality (see Sect. 4.4).

4.3 Shapley Value-Based Centrality

Towards evaluating the users in terms of the influence/impact they had on the retweet cascades, we have to create a consistent ranking where the top-k users are the most influential ones. One way to do so is to use a centrality measure that fits well in our problem. Here, we apply the Shapley Value-based degree centrality [1, 2,16] one of the game-theory inspired methods of identifying influential nodes in networks [19,20,23]. These methods are based on the Shapley Value [21], a division scheme for the fair distribution of gains or costs in each player of a cooperative game. The Shapley Value of each player in the game is the average weighted marginal contribution of the player over all possible coalitions. Hence, the problem of computing the Shapley Value in a N player game has, in most cases, exponential complexity since the possible coalitions are 2^N.

We apply the Shapley Value-based degree centrality introduced in [1,16], which is further refined in [2]. First, in [1,16], the authors provide a linear time algorithm for the exact computation of the Shapley Value in the following game. Given a directed graph $G(V, E)$, with V nodes and E edges, the set of players are the nodes in V, and each coalition is a subset of V. The value of a coalition C is defined by the size of the set $fringe(C)$, i.e., the set that consists of the members of C along with their out-neighbors. This set represents the sphere of influence of the coalition C. Moreover, we define that the value of the empty coalition is always zero. The exact closed-form solution of the Shapley Value of a node u_i is $V(u_i) = \displaystyle\sum_{u_j \in \{u_i\} \cup N_{out}(u_i)} \frac{1}{1 + \text{indegree}_G(u_j)}$.

Hence, the algorithm for computing the Shapley Values has running time $O(|V| + |E|)$ (see Algorithm 1 in [1,16]). In fact, the Shapley Value is the sum of probabilities that the node contributes to each of its neighbors and also itself.

This formulation is very similar to what we want to measure in the flow graphs. In our case, the value of a coalition is the set of users that have been informed by the members of the coalition about a given root-tweet. Having said that, we cannot directly apply the above formulation since a node cannot inform itself. This very problem has been addressed by the authors in [2] to solve the influence maximization problem. They refined the previous formulation so that the value of a coalition C is the size of the out-neighbors of the member in C, i.e., the number of nodes that can be directly influenced by C. In conclusion, we compute the Shapley Value for all nodes in any flow graph using the following formula (see [2]):

$$SV(u_i) = \sum_{u_j \in N_{out}(u_i)} \frac{1}{1 + \text{indegree}_G(u_j)} \tag{1}$$

In this way, the "leaf" nodes always have zero Shapley Value since they did not inform anyone in the flow graph. The advantage of this approach is that it provides a linear time computation of Shapley Values and also works for disconnected graphs. In fact, this is the case that we face here since the overall information flow is represented by the flow graphs, i.e., a set of disjoint graphs. Moreover, we can compute the overall Shapley Value for any subset of retweet cascades that a user is a part of. We will use this property in order to evaluate trolls and regular users together only in a subset of retweet cascades. The intuition of this approach is that Eq. 1 computes in a fair way the users' contribution in informing the other members of the graph for a given piece of information, which in our case is the original root-tweet and the URL it contains. We note that from the method in [2], we use only the part that computes the Shapley Values and not the whole process (influence maximization). Our goal is to compute the users' contribution without assumptions regarding the influence process.

Finally, the global Shapley Value of a user in the overall information exchange is the summation of his Shapley Values in the flow graphs (FG) the user participates in. Hence:

$$SV_{global}(u) = \sum_{FG \in \{FG\}_u} SV(u, FG) \tag{2}$$

4.4   Structural Virality and Influence-Degree

Structural virality evaluates how viral a retweet cascade tree is [9]. The structural virality of a cascade tree T with $n > 1$ nodes is the average distance between all pairs of nodes in a cascade. That is:

$$\nu(T) = \frac{1}{n(n-1)} \sum_{i=1}^{n} \sum_{j=1}^{n} d_{ij} \tag{3}$$

where d_{ij} is the shortest path between the nodes i and j. The $\nu(T)$ represents the average depth of nodes when we consider all nodes as the root of the cascade.

We expect the tree of a viral cascade will have many sub-trees, representing many generations of a viral diffusion process on a smaller scale. On the other hand, a cascade tree with many leaves directly connected with the root represents a "broadcast" – where in a single diffusion process, the material has been transmitted to many nodes (see an example of a broadcast in Fig. 1a). Even though the structural virality is a measure for the cascade tree, it also reflects the collective influence of the nodes in the tree, meaning that not only the root but also other intermediate nodes should have been influential since the material has been transmitted in several regions of the network. So, we expect to find influential nodes in cascades with large structural virality. Hence, in order to measure the influence on an individual level, we define the *influence-degree*. The influence-degree measures the direct influence a node had on a cascade tree. It is defined as the number of users that have been influenced by a given user i in the cascade tree. For instance, in Fig. 1c, the influence-degree of node a is two because he has influenced both b and e. The global *influence-degree* is the total number of users that have been influenced by i in all the cascade trees that i has participated in.

5 Results

The analysis is based on comparing the influence of two groups of users; the trolls and the regular users. First, we provide general topological features of the interaction-graph, as well as the follower-graph. Next, we focus on the retweet cascades. We compute the users' Shapley Value and influence-degree along with the Structural Virality of the cascade trees. Finally, we provide global rankings where we identify the top-k influential users.

5.1 Graph Topology

Degree Distribution. In both interaction-graph and follower-graph, the in-degree represents the user's popularity, i.e., the overall activity of his followers on his posts. On the other hand, the out-degree is a measure of a user's sociability/extroversion, i.e., how active a given user is by interacting with other Twitter accounts. We compare the degree distributions of both graphs, since users with a high degree in the interaction-graph do not necessarily have a large degree in the follower-graph; for instance, users who are highly popular in a small group of followers. The results show that the degree distributions for both graphs are very similar; thus, we discuss the findings only for the interaction-graph which depicts the overall users' activity. Figure 2 presents the empirical complementary cumulative distribution (CCDF) of in-degree and out-degree for regular

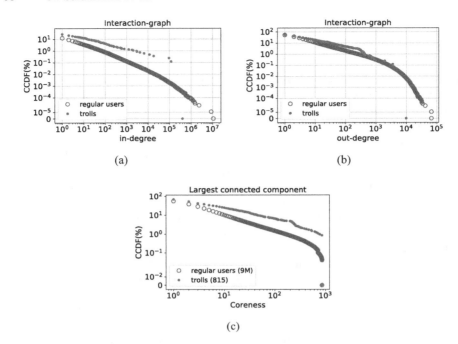

Fig. 2. (a) & (b) CCDF of in-degree and out-degree for trolls and regular users; (c) CCDF of coreness for the nodes in the largest connected component.

users and trolls. In summary: (i) 285 trolls and 2.3M regular users have non-zero in-degree; (ii) 675 trolls and 8.5M regular users have non-zero out-degree.

In-degree (Fig. 2a): (i) 12 troll accounts have in-degree larger than 1K. The top-3 trolls have 396K, 119K, and 95K in-degrees. On the other hand, we have 12K and 1.8K regular users with in-degrees larger than 1K and 10K, respectively. The top-3 regular users have 10.8M, 8.6M, and 2.3M in-degrees.

Out-degree (Fig. 2b): (i) the troll activity is not substantial, i.e., three accounts have out-degree larger than 1K, and the top-3 trolls have 9.8K, 3.5K, and 1.9K out-degrees; (ii) the regular users appear to be considerably more active, i.e., 29.6K and 594 accounts have out-degree larger than 1K and 10K, respectively. In conclusion, it seems that in our dataset the troll activity is not dominant compared to the activity of regular users.

Finally, Table 2 presents the average values for in-degree and out-degree for trolls and regular users in interaction-graph and follower-graph. Even though regular users are the dominant part of the population, the trolls attracted on average, a considerably large amount of traffic. For instance, the trolls' average in-degree is 45 times higher than the regular users' average in-degree.

Table 2. Average values: Regular Users vs Trolls

		Regular Users	Trolls
Interaction-graph	In-degree	18.16	821.22
	Out-degree	18.23	38.97
Follower-graph	In-degree	8.99	258.63
	Out-degree	9.02	22.48
Largest Comp.	Coreness	9.22	31.75
RT Cascades	Shapley Value	3.21	269.02
	Infl. Degree	5.35	382.71
	Ranking by Shapley	$1,82 \cdot 10^6$	$1,61 \cdot 10^6$

K-Core Decomposition. First, we identify the connected components of the undirected version of the follower-graph – 9.32M nodes and 82.8M reciprocal edges. We identified 104,954 connected components. The largest connected component consists of 9M nodes and 82,7M edges while the second largest has only 223 nodes. Hence, the largest part of the graph is well-connected. Then, we compute the *k-core decomposition* of the nodes in the largest connected component. The k-core decomposition is the process of computing the cores of a graph G. The k-core is the maximal subgraph of G where each node has a degree of at least k. The k-shell is the subgraph of G that consists of the nodes that belong to k-core but not to $(k+1)$-core. A node has *coreness* (or core number) k if it belongs to the k-shell. In other words, each node is assigned to a shell layer of the graph G. The graph k-core number is the maximum value of k where the k-core is not empty. Coreness is one of the most effective centrality measures for identifying the influential nodes in a complex network [13].

Figure 2c presents the CCDF of the coreness values for trolls and regular users. The graph k-core number is 854. The majority of nodes in the larger k-shells are the users since their population is larger than that of the troll accounts. There are only eight trolls with large coreness; seven accounts are part of the largest 854-shell, and one account is part of the second-largest 853-shell. This is an indication that these accounts were probably influential. Regarding the regular users, 3,710 and 250 of them belong to the largest and second-largest k-shell, respectively. Finally, from Table 2, we observe that the average coreness of trolls is three times larger than the coreness of regular users.

Summary of Results. Few trolls have a substantial number of followers (in-degree), activity on other accounts (out-degree), and structural position in the network (coreness). Generally, the dominant part of the population is the regular users. On the other hand, on average, the trolls attracted tens of times more traffic than the regular users.

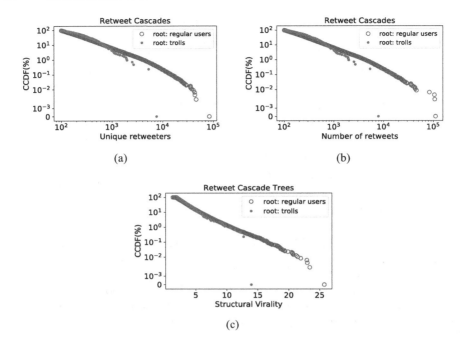

(a)   (b)

(c)

Fig. 3. (a) and (b) CCDF of retweet cascades in terms of the unique number of retweeters and the total number of retweets. The retweeters might have retweeted the same tweet more than once; hence the number of retweets is larger than the number of retweeters. (c) Structural Virality of the retweet cascade trees.

5.2   Retweet Cascades and Structural Virality

We now turn our attention to the retweet cascades and provide general statistics about the popularity of the root tweets posted by regular users and trolls. In Fig. 3 we present the CCDF of the number of unique retweeters and the CCDF of the total number of retweets per retweet cascade. From the 423 retweet cascades that have been initiated by troll accounts, 18 of them have more than 1K retweeters. In addition, the two largest cascades have 5.2K and 7.5K retweeters (Fig. 3a). Regarding the cascades that were initiated by regular users, in 2,890 of them the number of retweeters is larger than 1K; 101 cascades have more than 10K retweeters, and the top-5 have between 40K to 83.2K. Regarding the number of retweets per cascade, the findings are similar to the previous ones. The most popular root tweets have been posted by regular users instead of trolls (Fig. 3b). Moreover, in the largest four cascades, the number of retweets is between 83K to 111K, which renders them considerably larger than the number of unique retweeters. This indicates that the root tweets of these four cascades were very popular and they have been retweeted multiple times by the same users.

Structural Virality. The previous results depict that the cascades initiated by trolls were not very large. However, the results are based on the unstructured raw data provided by Twitter API, where all the retweets point to the original tweet (see the example in Fig. 1a). Here, we aim to measure how viral the cascades were by using the measure of structural virality (see Sect. 4.4). For the computation of Eq. 3, we use the networkx[7] Python package (Dijkstra's algorithm). In Fig. 3c, we compare the structural virality of cascade trees for: (i) the cascades initiated by trolls (423 root-tweets, see Table 1); and (ii) the 45,986 cascades initiated by regular users. We can see that regular users were the source of the most viral cascades. The top troll cascade has 13.95 structural virality. On the other hand, 138 user cascades have structural virality larger than 13.95.

Summary of Results. The vast majority of viral cascades were initiated by regular users and very few by troll accounts. Moreover, retweet cascades with thousands of retweets have very small structural virality, which indicates that their root users were the main source of influence.

5.3 Top-k Influential Users

We conclude the analysis by identifying the most influential Twitter accounts based on two measures, the Shapley Value-based centrality and the influence-degree. We produce the global ranking of all accounts (trolls and regular users) that are part of the retweet cascades (see Table 1; 233 trolls; 3.63M regular users). In addition, we measure how close to a Twitter bot the profiles of the top-1000 regular users are. Our goal is to examine whether the behavior of top-ranked accounts deviates from a human-operated account. As we mentioned in Sect. 1, an account can be automated (having a high Botometer score) and, at the same time, can be benign. On the other hand, a high bot-score raises questions about the authenticity of an account.

Shapley Value-Based Centrality and Influence-Degree. Here, based on the flow graphs and the Eqs. 1 and 2, we compute the global Shapley Value of every user who participated in the retweet cascades. Moreover, having the URLs that are embedded in the root-tweets as identifiers of the web and media material that has been diffused in the network, we collect only the cascades that refer to URLs that have been spread by trolls – either by posting an original root tweet or by retweeting. For simplicity, we call these URLs as *URLs-troll*.

In Fig. 4a, we plot the CCDF of the global Shapley Values. We have 27 out of 233 trolls and 161,513 out of 3.6 million regular users with non-zero Shapley Value. In other words, only 27 trolls have a non-zero contribution to the diffusion of information by the retweet cascades. Subsequently, based on the global Shapley Values, we get the global ranking, where the rank for the trolls is [27, 150, 181, 769, 1649, 1797, 2202, 3273, 3964, 4424, 10017, 12263,

---

[7] https://networkx.github.io/.

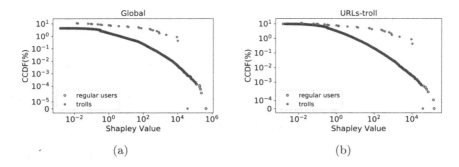

Fig. 4. CCDF of the Shapley Values for trolls and regular users.eps

12939, 22706, 23858, 38246, 58516, 58524, 64181, 90589, 114414, 124387, 139794, 142181, 146944, 158378, 158960]. Hence, only four troll accounts are in the top-1000, and one is in the top-100 (see Table 3). Moreover, the average ranking of trolls is not significantly larger than the rest of the population (see Table 2). At the same time, the average Shapley Value (global) for troll accounts is 83.8 times larger than the regular users' Shapley Value, which indicates that the troll accounts were quite effective in spreading information. Furthermore, Fig. 4b reports the Shapley Values only for the retweet cascades of *URLs-troll*. We have 2,723 URLs that appear in 3,924 cascades of 934K regular users and 233 trolls. Twenty-seven trolls and 91,572 regular users have non-zero Shapley Value. The distribution for the trolls is the same as the global one since the retweet cascades of *URLs-troll* are the only ones with troll accounts present. Regarding the regular users, we recompute their total Shapley Value by Eq. 2 and only for the subset of retweet cascades that correspond to *URLs-troll*. Again, we reach a final ranking, where the ranking of trolls in the top-1000 is [7, 28, 32, 125, 335, 361, 444, 697, 864, 981]; namely, only ten trolls appear in the top-1000 and three of them in the top-100.

Finally, we use the influence-degree as a measure to rank regular users and trolls according to the effect they have on the retweets cascade trees (see Sect. 4.4). In summary, we have 21 trolls and 118,960 regular users with non-zero influence (we omit the plot). We found four troll accounts in the top-1000 with rankings [34, 201, 241, 899] and one of them in the top-100 (see also Table 3). On the other hand, the influence-degree of trolls is more than 71.5 times larger than regular users' influence, on average, a similar result to the one for the Shapley Value (see Table 2).

Bots and Suspended Accounts. How similar to bot accounts are the top-k users? In order to estimate this, we use the Botometer scores for the top-1000 regular users (ranking by Shapley Values). Botometer[8] classifies Twitter accounts as a bot or human with 0.95 AUC classification performance [24,27]. It uses

---

[8] https://botometer.iuni.iu.edu.

Table 3. Top-k Twitter accounts. (We use bold for the suspended accounts)

Account-info User screen-name (User-ID)	Ranking (by-Shapley, by-Infl.)	Coreness	CAP (eng., univ.)
Top-10 influential accounts			
HillaryClinton (1339835893)	(1, 1)	854	(0.0015, 0.0019)
LindaSuhler (347627434)	(2, 2)	854	(0.0068, 0.019)
realDonaldTrump (25073877)	(3, 4)	854	(0.0015, 0.0022)
TeamTrump (729676086632656900)	(4, 5)	854	(0.0014, 0.0019)
wikileaks (16589206)	(5, 6)	854	(0.0013, 0.0019)
WDFx2EU7 (**779739206339928064**)	(6, 13)	854	N/A
PrisonPlanet (18643437)	(7, 9)	854	(0.0012, 0.0020)
FoxNews (1367531)	(8, 7)	854	(0.0028, 0.0026)
magnifier661 (**431917957**)	(9, 11)	854	N/A
CNN (759251)	(10, 8)	854	(0.0031, 0.0027)
ChristiChat (**732980827**)	(11, 10)	854	N/A
StylishRentals (**355355420**)	(13, 3)	96	N/A
Troll accounts in top-1000			
TEN_GOP (**4224729994**)	(27, 34)	854	N/A
Pamela_Moore13 (**4272870988**)	(150, 201)	854	N/A
America_1st_(**4218156466**)	(181, 241)	854	N/A
tpartynews (**3990577513**)	(769, 899)	854	N/A
Potentially Bot accounts in top-1000			
rsultzba (3248410062)	(275, 412)	854	(0.565, 0.297)
TrumpLadyFran (717627639159128064)	(311, 355)	854	(0.847, 0.446)
edeblazim (429229693)	(531, 571)	854	(0.892, 0.812)
WORlDSTARHIPHOP (2913627307)	(643, 552)	46	(0.511, 0.385)

various machine-learning models and more than a thousand features that have been extracted from the publicly available data of the account in question. For a given account, the Botometer API returns various scores where the more general one is the *Complete Automation Probability* (CAP) – the probability that a given account is completely automated. Two CAP scores are provided, one based on its English language tweets and one for universal features. Generally, CAP scores above 0.5 indicate a bot account [7].

In top-1000, four regular users have either CAP(english) or CAP(universal) score larger than 0.5, so they are potentially bots (see Table 3). On the other hand, only 22 and 21 users have CAP scores larger than 0.2. Moreover, 263 accounts were inactive. In order to verify the reasons for inactivity, we get the account information of the regular users in the top-10000, using Tweepy. When an account is not accessible, then Tweepy returns an error message[9] either "User not found" (code 50; corresponds with HTTP 404; deleted account by the user

---

[9] https://developer.twitter.com/en/support/twitter-api/error-troubleshooting.

itself) or "User has been suspended" (code 63; corresponds with HTTP 403; suspended account by Twitter due to violation of Twitter Rules[10]). In summary, we found that (i) in top-100: 23 suspended accounts out the of 26 inactive ones; (ii) in top-1000: 220 suspended out of the 263 inactive; (iii) in top-10000: 1,836 suspended out of the 2,508 inactive.

Lastly, Table 3 shows the account information for the top-10 influential users based on the Shapley Value. We also present the corresponding rankings in terms of influence-degree and coreness along with the Botometer scores. Two accounts in top-10 are suspended, which raises serious doubts about the authenticity of these users. The top-10 users are part of the largest 854-shell. In addition, we report the four trolls in top-1000 along with their rankings and coreness. All four of them are part of the largest 854-shell. Moreover, in retweet cascades initiated by them, more than 1.1% of the retweets were from regular users belonging to the top-1000 group.

Summary of Results. Four troll accounts were amongst the most influential users. Their tweets have been retweeted tens of times by top-1000 influential regular users. Four regular users in the top-1000 exhibit bot behavior. In addition, 23% and 22% of regular accounts in the top-100 and top-1000 respectively, have been suspended by Twitter, something that raises questions about their authenticity and practices overall.

6   Conclusion

In this paper, we have extensively studied the influence that state-sponsored trolls had during the 2016 US presidential election by analyzing millions of tweets from that period. We first constructed the interaction-graph between trolls and regular users, and then we concentrated our analysis on the retweet cascades. In order to measure the users' impact on the diffusion of information, we introduce the notion of *flow graph*, where we apply a game theoretic-based centrality measure. Moreover, we estimate the retweet paths by constructing the retweet cascade trees where we measure the users' direct influence. The results indicate that although the trolls initiated some viral cascades, their role was not dominant and the source of influence was mainly the regular users. On the other hand, the average influence of trolls was considerably larger than the average influence of regular users. This indicates that the strategies these trolls followed in order to attract and engage regular users were sufficiently effective. Furthermore, 23% and 22% of regular accounts in the top-100 and top-1000, respectively, have now been suspended by Twitter. This raises questions about the authenticity of these accounts.

Acknowledgement. We are grateful to Twitter for providing access to the trolls' ground truth dataset. We thank Nikolaos Laoutaris for his insightful comments about

---

[10] https://help.twitter.com/en/managing-your-account/suspended-twitter-accounts.

the Shapley Value. This project has received funding from the European Union's Horizon 2020 Research and Innovation program under the Cybersecurity CONCORDIA project (Grant Agreement No. 830927) and under the Marie Skłodowska-Curie INCOGNITO project (Grant Agreement No. 824015).

References

1. Aadithya, K.V., Ravindran, B., Michalak, T.P., Jennings, N.R.: Efficient Computation of the Shapley Value for Centrality in Networks. In: Saberi, A. (ed.) WINE 2010. LNCS, vol. 6484, pp. 1–13. Springer, Heidelberg (2010). https://doi.org/10.1007/978-3-642-17572-5_1
2. Adamczewski, K., Matejczyk, S., Michalak, T.: How good is the shapley value-based approach to the influence maximization problem? Front. Artif. Intell. Appl. **263** (2014)
3. Badawy, A., Ferrara, E., Lerman, K.: Analyzing the digital traces of political manipulation: The 2016 Russian interference twitter campaign. In: Proceedings of the 2018 IEEE/ACM International Conference on Advances in Social Networks Analysis and Mining. pp. 258–265. ASONAM 2018 (2018)
4. Badawy, A., Lerman, K., Ferrara, E.: Who falls for online political manipulation? In: Companion Proceedings of The 2019 World Wide Web Conference. pp. 162–168. WWW 2019, ACM (2019)
5. Benkler, Y., Faris, R., Roberts, H.: Network Propaganda: Manipulation, Disinformation, and Radicalization in American Politics. Oxford University Press (2018)
6. Bovet, A., Makse, H.A.: Influence of fake news in twitter during the 2016 us presidential election. Nat. Commun. **10**(7) (2019)
7. Bovet, A., Morone, F., Makse, H.A.: Validation of twitter opinion trends with national polling aggregates: Hillary clinton vs donald trump. Sci. Rep. **8**(1) (2018)
8. Davis, C.A., Varol, O., Ferrara, E., Flammini, A., Menczer, F.: Botornot: A system to evaluate social bots. In: Proceedings of the 25th International Conference Companion on World Wide Web. pp. 273–274. WWW 2016 Companion (2016)
9. Goel, S., Anderson, A., Hofman, J., Watts, D.J.: The structural virality of online diffusion. Manag. Sci. **2**(1) (2015)
10. Grinberg, N., Joseph, K., Friedland, L., Swire-Thompson, B., Lazer, D.: Fake news on twitter during the 2016 u.s. presidential election. Science **363**(6425), 374–378 (2019)
11. Jamieson, K.H.: Cyberwar: How Russian Hackers and Trolls Helped Elect a President What We Don't, Can't, and Do Know. Oxford University Press (2018)
12. Jensen, M.: Russian trolls and fake news: Information or identity logics? J. Int. Affairs **71**(1.5), 115–124 (2018)
13. Kitsak, M., et al.: Identification of influential spreaders in complex networks. Nat. Phys. **6**, 888–893 (2010)
14. Le, H., Boynton, G.R., Shafiq, Z., Srinivasan, P.: A postmortem of suspended twitter accounts in the 2016 U.S. presidential election. In: Proceedings of the 2019 IEEE/ACM International Conference on Advances in Social Networks Analysis and Mining. pp. 258–265. ASONAM 2019, ACM (2019)
15. Mazarr, M., et al.: Hostile Social Manipulation: Present Realities and Emerging Trends. Santa Monica: Rand Corporation (March 2019). https://www.rand.org/pubs/research_reports/RR2713.html

16. Michalak, T., Aadithya, K., Szczepański, P., Ravindran, B., Jennings, N.: Efficient computation of the shapley value for game-theoretic network centrality. J. Artif.l Intelll. Res **46**(2014)
17. Morone, F., Makse, H.A.: Influence maximization in complex networks through optimal percolation. Nature **524**(7563), 65–68 (2015)
18. Mueller, R.S.: Report on the Investigation into Russian Interference in the 2016 Presidential Election. Washington, DC: Department of Justice (2019). https://www.justice.gov/storage/report.pdf
19. Narayanam, R., Narahari, Y.: A shapley value-based approach to discover influential nodes in social networks. IEEE Trans. Autom. Sci. Eng. **8**(1), 130–147 (2011)
20. Papapetrou, P., Gionis, A., Mannila, H.: A shapley value approach for influence attribution. In: Gunopulos, D., Hofmann, T., Malerba, D., Vazirgiannis, M. (eds.) ECML PKDD 2011. LNCS (LNAI), vol. 6912, pp. 549–564. Springer, Heidelberg (2011). https://doi.org/10.1007/978-3-642-23783-6_35
21. Shapley, L.S.: A value for n-person games. In: Kuhn, H.W., Tucker, A.W. (eds.) Contributions to the Theory of Games II, pp. 307–317. Princeton University Press, Princeton (1953)
22. Sides, J., Tesler, M., Vavreck, L.: Identity Crisis: The 2016 Presidential Campaign and the Battle for the Meaning of America. Princeton University Press (2018)
23. Suri, N.R., Narahari, Y.: Determining the top-k nodes in social networks using the shapley value. In: Proceedings of the 7th International Joint Conference on Autonomous Agents and Multiagent Systems - Volume 3. pp. 1509–1512. AAMAS 20'08 (2008)
24. Varol, O., Ferrara, E., Davis, C., Menczer, F., Flammini, A.: Online human-bot interactions: detection, estimation, and characterization. Proceedings of the International AAAI Conference on Web and Social Media **11**(1), 280–289 (2017). https://doi.org/10.1609/icwsm.v11i1.14871
25. Vosoughi, S., Mohsenvand, M.N., Roy, D.: Rumor gauge: predicting the veracity of rumors on twitter. ACM Trans. Knowl. Discov. Data **11**(4) (2017)
26. Vosoughi, S., Roy, D., Aral, S.: The spread of true and false news online. Science **359**(6380), 1146–1151 (2018)
27. Yang, K.C., Varol, O., Hui, P.M., Menczer, F.: Scalable and generalizable social bot detection through data selection (2019)
28. Zannettou, S., Caulfield, T., De Cristofaro, E., Sirivianos, M., Stringhini, G., Blackburn, J.: Disinformation warfare: Understanding state-sponsored trolls on twitter and their influence on the web. In: Workshop on Computational Methods in Online Misbehavior, pp. 218–226. ACM (2019)
29. Zannettou, S., Caulfield, T., Setzer, W., Sirivianos, M., Stringhini, G., Blackburn, J.: Who let the trolls out?: Towards understanding state-sponsored trolls. In: Proceedings of the 10th ACM Conference on Web Science, pp. 353–362. WebSci '19, ACM (2019)

Attacks

Data Reconstruction Attack Against Principal Component Analysis

Saloni Kwatra[(✉)][ID] and Vicenç Torra[ID]

Department of Computing Science, Umeå University, Umeå, Sweden
{salonik,vtorra}@cs.umu.se

Abstract. Attacking machine learning models is one of the many ways to measure the privacy of machine learning models. Therefore, studying the performance of attacks against machine learning techniques is essential to know whether somebody can share information about machine learning models, and if shared, how much can be shared? In this work, we investigate one of the widely used dimensionality reduction techniques Principal Component Analysis (PCA). We refer to a recent paper that shows how to attack PCA using a Membership Inference Attack (MIA). When using membership inference attacks against PCA, the adversary gets access to some of the principal components and wants to determine if a particular record was used to compute those principal components. We assume that the adversary knows the distribution of training data, which is a reasonable and useful assumption for a membership inference attack. With this assumption, we show that the adversary can make a data reconstruction attack, which is a more severe attack than the membership attack. For a protection mechanism, we propose that the data guardian first generate synthetic data and then compute the principal components. We also compare our proposed approach with Differentially Private Principal Component Analysis (DPPCA). The experimental findings show the degree to which the adversary successfully attempted to recover the users' original data. We obtained comparable results with DPPCA. The number of principal components the attacker intercepted affects the attack's outcome. Therefore, our work aims to answer how much information about machine learning models is safe to disclose while protecting users' privacy.

Keywords: Principal Component Analysis · Privacy · Data reconstruction attack · Membership Inference Attack · Generative Adversarial Networks

1 Introduction

It is well known that Machine Learning (ML) models can memorize the training data [5,6]. The more the accuracy of the ML models, the more is their ability

This study was partially funded by the Wallenberg AI, Autonomous Systems and Software Program (WASP) funded by the Knut and Alice Wallenberg Foundation.

B. Arief et al. (Eds.): SocialSec 2023, LNCS 14097, pp. 79–92, 2023.
https://doi.org/10.1007/978-981-99-5177-2_5

to memorize [3]. Therefore, sharing such ML models leads to privacy violations. In order to share or deploy privacy-preserving machine learning models, it is important to understand how information leakage occurs and how much information ML models leak about individuals. For frameworks like Federated Learning (FL) [10], where the distributed devices share ML models trained on their local data with the aggregation server or with other distributed devices, knowing how much information machine learning models leak is an important question to address, especially when the ML models are trained on sensitive data. For example, medical data.

Different kinds of attacks are studied to evaluate the robustness of machine learning applications, including data poisoning attacks, model inversion attacks, and backdoor attacks. Membership Inference Attacks (MIA) [11] are the most relaxed attack, in the sense that it reveals minimal information about the individuals: whether or not a target sample is included in the training dataset on which the ML model was trained. MIA on medical data is harmful. For e.g., if the membership information is leaked from the ML model trained on Alzheimer's data. Data reconstruction attack lies at the other extreme of the information disclosure span. It is the most strict attack, as an adversary's successful data reconstruction attack can disclose all the information about an individual, which a machine learning model may have seen during its training.

In our work, we focus on Principal Component Analysis (PCA), which is a popular dimensionality reduction technique. In [15], the authors studied MIA against PCA, where the adversary intercepts some of the principal components and infer whether a particular sample participated in the computation of principal components. We show that the adversary can conduct a data reconstruction attack against PCA if the adversary intercepts some of the principal components obtained from the synthetic data generated using Conditional Tabular Generative Adversarial Network (CTGAN) [13]. Therefore, we show that even if the adversary has access to the principal components obtained from the synthetic data, which is considered safe for sharing, the adversary can attempt an extreme attack, like a data reconstruction attack, with considerable success. Differentially Private Principal Component Analysis (DPPCA) was already studied in the works [15], and [8]. In [15], the data curator adds Laplacian or Gaussian noise to the coefficients of the covariance matrix as a protection mechanism against privacy leakage. In our work, we generate a synthetic dataset before computing the principal components. The message of our work is as follows:

- In our work, we study the efficacy of synthetic datasets in combating attacks against machine learning models.
- If some of the principal components are leaked, we show that the membership attack (a less powerful attack) against PCA shown in work [15] can be converted into a more powerful attack, like a data reconstruction attack if the attacker has knowledge about the distribution of training data.
- From our work, we motivate to use protection mechanisms like generating synthetic data before training and sharing of machine learning/deep learning models.

– We also analyze the reconstruction attack's success when Differentially Private Principal Component Analysis (DPPCA) [8] is used.

The paper is organized as follows. Section 2 reviews some concepts needed in the rest of the paper. In particular, we discuss PCA, MIA against PCA, and CTGAN. Our suggested attack strategy is described in Sect. 3. Section 4 describes the approaches that were compared, including DPPCA. In Sect. 5, we provide and discuss the results. Section 6 gives the conclusion and future directions.

2 Related Work

2.1 Principal Component Analysis

Given a set $\mathcal{D} = \{x_n \in R^d : n = 1 : N\}$ comprising N raw data samples corresponding to N individuals of dimension d. After subtracting the mean from the data, we obtain the centered data matrix and denote it as X. The PCA technique aims to determine a p dimensional subspace that approximates each sample x_n [1]. The formulation of PCA is as follows:

$$\min_{\pi_p} E = \frac{1}{N} \sum_{n=1}^{N} E_n = \frac{1}{N} \sum_{n=1}^{N} \frac{1}{N} ||x_n - \pi_p x_n||_2^2 \tag{1}$$

where E is the average reconstruction error and π_p is an orthogonal projector, which approximates each sample x_n by $\hat{x_n}$. The solution to the PCA problem can be obtained via the Singular Value Decomposition (SVD) of a sample covariance matrix Σ_{cov}, a positive semi-definite matrix. Therefore, its singular value decomposition is equivalent to spectral decomposition. SVD of Σ_{cov} is given by $\sum_{i=1}^{d} \lambda_i v_i v_i^T$, where $\lambda_1 \geq \lambda_2 \ldots \lambda_d$ are the eigenvalues, and $v_1, v_2 \ldots v_d$ are the corresponding eigenvectors of Σ_{cov}, respectively. Let V_p denote the matrix whose columns are the top p eigenvectors. $\pi_p = V_p V_p^T$ is the solution to the problem in (1).

2.2 Membership Inference Attack Against Principal Component Analysis

Membership Inference attack (MIA) infers whether a particular record is part of the training dataset on which the machine learning algorithm was trained. The authors of [15] addressed MIA against PCA for the first time. In [15], the authors assume that the adversary intercepts some of the principal components. Using the intercepted principal components, the adversary computes the reconstruction error of the target sample (a sample whose membership is to be determined by the attacker). The concept is that the samples belonging to the training set will incur lower reconstruction error in comparison with the samples not belonging to the training set. Hence, on the basis of a tunable threshold value t, the adversary can distinguish between the members and the non-members of the training set.

It is quite interesting to know why membership attacks work. Previous works, including [2,4,9], and [14] identified that the overfitting of machine learning models is a reason behind the success of membership attacks. The overfitting of ML models is usually because of high model complexity and the limited size of the training dataset. Deep learning models are overparameterized and complex, which, on the one hand, enables them to learn successfully from big data, but, on the other hand, may cause them to have an unreasonably high capacity of retaining the noise or the details of a specific training dataset. Moreover, ML models are trained in a lot of (often tens to hundreds) epochs on the same instances repeatedly, making the training instances very susceptible to model memorization. Also, in [2], Bentley et al. presented a theorem that says that the overfitting of the target models can lead to the performance of an MIA better than randomly guessing (i.e., 50% attack success rate (ASR)).

2.3   Conditional Tabular Generative Adversarial Network (CTGAN)

GANs learn to generate fake samples that mimic the real ones. GANs have two neural networks. One is the generator, which generates new data, while the other is the discriminator, which aims to correctly classify the real and fake data. GANs face certain challenges when applied to tabular data, including the need to simultaneously model discrete and continuous columns, the multi-modal non-Gaussian values within each continuous column, and the imbalance in categorical columns. CTGAN [13] proposed two modifications to tackle the issues faced by GANs when applied to generate tabular data. The first problem that CTGANs solved is finding the representative normalization of continuous data. A discrete variable can be represented using one-hot encoding. For example, to represent the working days of a week, we can use one-hot encoding with five columns. Mondays can be represented as {1,0,0,0,0}. Tuesdays can be represented as {0,1,0,0,0}, and so on. However, when dealing with continuous data, it is challenging to represent all the information carried by the continuous variable. A continuous variable has multiple modes. Therefore by merely feeding the model the value of the continuous variable at our sample, we risk losing information, such as what mode the sample belongs to? and what is its importance within that mode? CTGAN proposed using mode-specific normalization to avoid losing information, which first fits a VGM (Variational Gaussian Mixture model) to each continuous variable. A Gaussian mixture model finds the optimal k Gaussians to represent the data through expectation maximization. To handle an imbalance in discrete columns, CTGANs designed a conditional vector *cond*, and a training-by-sampling technique. The conditional generator can generate synthetic rows conditioned on one of the discrete columns. Using training-by-sampling, the *cond* and training data are sampled according to the log frequency of each category. Therefore, CTGAN can explore all possible discrete values.

3   Proposed Work: Threat Model and Attack Methodology

In our attack setting, the data curator/guardian generates synthetic/fake data $\mathcal{D}_{syn}$ using different percentages (10%, 30%, 50%, 70%,100%) of samples from the original data $\mathcal{D}$. The synthetic data is generated using CTGAN, as described in Sect. 2.3. The curator then computes the principal components P_k of the synthetic data $\mathcal{D}_{syn}$, and sends these to a reliable party. We suppose that the attacker $\mathcal{A}$ intercepts some or all of the Principal Components (PCs) computed on the synthetic data by eavesdropping on the communication channel. The previous works regarding MIA are reviewed in [7], there are two kinds of knowledge useful for attackers to implement MIAs against ML models: knowledge of **data distribution**, and knowledge of **machine learning model/algorithm**, which learns about the patterns in the training data. Knowledge of training data refers to the knowledge of the data distribution, which means that the attacker has access to the shadow dataset, which has the same distribution as the original data. This is a reasonable assumption, as the attacker can obtain the shadow dataset using statistics-based synthesis when the data distribution is known and model-based synthesis when the data distribution is unknown [11]. Hence, in our attack setting, we assume that the attacker can synthesize the shadow dataset using CTGAN. By knowing some of the principal components, and the constructed shadow dataset using CTGAN, the attacker can make a data reconstruction attack as follows.

Suppose we have an original data matrix X_{orig} of size $n \times p$. We obtain a data matrix X, after subtracting the mean vector μ from each row of X_{orig}. Let V be the $p \times k$ matrix of some k eigenvectors to reduce the dimension; these would most often be the k eigenvectors with the largest eigenvalues. Then the $n \times k$ matrix of PCA projection scores (Z) will be given by $Z = XV$. In order to be able to reconstruct all the original variables from a subset of principal components/eigenvectors, we can map it back to p dimensions with V^T. The result is then given by $\hat{X} = ZV^T$. Since we have a projection scores matrix, $Z = XV$, we obtain $\hat{X} = XVV^T$. We do not have access to the original data X; we assume that the attacker has knowledge about the distribution of X. Therefore, the attacker can synthesize the data X_{syn} with a similar distribution as X, and reconstruct the original data using $\hat{X} = ZV = X_{syn}V^TV$. We assume the attacker can access the synthetic data generated using the Conditional Tabular Generative Adversarial Network (CTGAN) to show experimental results. We generate the synthetic data using different percentages of records from the original data, including {10%, 30%, 50%, 70%, 100%}. To show the degree of success of the data reconstruction attack, we show the Reconstruction Accuracy (R.A.) in estimating the original data. We define R.A. as follows.

Definition 1. *Suppose R is the reconstructed data, which is the estimator for the original data O, where $R = \{R_1 \ldots R_d\}$, and $O = \{O_1, \ldots O_d\}$. Let δ be a reconstruction error, which can be tolerated to measure the level of reconstruction for a record. The reconstruction accuracy, R.A. is defined as follows:*

$$R.A. = \frac{\#\left\{\hat{R}_j : |\frac{O_j - R_j}{O_j}| \leq \delta, j = 1 \ldots d\right\}}{n} \qquad (2)$$

where $\#$ means count, and n is the number of records. Hence, R.A. is the percentage of reconstructed entries for which the relative errors are within δ. The diagram of our proposed attack is shown in Fig. 1, which explains our methodology.

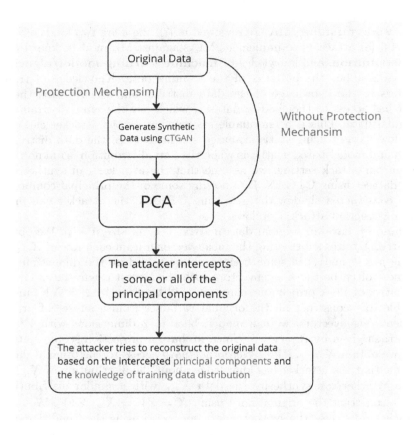

Fig. 1. Data reconstruction attack against Principal Component Analysis

4   Compared Methodologies

We compared our approach with two alternative strategies. In one strategy, we use no protection mechanism before computing the principal components. In the other strategy, we use Differentially Private Principal Component Analysis (DPPCA) for computing the principal components. In this section, we describe these alternative strategies. The results are presented in Sect. 5.

4.1 No Protection Mechanism

We first compare our proposed methodology with the case when the data curator uses no protection mechanism at all, computes the principal components of the original data, and shares these principal components with a reliable third party. Nevertheless, the attacker eavesdrops on the communication channel and obtains some or all of the principal components. Based on the knowledge of the training data distribution and the intercepted principal components, the attacker tries to reconstruct the original data of users. To be noted, the difference between our proposed methodology and the compared methodology is that in the proposed methodology, the principal components computed on the synthetic data are leaked, and in the compared methodology, the principal components computed on the original data are leaked.

4.2 Differentially Private Principal Component Analysis

The goal of PCA is to find the principal components of a dataset, which are the directions in which the data varies the most. In [8], the authors proposed a new approach to perform differentially private PCA (DPPPCA) on high-dimensional datasets. The algorithm in this paper involves perturbing the covariance matrix of the dataset in a differentially-private manner to ensure that the PCA output is also differentially-private. Specifically, the algorithm takes as input a dataset X with n samples and d dimensions and a privacy parameter ϵ. It then computes the covariance matrix S of the dataset, which is a $d \times d$ symmetric matrix. To perturb the covariance matrix while maintaining privacy, the algorithm adds a noise matrix N to S, where N is also a symmetric matrix. The noise matrix is generated using the Laplace mechanism, which adds independent Laplace noise to each entry of N, scaled by the privacy parameter ϵ. The algorithm then performs eigendecomposition on the perturbed covariance matrix $S+N$ to obtain the principal components of the dataset. The eigendecomposition is performed using a numerical algorithm, such as the power iteration method. Finally, the algorithm outputs the top k principal components of the dataset, where k is a user-specified parameter. The output is also differentially-private, as the added noise ensures that the output does not reveal information about any individual sample in the dataset. They also provide theoretical bounds on the privacy loss and the accuracy of the method.

Table 1. Description of datasets

Dataset	Number of Samples	Number of Attributes
Heart-scale	270	13
a9a	32561	123
Mushrooms	8124	112

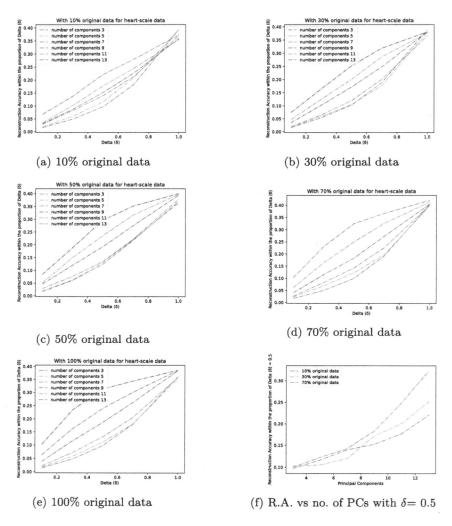

(a) 10% original data

(b) 30% original data

(c) 50% original data

(d) 70% original data

(e) 100% original data

(f) R.A. vs no. of PCs with $\delta = 0.5$

Fig. 2. R.A. within the limit Delta (δ) for heart-scale data

5   Experimental Results and Analysis

We experimented on three publicly available binary classification datasets: Heart-scale, a9a, and mushrooms. The datasets can be found on[1]. The number of samples and the number of attributes of these datasets are described in Table 1. It can be seen that the range for the number of samples is from 270 to 32,561, and the number of attributes is from only 13 to 123. Each dataset has some preprocessing steps involved. The scale for the heart-scale dataset is

---

[1] https://www.csie.ntu.edu.tw/~cjlin/libsvmtools/datasets/binary.html.

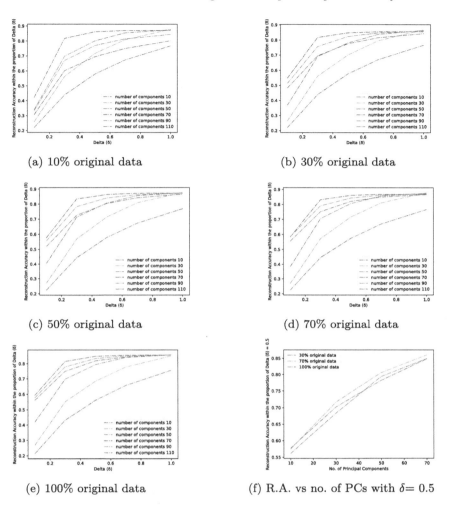

(a) 10% original data   (b) 30% original data

(c) 50% original data   (d) 70% original data

(e) 100% original data   (f) R.A. vs no. of PCs with $\delta= 0.5$

Fig. 3. R.A. within the limit Delta (δ) for a9a data

$[-1,1]$. After preprocessing, the adult dataset is converted into the a9a dataset. There are 14 features in the original adult data set, eight of which are categorical and six of which are continuous. The continuous features in this data set are discretized into quantiles, and a binary feature represents each quantile. In addition, a categorical feature with m categories is converted to m binary features. In the mushrooms dataset, each nominal attribute is expanded into several binary attributes. Also, the original attribute 12 has missing values and is not used.

In our experiments, we generated synthetic datasets using different percentages of original data. We apply PCA to the generated synthetic datasets. Assuming that the adversary intercepted some of these principal components, we try to reconstruct the data from which the principal components were computed.

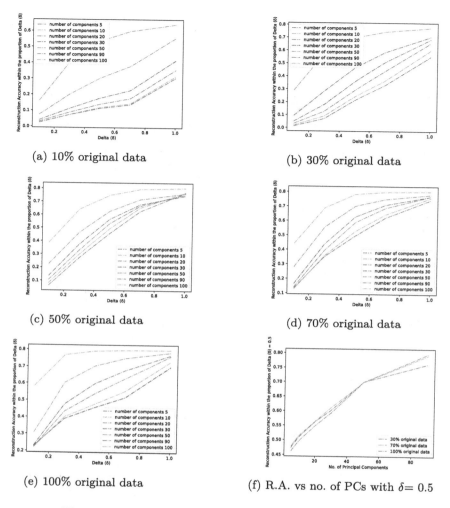

(a) 10% original data

(b) 30% original data

(c) 50% original data

(d) 70% original data

(e) 100% original data

(f) R.A. vs no. of PCs with $\delta = 0.5$

Fig. 4. R.A. within the limit Delta(δ) for mushrooms data

We obtain the reconstruction accuracy, as shown in Fig. 2, 3, and 4, respectively. We have an upper cap for the Reconstruction Accuracy (R.A.), as the maximum reconstruction error we can obtain is the difference between the original and synthetic data generated using CTGAN using all the original data records. We are measuring the capability of CTGANs to generate a different-looking but similar distribution of synthetic data and the privacy breach caused by the leakage done by the principal components. We summarize our main findings as follows.

1. We found that even after using just 10% samples from the original data, the R.A. is close to 90% when the attacker intercepted 110 principal components.

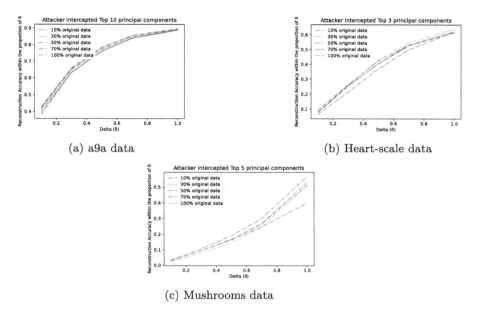

(a) a9a data   (b) Heart-scale data

(c) Mushrooms data

Fig. 5. R.A. without protection mechanism prior to the computation of PCs

R.A. is close to 70% when the attacker intercepted 10 principal components, as shown in Fig. 3a for the a9a dataset.

2. For the a9a dataset, the R.A. is more in comparison with the heart-scale data in Fig. 2 and mushrooms data in Fig. 4 dataset. The reason behind more R.A. in the case of the a9a dataset is that a9a has more categorical features. Hence, the generation of synthetic data using CTGAN could provide less protection in the case of the a9a dataset.

3. The maximum R.A. for heart-scale data, as shown in Fig. 2 is close to 40%. It is less because we have a protection mechanism using synthetic data generation before the computation of principal components.

4. The minimum reconstruction in the case of mushroom data in Fig. 4a is close to 20% when the attacker intercepted 5 or 10 principal components and only 10% of the original data was used in constructing the synthetic data.

5. In Figs. 2f, 3f, and 4f for heart-scale, a9a, and mushrooms dataset, respectively, we show a trend between R.A. and the number of principal components intercepted by the attacker. Our results show that R.A. increases as the number of principal components increases, which is also expected from theory.

6. We generated synthetic datasets from different percentages of original data. From Figs. 3a to 3e, we observe that as we increase the percentage of samples used in generating the synthetic data, the gap between the lines for R.A. in the graph widens, indicating the increase in R.A. with the increase in the

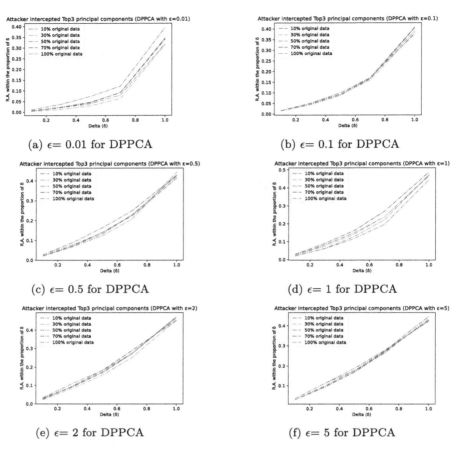

(a) ϵ= 0.01 for DPPCA

(b) ϵ= 0.1 for DPPCA

(c) ϵ= 0.5 for DPPCA

(d) ϵ= 1 for DPPCA

(e) ϵ= 2 for DPPCA

(f) ϵ= 5 for DPPCA

Fig. 6. R.A. using DPPCA on heart-scale data when the attacker intercepted Top 3 PCs

percentage of samples used from original data for generating synthetic data using CTGAN.

7. It is noted that there is not much difference in the R.A. when the CTGAN uses less percentage (e.g., 10%) of samples from the original data compared to using all the samples from the original data for generating the synthetic data. This shows the capability of CTGAN in successfully generating synthetic data similar to the original data using fewer samples from the original data.

8. When no protection mechanism is used, we show that the R.A. increases. For e.g., in Fig. 5b, the R.A. for the heart-scale data approaches 60%, which is higher in comparison with the case when DPPCA is used (Refer Fig. 6), and when the principal components were computed on the synthetic data (Refer Fig. 2).

9. In Fig. 6, we use DPPCA on the heart-scale data. We observe that the lesser the value of ϵ, the shallower the graph for R.A.
10. Both DPPCA and the generation of synthetic data technique outputs comparable R.A. The performance of DPPCA depends on the value of a privacy parameter ϵ. The lower the value of ϵ, the higher the privacy.
11. Therefore, from our experiments, we can conclude that generating synthetic data from the original data and then training machine learning models on the synthetic data is a good way to combat attacks against machine learning models to an extent.

6   Conclusion and Future Works

We proposed a data reconstruction attack against PCA by extending the work related to membership inference attacks in [15] and [7]. Specifically, we made two assumptions for attempting a data reconstruction attack against PCA; one is that the attacker knows some of the principal components computed on the synthetic dataset generated by the data curator, and the other is that the attacker has knowledge about the data distribution. Knowing that the data reconstruction attack is more harmful than the membership attack, we obtained reasonably good results in terms of reconstruction accuracy. We studied the efficacy of synthetic datasets generated using Conditional Tabular Generative Adversarial Networks as a protection mechanism in combating data reconstruction attacks. In the future, we would like to explore the behavior of other machine learning models against MIA and data reconstruction attacks. In the work [12], it is shown that synthetic data cannot protect the outlier records but performs well in terms of utility, whereas DP synthetic data provides high privacy gains but at the cost of degrading the utility of data. Hence, we would also like to conduct the privacy and utility analysis of synthetic and DP synthetic datasets.

References

1. Abdi, H., Williams, L.J.: Principal component analysis. Wiley Interdiscip. Rev. Comput. Stat. **2**(4), 433–459 (2010)
2. Bentley, J.W., Gibney, D., Hoppenworth, G., Jha, S.K.: Quantifying membership inference vulnerability via generalization gap and other model metrics. arXiv preprint arXiv:2009.05669 (2020)
3. Brown, G., Bun, M., Feldman, V., Smith, A., Talwar, K.: When is memorization of irrelevant training data necessary for high-accuracy learning? In: Proceedings of the 53rd Annual ACM SIGACT Symposium on Theory of Computing, pp. 123–132 (2021)
4. Farokhi, F., Kaafar, M.A.: Modelling and quantifying membership information leakage in machine learning. arXiv preprint arXiv:2001.10648 (2020)
5. Feldman, V.: Does learning require memorization? A short tale about a long tail. In: Proceedings of the 52nd Annual ACM SIGACT Symposium on Theory of Computing, pp. 954–959 (2020)

6. Feldman, V., Zhang, C.: What neural networks memorize and why: discovering the long tail via influence estimation. Adv. Neural. Inf. Process. Syst. **33**, 2881–2891 (2020)
7. Hu, H., Salcic, Z., Sun, L., Dobbie, G., Yu, P.S., Zhang, X.: Membership inference attacks on machine learning: a survey. ACM Comput. Surv. (CSUR) **54**(11s), 1–37 (2022)
8. Imtiaz, H., Sarwate, A.D.: Symmetric matrix perturbation for differentially-private principal component analysis. In: 2016 IEEE International Conference on Acoustics, Speech and Signal Processing (ICASSP), pp. 2339–2343. IEEE (2016)
9. Jha, S.K., et al.: An extension of Fano's inequality for characterizing model susceptibility to membership inference attacks. arXiv preprint arXiv:2009.08097 (2020)
10. McMahan, B., Moore, E., Ramage, D., Hampson, S., Arcas, B.A.: Communication-efficient learning of deep networks from decentralized data. In: Artificial Intelligence and Statistics, pp. 1273–1282. PMLR (2017)
11. Shokri, R., Stronati, M., Song, C., Shmatikov, V.: Membership inference attacks against machine learning models. In: 2017 IEEE Symposium on Security and Privacy (SP), pp. 3–18. IEEE (2017)
12. Stadler, T., Oprisanu, B., Troncoso, C.: Synthetic data-anonymisation groundhog day. In: 31st USENIX Security Symposium (USENIX Security 2022), pp. 1451–1468 (2022)
13. Xu, L., Skoularidou, M., Cuesta-Infante, A., Veeramachaneni, K.: Modeling tabular data using conditional GAN. In: Advances in Neural Information Processing Systems, vol. 32 (2019)
14. Yeom, S., Giacomelli, I., Fredrikson, M., Jha, S.: Privacy risk in machine learning: analyzing the connection to overfitting. In: 2018 IEEE 31st Computer Security Foundations Symposium (CSF), pp. 268–282. IEEE (2018)
15. Zari, O., Parra-Arnau, J., Ünsal, A., Strufe, T., Önen, M.: Membership inference attack against principal component analysis. In: Domingo-Ferrer, J., Laurent, M. (eds.) PSD 2022. LNCS, vol. 13463, pp. 269–282. Springer, Cham (2022). https://doi.org/10.1007/978-3-031-13945-1_19

The Impact of Synthetic Data
on Membership Inference Attacks

Md Sakib Nizam Khan$^{(\boxtimes)}$ and Sonja Buchegger

KTH Royal Institute of Technology, Stockholm, Sweden
{msnkhan,buc}@kth.se

Abstract. Privacy of machine learning on Big Data has become a prominent issue in recent years due to the increased availability and usage of sensitive personal data to train the models. Membership inference attacks are one such issue that has been identified as a major privacy threat against machine learning models. Several techniques including applying differential privacy have been advocated to mitigate the effectiveness of inference attacks, however, they come at a cost of reduced utility/accuracy. Synthetic data is one approach that has been widely studied as a tool for privacy preservation recently but not much yet in the context of membership inference attacks. In this work, we aim to deepen the understanding of the impact of synthetic data on membership inference attacks. We compare models trained on original versus synthetic data, evaluate different synthetic data generation methods, and study the effect of overfitting in terms of membership inference attacks. Our investigation reveals that training on synthetic data can significantly reduce the effectiveness of membership inference attacks compared to models trained directly on the original data. This also holds for highly overfitted models that have been shown to increase the success rate of membership inference attacks. We also find that different synthetic data generation methods do not differ much in terms of membership inference attack accuracy but they do differ in terms of utility (i.e., observed based on train/test accuracy). Since synthetic data shows promising results for binary classification-based membership inference attacks on classification models explored in this work, exploring the impact on other attack types, models, and attribute inference attacks can be of worth.

Keywords: Synthetic Data · Machine Learning · Membership Inference Attack · Accuracy

1 Introduction

Machine learning has become one of the most essential elements of many technological solutions in recent years due to its huge benefits. The increasingly common applications of machine learning include image and speech recognition, predictive analytics, natural language processing, behavioral analysis, recommender systems, etc. In the majority of these scenarios, the data that the

B. Arief et al. (Eds.): SocialSec 2023, LNCS 14097, pp. 93–108, 2023.
https://doi.org/10.1007/978-981-99-5177-2_6

machine learning models build upon contains privacy-sensitive data of individuals. Privacy of machine learning has become a concerning issue recently due to the rapid increase in the use of personal and thus potentially privacy-sensitive data to train machine learning models. The problem of models with sufficient capacity (i.e., especially deep neural networks (DNN)) is that they tend to memorize the training data [35]. Several attacks have been developed that are capable of revealing information about the training data by exploiting the memorization capability of machine learning models.

Membership inference is one of the most prominent privacy vulnerabilities of machine learning models [24]. The goal of the attacker in the case of membership inference is to identify whether a given record is used to train the machine learning model or not which can eventually leak privacy-sensitive information. For instance, just revealing membership in a set used to train a target model related to a certain disease can reveal that a person has the disease which is a severe violation of privacy. Moreover, the attack can be carried out with minimal information in a black-box manner which increases the severity of the attack further. Shokri et al. [25] first proposed the black-box membership inference attack (MIA) which utilized a neural network-based binary classifier for detecting membership. Since then a plethora of attacks both black-box and white-box have been proposed for membership inference [10].

Model overfitting has been identified as one of the prime reasons for membership inference [25]. The machine learning models overfit when the model accuracy on the training data is significantly better compared to the accuracy on the unseen test data. This difference in accuracy is also termed as generalization error. Many different mitigation techniques have been proposed to solve the problem of membership inference mainly to achieve indistinguishability between the model's behavior on training and unseen test data. The mitigation strategies include the use of differential privacy [20], adding inference attack as a regularization term during model training [17], adding perturbed noise to models prediction outputs [13], etc. Nonetheless, it has been shown in some recent works that these defense strategies are not effective enough for some novel membership inference attacks (MIAs) [24].

The use of synthetic data for disclosure protection has gained significant attention in recent years. It has been widely studied as a measure of privacy protection for data release and analysis. The benefit of synthetic data is that there is no given direct linkability between the records and individuals since the data is not real. Furthermore, several works have shown that in terms of utility for machine learning tasks, synthetic data can also achieve acceptable accuracy close to original data, e.g., for tabular data [14] and image data [30]. However, more research is needed to understand what happens to MIAs if we train machine learning models using synthetic data instead of original data.

In this work, we thus investigate the impact of synthetic data on membership inference attacks against machine learning models where the target models are mainly classification models with supervised learning. First, we compare the membership inference attack accuracy between models trained on synthetic data and original data using four publicly available datasets. Second, we compare different synthetic data generation methods in terms of MIAs. Third, we also study the effect of overfitting on models trained on original and synthetic data concerning membership inference attack accuracy by reducing the number of training data to intentionally overfit the model.

Organization. The rest of the paper is organized as follows. In Sect. 2, we discuss the related work, followed by an overview of the membership inference attack in Sect. 3. In Sect. 4, we briefly discuss synthetic data generation methods. We then present our experimental setup in Sect. 5 followed by the experimental results in Sect. 6. Finally, we conclude our work in Sect. 7.

2 Related Work

Since the inception of membership inference attacks against machine learning models, there has been a lot of work focusing on the mitigation of such attacks. Overfitting has been one of the prime reasons for membership inference. Thus, several works [17,23,25,27,33] focused on reducing the overfitting of machine learning models to defend against membership inference attacks. The works mainly utilized various regularization techniques such as l2 regularization [25], dropout [23], and adversarial regularization [17] to reduce the overfitting of machine learning models. Besides this, several mechanisms leveraged differential privacy [1,12,29,34] for mitigating the risk of membership inference attacks. The problem with employing these mitigation strategies is that besides reducing the privacy risks typically they reduce the performance of the target model as well.

We also consider some related works that look into different aspects of synthetic data concerning inference attacks. For instance, in a recent work, Stadler et al. [28] performed a quantitative evaluation of the privacy gain of synthetic data publishing and compared it with other anonymization techniques. The authors first empirically evaluated whether synthetic data generated by a wide range of generative models without any additional privacy measures provide robust protection against linkage attacks for all target records or not. Based on their experiments, the authors concluded that synthetic data does not provide uniform protection for all records and cannot protect some outlier records from linkage attacks. Next, the authors also show that differentially private synthetic data can protect such records from inference attacks but at a high utility cost. According to the author's findings, synthetic data cannot provide transparency about the privacy-utility tradeoff, unlike traditional anonymization techniques. It is impossible to predict what features of the original data will be preserved or suppressed in the synthetic data. Lastly, the authors also provide a framework as an open-source library to quantify the privacy gain of synthetic data publishing and compare the quality with different anonymization techniques.

Slokom et al. [26] investigated whether training a classifier on synthetic data instead of original data can mitigate the effectiveness of attribute inference attacks. The authors first demonstrate with a model trained on original data that by performing the attack an attacker can learn sensitive attributes both about individuals present in the training data and also about previously unseen individuals. Then they replicated the attack on a model trained on synthetic data instead of the original data and found that the synthetic model is also as susceptible to attribute inference as the original model. According to the authors, this finding relates to the success of an attack inferring sensitive information from individuals using priors and not the machine learning model itself.

Zhang et al. [36] proposed a novel approach for membership inference against synthetic health data that tries to infer whether specific records are used for generating synthetic data or not. The authors evaluate fully synthetic and partially synthetic data based on their proposed approach for membership inference. According to the authors, their experimental results show that partially synthetic data are susceptible to membership inference whereas fully synthetic data are substantially more resilient against such inference attacks. The authors believe that their method can be used for preliminary risk evaluation of releasing any partially synthetic data.

Hu et al. [11] proposed to use data generated by Generative Adversarial Network (GAN) based on original data (i.e., synthetic data) for training machine learning models to defend against membership inference attacks. To ensure high utility, the authors utilize two different GAN structures with special training techniques for image and tabular data types respectively. For the generation of image data, the truncation technique is used whereas for tabular data clustering is used to ensure the quality of the generated data. Their empirical evaluation show that the proposed approach is effective against existing attack schemes and more efficient than existing defense mechanisms.

Though not focusing directly on membership attacks, another relevant related work for the potential privacy-protecting properties of synthetic data for data analysis, Ruiz et al. [22] investigate the linkability of synthetic to original data and argue that, based on a scenario where the attacker has access to the original dataset in its entirety, individuals' representations in synthetic and original datasets remain linked by the information they convey. Nonetheless, a contrasting finding was reported by Giomi et al. in [8] where the authors evaluated three types of privacy risk namely singling out, linkability, and inference risks of synthetic data using their proposed framework called Anonymneter. From their experiments, the authors observed that synthetic data is the least vulnerable to linkability. The findings indicate that one-to-one relationships between the original and generated records are not preserved in synthetic data.

The main difference between these works and our work is that none of the works perform a thorough investigation of the effect of synthetic data on the overall accuracy of membership inference attacks compared to the original data when using the synthetic data as training data, in contrast to publishing synthetic data in an effort to protect the privacy of the original data. For example, [28] investigates whether synthetic data can protect outliers equally as other records from inference attacks, [26] looks into attribute inference attacks, [36] focused on inference attacks against synthetic data generation process, and [11] only focused on GAN based methods for synthetic data generation and did not investigate the effect of different synthesizers or overfitting on membership inference attack accuracy in the context of synthetic data. There exists a research gap regarding the impact of training machine learning models on synthetic data instead of original data on membership inference attacks which we try to bridge in this work.

3   Membership Inference Attacks (MIA)

The attack mechanism for membership inference can vary depending on the adversarial knowledge of the attacker. In this section, we provide a brief overview of adversarial knowledge and attack types and then discuss the attack mechanism used in this work in detail.

Adversarial Knowledge. The knowledge of an attacker can vary depending on how much information the attacker has access to about the machine learning model they are trying to attack. With regards to membership inference, there are two types of information that are beneficial for the attacker, namely information about the training data and information about the target model. The information about the training data refers to knowing the distribution of the training data. It is assumed in most of the membership inference attack settings that the distribution of the training data is known to the attacker which means that the attacker can obtain a so-called shadow dataset from the same distribution as the training data. To be realistic, it is also assumed that the training dataset and the shadow dataset are disjoint. The information about the target model refers to knowing the learning algorithm, model architecture, and parameters of the model. Depending on the knowledge of the attacker, MIAs are divided into two categories which are white-box attacks and black-box attacks.

White-Box Attack. In this type of attack, it is assumed that the attacker has knowledge about the training data and also about the target model. The knowledge that the attacker possesses in this setting includes information about the training data distribution, learning algorithm, model architecture, and parameters of the target model.

Black-Box Attack. In the case of black-box, it is assumed that the attacker only has information about the training data distribution and can query the target model in a black-box manner. For instance, in the case of the classification model, the attacker can provide an input record as a query to the model and can obtain the corresponding prediction output from the model. Nonetheless, the attacker does not have any information about the target model architecture, parameters, or the learning algorithm.

Approaches of Attack. Due to overparameterization, machine learning models such as DNN sometimes achieve the capacity to memorize features about the data that they are trained on [4]. As a result, the models behave differently on training data (i.e., members) versus the test data (i.e., nonmembers) that they have never seen. For instance, if the target model is a classification model, then it

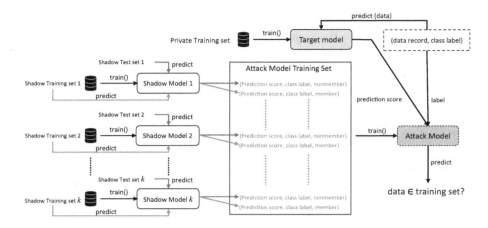

Fig. 1. Binary Classifier-based Membership Inference Attack

would classify the true class of training data with a higher confidence score than it would do for the unseen test data. This differentiation allows an attacker to build an attack model that can distinguish between members and nonmembers of a training dataset. Depending on how an attack model is created, the approach of membership inference attack can be divided into two major categories which are, binary classifier-based approach and metric-based approach. In this work, we use a binary classifier-based membership inference attack on classification models which is discussed in the following section. For more details on membership inference attacks based on other approaches and other models see [10].

3.1   Binary Classifier-Based Black-Box Attack

The basic idea of this approach for MIA is to train a binary classifier (i.e., attack model) capable of distinguishing the behavior of a target model on the members of the training set from nonmembers. The very first and most popular binary classifier-based membership inference attack technique (also termed shadow training) was proposed by Shokri et al. [25]. The main idea of the attack technique proposed by the authors is that the attacker trains multiple shadow models to imitate the behavior of the target model. Figure 1 shows an overview of the attack process. The shadow models are trained using shadow datasets which are drawn from a similar distribution as the training dataset of the target model. The assumption here is that the attacker knows the distribution of the training data which can be used to generate the shadow datasets. It is also assumed for non-triviality that the target model's training dataset and the shadow datasets are disjoint.

For each shadow model, the shadow dataset is divided into a shadow train set and a shadow test set. The shadow models are then trained using their corresponding train sets. Once the models are trained, prediction outputs are generated using each trained model for both their own train set and the unseen test set. The obtained output vectors for each shadow model are then labeled as *members* for the model's own train set and as *non-members* for the unseen test set. The resulting labeled data make up the training data for the attack model which is the binary classifier inferring membership status. It is important to note that for each class of the target model, a separate attack model is trained to infer membership for the particular class. Once the attack model is trained, for the membership inference, the attacker first queries the target model with a particular record and obtains the prediction vector. Then the attacker passes the prediction vector value to the trained attack model with its true class to obtain the membership status.

4   Synthetic Data Generation

The idea of synthetic data as a confidentiality measure was introduced first in 1993 by Rubin [21], where the proposal was to use multiple imputation on all variables to generate fully synthetic data such that no original data is released. Since then multiple approaches such as parametric, non-parametric (e.g., classification and regression trees (CART) [3], random forest [2], etc.), saturated model, and so on have emerged for generating synthetic data. Recently, due to the advancement of machine learning, deep learning-based methods such as Generative Adversarial Networks (GANs) [9] are also getting widely used for generating fully synthetic data.

Synthpop is an open-source R package developed by Nowok et al. [18] for generating synthetic data based on the original data. The package provides the possibility of choosing parametric and non-parametric methods for synthetic data generation. The non-parametric method is mainly based on classification and regression tree (CART) which is capable of handling any type of data. For parametric the available methods include linear regression and predictive mean matching for numerical variables and logistic regression for categorical variables.

Synthetic Data Vault (SDV) is a python-based library also for generating synthetic data developed by Patki et al. [19]. Besides statistical approaches, SDV also includes GAN-based approaches to generate synthetic data. Conditional Tabular GAN (CTGAN) developed by Xu et al. [31] is a popular GAN-based approach capable of handling and achieving good performance for the mixed type of data. Apart from CTGAN, SDV also has another GAN-based approach called CopulaGAN which is a variation of CTGAN that utilizes cumulative distribution function (CDF) based transformations for making the learning process easier. In this work, we use different methods from *Synthpop* and *SDV* libraries for generating synthetic datasets.

5   Experimental Setup

This Section discusses the experimental setup. Table 1 provides a brief overview of the datasets used in this work for the empirical evacuation.

The goal of the experiments is to find out whether, given the synthetic data, the attacker can infer whether a particular record (e.g. an individuals data) was used to generate the synthetic data that, in turn, was used to train the model as opposed to whether the record was a member of the dataset that was used to train the model directly. The inferred membership is thus an indirect one. Our codes for the experiments are available on GitHub[1].

As shown in Table 1, we use four publicly available datasets for our experiments which are Adult [15] and Avila [6] from UCI Machine Learning Repository [7], Polish quality of life dataset (SD2011) [5] from Synthpop example datasets, and Location-30 dataset created by Shokri et al. [25] based on location check-ins in the Foursquare social network, restricted to the Bangkok area and collected from April 2012 to September 2013 [32]. The classification task for the Adult dataset is to classify if the income of a person is above or below 50K and for Avila, it is to classify the author based on the patterns. For Location-30, the task is to predict the user's geosocial type based on their geographical profile. For the Polish dataset, there is no such common classification task. However, since it is a census dataset similar to Adult and has an income variable, we predict whether the income of a person is above or below 1K.

For the target model architecture of Adult, Avila, and Polish datasets, we use a fully connected deep neural network (DNN) model with layer sizes 600, 512, 256, and 128 before the final output layer. We use Adam optimizer for the learning with 200 epochs. For the Location-30 dataset, we also use a fully connected DNN but with layer sizes 512, 248, 128, and 64 before the output layer. Adam optimizer with 100 epochs is used for learning. For Location-30, we use l2 regularization with a weight of 0.0007 whereas for the other three datasets weight of 0.00003 is used. Tanh is used as the activation function for all of the datasets. We train 20 shadow models for each of the datasets.

For synthetic models, we generate synthetic data using the original records sequentially starting from 1. For instance, in the case of Adult, we use original records from 1 to 10000 for synthetic data generation. Similarly, for Polish original records 1–2500 is used for generating synthetic data. The data for the shadow model and nonmember test set for the attack model is randomly drawn from the remaining original dataset whereas the member test set for the attack model is drawn randomly from the original records used for synthetic data generation.

6   Experimental Results

6.1   Membership Inference Accuracy Comparison

In this experiment, we evaluate the impact of synthetic data on membership inference by comparing membership inference attack accuracy between the model trained on original data versus the model trained on synthetic data. As mentioned previously, we use the binary classification-based attack technique proposed by Shokri et al. [25] for membership inference.

For this experiment, for each of the four datasets, we train an original target model and a synthetic target model. We divide the original dataset by drawing

---

[1] https://github.com/sakib570/mia-synthetic-data.

Table 1. Dataset Description

Dataset	Total Instances	No. Classes	Model Type	Data Type	Synthetic Data Gen.	Target Model Train Set	Target Model Test Set	Shadow Train Size	Attack Model Member	Attack Model Non-member
Adult	48842	2	Original	Original	-	7000	3000	7000	2500	2500
			Synthetic	Original	10000	-	-	7000	2500	2500
				Synthetic	-	7000	3000	-	-	-
Polish	5000	2	Original	Original	-	840	360	840	600	600
			Synthetic	Original	2500	-	-	840	600	600
				Synthetic	-	840	360	-	-	-
Location-30	5010	30	Original	Original	-	840	360	840	600	600
			Synthetic	Original	2500	-	-	840	600	600
				Synthetic	-	7000	3000	-	-	-
Avila	20867	12	Original	Original	-	7000	3000	7000	2500	2500
			Synthetic	Original	10000	-	-	7000	2500	2500
				Synthetic	-	7000	3000	-	-	-

three disjoint datasets where one dataset is used for training and testing the target model, one is for training and testing the shadow model, and the remaining one is for testing the attack model. However, for the synthetic model, we first generate a synthetic dataset based on the original dataset. The portion of the dataset used for generating synthetic data is similarly drawn from the original data as in the case of the original model. For generating synthetic data, we use *Synthpop* method *CART with Catall* for all of the datasets. In the case of the synthetic model, the data for the shadow model and testing the attack model are drawn from the original dataset similar to the original model. Thus, the only difference between the original and synthetic model is that, for synthetic, the target model is trained using the synthetic data that is generated based on original data instead of directly training on original data which is the case for the original model. This introduces an extra layer of indirection to the original data for the synthetic model and the goal of this experiment is to study the impact of this indirection on the membership inference accuracy. Table 1 depicts for each dataset the number of records used for the target, shadow, and attack model for both the original and the synthetic scenario.

For the evaluation, we measure the train and test accuracy of the target model and the attack accuracy and precision of the attack model. We use an equal number of members and nonmembers (i.e., 50% members and 50% nonmembers) for the validation of the attack model. Thus, attack accuracy close to 0.5 would indicate that the attack performance is as good as a random guess. The train and test accuracy comparison between the original and synthetic model provides an intuition of whether the synthetic model is behaving similarly to the original model or not. Table 2 depicts the results obtained from this experiment for each of the four datasets.

As shown in Table 2, concerning train and test accuracy, for all of the datasets, the original and synthetic models achieve similar results. The deviation in accuracy remains within ∼0%–5% except for the test accuracy in the case of the Location-30 dataset. The synthetic model for the Location-30 dataset achieves much better test accuracy (i.e., ∼14%) than the original model,

Table 2. Accuracy Comparison between Original and Synthetic Model

Dataset	Target Model	Train Accuracy	Test Accuracy	Attack Accuracy	Attack Precision
Adult	Original	92.84	80.73	0.545	0.524
	Synthetic	93.057	83.26	0.5042	0.5023
Polish	Original	97.38	55.83	0.66	0.59
	Synthetic	98.33	60.84	0.53	0.52
Location-30	Original	100	48.61	0.83	0.75
	Synthetic	100	64.44	0.54	0.57
Avila	Original	99.92	98.66	0.5108	0.5054
	Synthetic	99.95	99.15	0.4991	0.4992

however, both models achieve the same train accuracy (i.e., 100%). This indicates that the synthetic model for the Location-30 dataset generalizes better than the original model.

In terms of attack accuracy, we see that the synthetic models achieve lower attack accuracy than the corresponding original models as well as the accuracy values are close to the baseline accuracy of 0.5 for all of the datasets. The most significant reduction happens in the case of the Location-30 dataset where the accuracy drops from 0.83 for the original model to 0.54 for the synthetic model. Similarly, for the Polish dataset, we see that attack accuracy reduces from 0.66 to 0.53 for the synthetic model. In the case of Adult and Avila, even though the attack accuracy for the original model is already close to the baseline accuracy of 0.5, we still see that the synthetic model brings the accuracy further close to the baseline. One reason behind the significant reduction of attack accuracy for the synthetic model of the Location-30 dataset can be a better generalization. Since overfitting is one of the prime reasons for membership inference and the synthetic model for Location-30 on top of the indirection layer of synthetic data achieves better generalization (i.e., less overfitting), it is able to reduce the attack accuracy further. The attack precision scores also show a similar trend as the attack accuracy.

In summary, the experiment reveals that training on synthetic data instead of original data can significantly reduce the effectiveness of membership inference attacks. For all of the datasets we see that training on synthetic data is able to bring down the attack accuracy close to random guessing. The exact results for attack accuracy have been shown to not only depend on the dataset but also the bias of the samples used [24], and should thus be taken as approximations though we did not influence the sample selection in our experiments.

6.2 Evaluation of Synthetic Data Generation Methods

In this experiment, we evaluate different synthetic data generation methods concerning membership inference. We compare four different synthetic data

Table 3. Comparison of Synthetic Data Generation Methods

Dataset	Model	Train Accuracy	Test Accuracy	Generalization Error	Attack Accuracy
Adult	Original	92.84	80.73	12.11	0.545
	Synthpop CART+Catall	93.057	83.26	9.797	0.5042
	Synthpop Parametric	87.44	82.8	4.64	0.49
	SDV CTGAN	92.72	77.16	15.56	0.49
	SDV Copula GAN	84.11	81.86	2.25	0.498
Polish	Original	97.38	55.83	41.55	0.66
	Synthpop CART+Catall	98.33	60.84	37.49	0.53
	Synthpop Parametric	92.85	55.96	36.89	0.51
	SDV CTGAN	99.88	61.26	38.62	0.505
	SDV Copula GAN	99.76	50.48	49.28	0.49
Location-30	Original	100	48.61	51.39	0.83
	Synthpop CART+Catall	100	64.44	35.56	0.54
	Synthpop Parametric	100	24.16	75.84	0.534
	SDV CTGAN	100	8.33	91.67	0.506
	SDV Copula GAN	100	4.44	95.56	0.491
Avila	Original	99.92	98.66	1.26	0.5108
	Synthpop CART+Catall	99.95	99.15	0.8	0.4991
	Synthpop Parametric	98.04	39.6	58.44	0.45
	SDV CTGAN	99.028	64.033	34.995	0.5074
	SDV Copula GAN	96.785	35.06	61.725	0.4974

generation methods which are *Synthpop CART with Catall, Synthpop Parametric, SDV CTGAN*, and *SDV Copula GAN*. The reason behind choosing these methods is that we want to cover traditional approaches such as CART and parametric as well as more recent GAN-based approaches. For this experiment, we use the same attack technique and training/testing methods used in Sect. 6.1.

Table 3 shows the train and test accuracy, generalization error, and attack accuracy obtained for different synthetic data generation methods for each of the four datasets. For the Adult dataset, in terms of train/test accuracy and generalization error, all of the synthetic data generation methods obtain similar results as the original model. The attack accuracy for all of the methods is also very close to the baseline accuracy of 0.5 with negligible differences. *Synthpop CART with Catall* obtained the closest train/test accuracy and generalization error to the original model. For the Polish dataset, we also see a similar trend where all of the methods obtained similar results to the original model for train/test accuracy and generalization error. However, in terms of attack accuracy, we see more significant differences between the methods than in the case of Adult. For Polish, *SDV CTGAN* obtained the closest train/test accuracy to the original model and also achieved an attack accuracy value (i.e., 0.505) close to baseline accuracy.

For Location-30, the methods perform very differently than what we saw for Adult and Polish. In terms of test accuracy, *SDV CTGAN* and *Copula GAN* obtain only 8.33 and 4.44 respectively which are very poor compared to the test accuracy of 48.61 of the original model. *Synthpop Parametric* perform a bit better than the GAN methods and obtain a test accuracy value of 24.16 which is still far from the test accuracy of the original model. This can be an indication that the synthetic datasets generated by these methods are unable to capture the complete features of the original data. Nonetheless, *Synthpop CART with Catall* perform much better in terms of test accuracy than the other methods and obtain even better test accuracy value (i.e., 64.44) than the original model which indicates that the synthetic model generalizes better than the original model. In terms of attack accuracy even though *Synthpop CART with Catall* obtain 0.54 which is the highest attack accuracy value compared to other methods, it is still close to the baseline accuracy and not significantly far away from other methods. Thus, overall *Synthpop CART with Catall* performs best for the Location-30 dataset. For the Avila dataset, we also see a similar trend as the Location-30 dataset where *Synthpop Parametric, SDV CTGAN,* and *SDV Copula GAN* perform poorly in terms of test accuracy compared to the original model. Also, *Synthpop CART with Catall* performs best overall and achieves both train/test accuracy close to the original model and attack accuracy close to the baseline.

In summary, from this experiment, we see that the synthetic data generation method can perform differently depending on the dataset. The performance of the synthetic model can also vary depending on the method and some methods can imitate the original model better than others in terms of train and test accuracy. For attack accuracy, we do not see any significant differences between the methods. Finally, *Synthpop CART with Catall* performs best for the combination of train/test accuracy and attack accuracy for all of the datasets.

6.3   Effect of Overfitting

Model overfitting has been identified as one of the most common causes of membership inference by many studies [16,25]. Hence, in this experiment, we want to study whether synthetic data has any effect on membership inference of overfitted models and whether the reduction of the attack accuracy achieved remains robust even when the training process is biased in favor of the attacker. Since overfitting occurs when models have sufficient memorizing capacity, reducing the size (number of records) of the training dataset increases the memorizing capability which in turn increases the overfitting of a model. Thus, for this experiment, we varied the size of training datasets to intentionally overfit both the original and synthetic models and then measured the attack accuracy.

Table 4 shows the obtained results. For this experiment, we use the Adult and Location-30 datasets and reduce the number of training data to 100 for both the datasets to achieve overfitting. We compare the results of train size 100 with train size 7000 for Adult and 840 for Location-30, the same train sizes used in previous experiments. For the Adult dataset, when we reduce the train size from

7000 to 100 the generalization error increases from 12.11 to 28.01 respectively for the original model. This indicates that the original model with train size 100 overfits more on the training data. Due to this overfitting, the attack accuracy for the original model increases to 0.63 (train size 100) from 0.545 (train size 7000). However, when we look at the synthetic model attack accuracy, it only increases to 0.53 from 0.5042 for the same. The generalization error for the synthetic model also does not increase as much as the original model.

Table 4. Effect of Overfitting

Dataset	Train Size	Model Type	Train Accuracy	Test Accuracy	Generalization Error	Attack Accuracy
Adult	7000	Original	92.84	80.73	12.11	0.545
		Synthetic	93.057	83.26	9.797	0.5042
	100	Original	98	69.99	28.01	0.63
		Synthetic	95.99	75.99	20	0.53
Location-30	840	Original	100	48.61	51.39	0.83
		Synthetic	100	64.44	35.56	0.54
	100	Original	100	28.45	71.55	1
		Synthetic	100	56	44	0.55

For the Location-30 dataset, synthetic data shows an even more significant effect on attack accuracy. In the case of the original model, the generalization error increases to 71.55 (train size 100) from 51.39 (train size 840). Similarly, the attack accuracy increases to 1 (train size 100) from 0.83 (train size 840). The attack accuracy 1 for the model with train size 100 means that the attack model can successfully infer members and nonmembers with 100% accuracy. Nonetheless, for synthetic data, the attack accuracy for train size 100 is 0.55 which is not far from the baseline accuracy. The synthetic model significantly reduces the attack accuracy compared to the original model. In terms of the generalization error, we see a similar trend as the Adult dataset.

In summary, the experiment reveals that in scenarios where training on original data results in a highly overfitted model, training on synthetic data instead can significantly reduce the possibility of membership inference attacks.

7   Discussion and Conclusion

In this work, we investigate the impact of synthetic data on membership inference attacks. We also compare different synthetic data generation methods in terms of membership inference attack accuracy and study the effect of overfitting on the synthetic and original models. Our investigation reveals that training on synthetic data can effectively reduce the membership inference attack accuracy compared to the models trained on original data. The synthetic model can bring down the attack accuracy close to baseline accuracy which is as good as a random guess even for datasets that have significantly high attack accuracy. In the case of synthetic data generation methods, our experiments reveal that some methods generate synthetic data such that the models train on them imitate the original model better than others in terms of train and test accuracy. However, the attack accuracy does not vary significantly for any of the methods. Thus, the choice of synthetic data generation method should depend on the utility and one should choose a method that provides the best utility close to the original data. Furthermore, our investigation on overfitting reveals that training on synthetic data can significantly reduce the possibility of membership inference in scenarios where original data produces highly overfitted models. In this work, we just look at binary classification-based membership inference attacks. Nonetheless, there are other metric-based and also more advanced membership inference attacks. In future work, we, therefore, want to investigate whether synthetic data has a similar impact on such attacks. Additionally, further investigation can be done to understand if synthetic data can mitigate or reduce the effectiveness of attribute inference attacks on machine learning models.

Acknowledgment. This work was partially supported by the Wallenberg AI, Autonomous Systems & Software Program (WASP) funded by Knut & Alice Wallenberg Foundation.

References

1. Abadi, M., et al.: Deep learning with differential privacy. In: Proceedings of the 2016 ACM SIGSAC Conference on Computer and Communications Security, pp. 308–318 (2016)
2. Breiman, L.: Random forests. Mach. Learn. **45**(1), 5–32 (2001)
3. Breiman, L., Friedman, J., Olshen, R., Stone, C.: Classification and Regression Trees, vol. 37, no. 15, pp. 237–251. Wadsworth International Group (1984)
4. Carlini, N., Liu, C., Erlingsson, Ú., Kos, J., Song, D.: The secret sharer: evaluating and testing unintended memorization in neural networks. In: 28th USENIX Security Symposium (USENIX Security 2019), pp. 267–284 (2019)
5. Czapiński, J., Panek, T.: Social diagnosis 2011. Objective and subjective quality of life in Poland. Contemp. Econ. **5**(3) (2011)
6. De Stefano, C., Maniaci, M., Fontanella, F., di Freca, A.S.: Reliable writer identification in medieval manuscripts through page layout features: the "Avila" bible case. Eng. Appl. Artif. Intell. **72**, 99–110 (2018)
7. Dua, D., Graff, C.: UCI Machine Learning Repository (2017). http://archive.ics.uci.edu/ml
8. Giomi, M., Boenisch, F., Wehmeyer, C., Tasnádi, B.: A unified framework for quantifying privacy risk in synthetic data. In: Proceedings of Privacy Enhancing Technologies Symposium (2023). https://doi.org/10.56553/popets-2023-0055
9. Goodfellow, I., et al.: Generative adversarial networks. Commun. ACM **63**(11), 139–144 (2020)
10. Hu, H., Salcic, Z., Sun, L., Dobbie, G., Yu, P.S., Zhang, X.: Membership inference attacks on machine learning: a survey. ACM Comput. Surv. (CSUR) **54**(11s), 1–37 (2022)

11. Hu, L., et al.: Defending against membership inference attacks with high utility by GAN. IEEE Trans. Dependable Secure Comput. **20**(3), 2144–2157 (2023). https://doi.org/10.1109/TDSC.2022.3174569
12. Jayaraman, B., Evans, D.: Evaluating differentially private machine learning in practice. In: 28th USENIX Security Symposium (USENIX Security 2019), pp. 1895–1912 (2019)
13. Jia, J., Salem, A., Backes, M., Zhang, Y., Gong, N.Z.: Memguard: defending against black-box membership inference attacks via adversarial examples. In: Proceedings of the 2019 ACM SIGSAC Conference on Computer and Communications Security, pp. 259–274 (2019)
14. Khan, M.S.N., Reje, N., Buchegger, S.: Utility assessment of synthetic data generation methods. In: Privacy in Statistical Databases USB Proceedings (2022)
15. Kohavi, R., Becker, B.: Adult Dataset. UCI Machine Learning Repository, vol. 5, p. 2093 (1996)
16. Li, J., Li, N., Ribeiro, B.: Membership inference attacks and defenses in classification models. In: Proceedings of the Eleventh ACM Conference on Data and Application Security and Privacy, pp. 5–16 (2021)
17. Nasr, M., Shokri, R., Houmansadr, A.: Machine learning with membership privacy using adversarial regularization. In: Proceedings of the 2018 ACM SIGSAC Conference on Computer and Communications Security, pp. 634–646 (2018)
18. Nowok, B., Raab, G.M., Dibben, C.: Synthpop: bespoke creation of synthetic data in R. J. Stat. Softw. **74**, 1–26 (2016)
19. Patki, N., Wedge, R., Veeramachaneni, K.: The synthetic data vault. In: 2016 IEEE International Conference on Data Science and Advanced Analytics (DSAA), pp. 399–410. IEEE (2016)
20. Rahman, M.A., Rahman, T., Laganière, R., Mohammed, N., Wang, Y.: Membership inference attack against differentially private deep learning model. Trans. Data Priv. **11**(1), 61–79 (2018)
21. Rubin, D.B.: Statistical disclosure limitation. J. Off. Stat. **9**(2), 461–468 (1993)
22. Ruiz, N., Muralidhar, K., Domingo-Ferrer, J.: On the privacy guarantees of synthetic data: a reassessment from the maximum-knowledge attacker perspective. In: Domingo-Ferrer, J., Montes, F. (eds.) PSD 2018. LNCS, vol. 11126, pp. 59–74. Springer, Cham (2018). https://doi.org/10.1007/978-3-319-99771-1_5
23. Salem, A., Zhang, Y., Humbert, M., Berrang, P., Fritz, M., Backes, M.: Ml-leaks: Model and Data Independent Membership Inference Attacks and Defenses on Machine Learning Models. arXiv Preprint arXiv:1806.01246 (2018)
24. Senavirathne, N., Torra, V.: Dissecting membership inference risk in machine learning. In: Meng, W., Conti, M. (eds.) CSS 2021. LNCS, vol. 13172, pp. 36–54. Springer, Cham (2022). https://doi.org/10.1007/978-3-030-94029-4_3
25. Shokri, R., Stronati, M., Song, C., Shmatikov, V.: Membership inference attacks against machine learning models. In: 2017 IEEE Symposium on Security and Privacy (SP), pp. 3–18. IEEE (2017)
26. Slokom, M., de Wolf, P.P., Larson, M.: When machine learning models leak: an exploration of synthetic training data. In: Domingo-Ferrer, J., Laurent, M. (eds.) PSD 2022. LNCS, vol. 13463, pp. 283–296. Springer, Cham (2022). https://doi.org/10.1007/978-3-031-13945-1_20
27. Song, L., Mittal, P.: Systematic evaluation of privacy risks of machine learning models. In: 30th USENIX Security Symposium (USENIX Security 2021), pp. 2615–2632 (2021)

28. Stadler, T., Oprisanu, B., Troncoso, C.: Synthetic data-anonymisation groundhog day. In: 31st USENIX Security Symposium (USENIX Security 2022), pp. 1451–1468 (2022)
29. Wang, D., Ye, M., Xu, J.: Differentially private empirical risk minimization revisited: faster and more general. In: Advances in Neural Information Processing Systems, vol. 30 (2017)
30. Wood, E., Baltrušaitis, T., Hewitt, C., Dziadzio, S., Cashman, T.J., Shotton, J.: Fake it till you make it: face analysis in the wild using synthetic data alone. In: Proceedings of the IEEE/CVF International Conference on Computer Vision, pp. 3681–3691 (2021)
31. Xu, L., Skoularidou, M., Cuesta-Infante, A., Veeramachaneni, K.: Modeling tabular data using conditional GAN. In: Advances in Neural Information Processing Systems, vol. 32 (2019)
32. Yang, D., Zhang, D., Qu, B.: Participatory cultural mapping based on collective behavior data in location-based social networks. ACM Trans. Intell. Syst. Technol. (TIST) **7**(3), 1–23 (2016)
33. Yin, Y., Chen, K., Shou, L., Chen, G.: Defending privacy against more knowledgeable membership inference attackers. In: Proceedings of the 27th ACM SIGKDD Conference on Knowledge Discovery & Data Mining, pp. 2026–2036 (2021)
34. Yu, L., Liu, L., Pu, C., Gursoy, M.E., Truex, S.: Differentially private model publishing for deep learning. In: 2019 IEEE Symposium on Security and Privacy (SP), pp. 332–349. IEEE (2019)
35. Zhang, C., Bengio, S., Hardt, M., Recht, B., Vinyals, O.: Understanding deep learning (still) requires rethinking generalization. Commun. ACM **64**(3), 107–115 (2021)
36. Zhang, Z., Yan, C., Malin, B.A.: Membership inference attacks against synthetic health data. J. Biomed. Inform. **125**, 103977 (2022)

Time Is on My Side: Forward-Replay Attacks to TOTP Authentication

Giuseppe Bianchi[1,2] and Lorenzo Valeriani[1,2]([⊠])

[1] University of Rome Tor Vergata, Rome, Italy
`lorenzo.valeriani@cnit.it`
[2] CNIT National Laboratory of Network Assessment, Assurance and Monitoring, Rome, Italy

Abstract. Time-based One-Time Password (TOTP) is a widely used method for two-factor authentication, whose operation relies on one-time codes generated from the device's clock and validated using the servers' clock. By introducing the notion of *forward-replay* attack, in this paper we underline an obvious (but somewhat overlooked) fact: a secure server's time reference is not sufficient when an attacker may maliciously set *future* time instants over the device, collect the relevant TOTPs, and play them back later on, when these time instants will be reached. Through examining viable attack scenarios, we present a concrete proof-of-concept implementation on Android mobile phones and three applications using TOTP, including the widely used TOTP-based Google Authenticator app. Our findings highlight the practicality of such threat and raise concerns about the security of TOTP, suggesting that hardened TOTP-based methods should be explored.

1 Introduction

In today's world, where personal data and online accounts are increasingly valuable targets for hackers, securing online accounts has become more critical than ever. Two-factor authentication (2FA) is a widely used method to add an extra layer of protection against unauthorized access or fraud. It is a security process that requires users to provide two forms of identification to access a system or account, typically a password and a second factor such as a fingerprint, security token, or verification code sent to a registered mobile device. In many regions, 2FA may also be explicitly imposed by regulation for selected online services. For instance, the EU regulation mandates two-factor authentication in the Second Payment Services Directive (PSD2) [3] for electronic payments within the European Economic Area (EEA).

One-time password (OTP) authentication is a very common second factor used in several online services since at least 20 years ago. In this paper we specifically focus on the Time-Based One-Time Password (TOTP) approach [19], which has gained popularity in more recent years due to its convenience and usability. TOTP requires the user to i) have a TOTP generator installed on their device, and ii) have preliminarily shared with the server a secret key. Using such key and the timestamp gathered on the device, the TOTP application generates time-based codes valid for a short period, usually 30 s. This is very practical and simple to use, as it just requires a loose time synchronization among the device and the server clocks, and ensures that even if an attacker obtains a TOTP code, it will be useless after a short time.

Other than the knowledge of a shared secret, the security of TOTP is reliant on the assumption that the server's clock is trustworthy, thereby preventing replay attacks where a previously used one-time password/code is reused to gain unauthorized access to the server.

However, what about the user device's clock? While it may be reasonable to assume that the server's time can be trusted, this is hardly the case for the user's device. Even the users themselves can easily manipulate the device time for their own purpose, such as cheating in time-based rewards apps or games. Just to mention one among the many examples, a widely popular game, Candy Crush Saga (an app with over 1 billion downloads), requires users to wait 30 min for game lives to replenish. By manipulating the internal clock settings on the phone, users can easily obtain free lives. In fact, such cheating techniques in time-based games inspired us to investigate whether the unreliability of a mobile device's clock could be further exploited for malicious purposes by an *external* attacker.

In this paper we introduce the notion of *forward-replay* attack, which exploits the obvious but somewhat overlooked vulnerability in the currently deployed TOTP security mechanism, namely the **sole** reliance on the device time. More specifically, the challenge addressed in this paper revolves around the possibility for an attacker to *practically* exploit device time manipulation for a concrete malicious purpose: collect and exfiltrate valid TOTPs by sampling future time instants on the victim's device. These TOTPs can be stored and used at such later time instants to gain unauthorized access to the user's account.

We prove the viability of such threat by discussing attack scenarios and by concretely presenting a proof-of-concept implementation against widely used TOTP-based authenticator applications for Android mobile phones. By examining the potential attack scenarios, we demonstrate the severity of the forward-replay threat, and its significant implications on the security of TOTP. In summary, this paper contributes as follows:

- we introduce the (perhaps obvious, but apparently overlooked) notion of *forward-replay attack*;
- we discuss relevant threat scenarios by detailing the possibilities and the capabilities needed by a third party malicious attacker to perform such attack;
- we show a preliminary experimental proof-of-concept of an actual attack over Android phones and three TOTP-based apps, including the massively employed TOTP-based Google Authenticator app;
- we discuss possible ways to mitigate such threat.

While TOTP has been a popular and effective security mechanism, we believe that our findings raise serious concerns regarding its overall security. Indeed, we remark that the attack pattern discussed in this paper is a foundational one and *not* an implementation issue, as pragmatically confirmed by the fact that we adapted it (with minimal effort) to operate on three different TOTP-based applications (Google Authenticator, Duo Mobile, and FreeOTP Authenticator). All this highlights the need for alternative TOTP-based methods that can provide a higher level of security and mitigate the risk of unauthorized access.

The rest of the paper is organized as follows. Section 2 introduces baseline TOTP concepts and discusses related works. In Sect. 3, we present and discuss the threat scenarios that are challenged by the forward replay attack. Section 4 offers a detailed overview of our preliminary proof-of-concept implementation over Android smartphones. In Sect. 5, we discuss alternative methods, extensions, and consequences of this threat. Finally, conclusions are drawn in Sect. 6.

2   Background and Related Work

HOTP, TOTP and Other Standardized Mechanisms

One-time password (OTP) authentication is a very common second factor used in several online services. The first IETF standard dealing with an OTP specification was issues almost 20 years ago in RFC 4226 [17], which documents the so-called HMAC-based One-Time Password (HOTP). In this first approach, the underlying usage model assumes that a user device such as the user smartphone or, preferably, a dedicated physical device such as a smart card or a USB dongle share a secret key K with the authentication server. In addition, the device must also be synchronized with the server by means of a counter C, which is increased at each new authentication. Using these two quantities, a same one time code at both ends is computed as:

$$\text{HOTP}(K, C) = \text{Truncate}(HMAC(K, C)),$$

i.e., by applying an HMAC [12] construction relying on a cryptographically secure hash function - SHA-1 in the original specification but today the de-facto standard being SHA-256 - and a subsequent truncation function which transforms the output of the hash function into a sequence of 6–8 digits that can be easily understood and handled by the end user.

Alternative mechanisms, such as the Time-Based One-Time Password (TOTP) approach [19] considered in this paper, have gained popularity in more recent years due to their convenience and usability. While HOTP generates one-time codes using increasing counters, TOTP generates time-based codes that are valid only for a short period, usually 30 s. This can be trivially accomplished, as specified in the IETF RFC 6238 [19], by reusing HOTP as follows:

$$\text{TOTP}(K, T) = \text{HOTP}\left(K, \left\lfloor \frac{\text{Current Unix time} - T_0}{X} \right\rfloor\right), \tag{1}$$

where T is an integer which represents the number of time steps, each of size X seconds, between the initial counter time T_0 and the current Unix time - i.e., the number of seconds elapsed since midnight UTC of January 1, 1970.

For example, if an authentication were to occur on Monday 3 April 2023 16:40:26 GMT, the number of seconds elapsed since T_0 would be 1.680.540.026. The division by $X = 30$ s and the relevant floor rounding would yield the integer 56.018.000 which would be used as counter within the HMAC+Truncate functions' invocation for computing the resulting OTP. This counter would increase by one once the time reaches 16:40:30 GMT.

TOTP therefore yields a very practical and simple to use approach, as it just requires a loose time synchronization among the device and the server clocks, and ensures that even if an attacker obtains a TOTP code, it will be useless after a short time.

Furthermore, TOTP is more convenient than challenge-response extensions such as OATH Challenge-Response Algorithm (OCRA) [18]. In OCRA, the client and server exchange a challenge that is used to generate a one-time password. This exchange can be time-consuming and requires direct online connectivity between client device and server. On the other hand, TOTP only requires the user to have a TOTP generator installed on their device. With TOTP, the client and server can independently calculate the expected code at any given time, without any interaction required, being confident that any non marginal time difference[1] between time of generation of the OTP on the device and its delivery to the server will result in the OTP being rejected.

Vulnerabilities in Time Sources

As very clear from the TOTP construction reported in the above Eq. 1, if the secret key K is fixed and set at registration time, the OTP codes generated over the user device **solely** depend on the local time reference. The *forward-replay* attack discussed in the remainder of this paper is enabled by the native insecurity of the time source in the user device. Not only such time can be trivially manipulated by having manual access to the smartphone, but can also be modified from the network.

Indeed, when automatic time setting is enabled over the smartphone, the loose time synchronization required by TOTP at the device level is usually gathered by a Network Time Protocol (NTP) server, or by the NITZ (Network Identity and Time Zone) broadcast by the cellular network operator, or by a GNSS (Global Navigation Satellite System) such as GPS.

The NTP protocol is known to be subject to several types of attacks. Many of these are described by Malhotra et al. [14], and tools such as Delorean [2,25] have been devised for specifically tampering with NTP.

An insecure clock source can lead to significant errors in time synchronization, which can affect various mobile applications that rely on time accuracy, such as location-based services and authentication protocols. Regarding this, Park et al. [22] investigated the impact of an insecure clock source on the time accuracy of smartphones. Their interest was not only related to the NTP protocol, but

---

[1] A server may consider valid not only an OTP generated in the latest time stamp but also OTPs generated in past timestamps that are within a given delay window. But in practice, as explicitly recommended in the specification [19], at most one time step is generally allowed.

they also focused on the NITZ protocol, which is part of the 3GPP standard and is used to automatically set the time in mobile devices via the cellular network.

During COVID pandemics, such techniques were practically exploited in [10] for proving that false proximity/contact alerts could be easily generated in about half a dozen national contact tracing apps deployed in Europe. While the *time travel* promoted in [10] brings the smartphone back to a past time, we exploit such induced time travel to bring the smartphone in the "future" so as to make it compute a TOTP yet to come.

Finally, a very recent work [15] has started to address formal models for adversaries equipped with a time machine along with their consequences for cryptography.

Vulnerabilities in Mobile TOTP Applications
Most scientific contributions dealing with TOTP applications for mobile devices address significantly more complex attack scenarios, by targeting weaknesses or privacy violations in storage and communication channels while seeking to obtain the secret used to generate the codes. Polleit and Spreitzenbarth [23] examined 16 Android TOTP apps based on user ratings. They analyzed the storage mechanism of TOTP secrets on the device and performed an analysis of network traffic. In a just appeared study, Gilsenan et al. [8] analyzed the backup process and the traffic generated by a dataset of 22 Android apps in significant detail. The authors inspected the entire backup and recovery workflow of the apps to assess the security of the stored data and how it was transmitted over the network. Ozkan and Bicakci [21] evaluated the security of 11 popular Android TOTP apps. The authors found that they could read the plaintext TOTP secrets from storage and from memory for many of the apps. However, in their work, they considered a threat model in which the attacker possessed the device and had root access. This means that the attacker had full control over the device and could bypass many security measures implemented by the app and by the operating system to protect the secrets.

In our study, we do not aim to attack the secret used to generate TOTPs, nor we require root access. We just need to have the permission to manipulate the date and time of the mobile phone, which is immediate in the case of physical access to the device, but can also be done, as demonstrated in Sect. 4, via a malicious app which simply has accessibility permissions. By trying to obtain future codes on a previously untampered device, we want to raise awareness about this weakness, which can be used by potential attackers to bypass the secondary authentication process and eventually gain access to sensitive information.

Positioning of this Work
The reliance of TOTP's security on trusted time sources is arguably obvious, and past works such as TrustOTP [26] have duly implemented a secure realtime clock for generating OTPs. Despite this, and despite some works give the clear impression that insecurity of the time reference is a well known issue, our initial literature review failed to identify papers that specifically address the methods by which an insecure user device time reference can be exploited for the purpose

of *future authentication breaches*, i.e. as an enabler for the forward replay attack scenario introduced and discussed in our work.

It was only during the review process that we were fortunate enough to have an anonymous reviewer bring to our attention two references to online blog posts [7,9], which adopt a conceptually similar approach to the one described in our paper. However, these references focus on very specific domains and specialized technologies. In contrast, our work deals with the more widespread and general case of TOTP usage by applications on Android smartphones.

Notably, our proof-of-concept does not require any modifications at the operating system level, such as root privileges, and once initiated, it operates seamlessly without any manual intervention. Even more important, we underline that the threat raised in our work should *not* be considered an implementation issue for a specific domain, but it is a general problem that transcends individual implementations and may hence affect any system which relies on TOTP as standardized in [19]. This is the main reason why we suggest to use a new term, *forward replay*, for this specific form of attack, so as to distinguish it from other different and/or more specialized forms of time traveler attacks, which e.g., may also refer to altering a server's clock to accept a replayed past token, or accept a time-dependent event such as a COVID-19 alert, as discussed in [10].

3 General Idea and Threat Scenarios

3.1 Forward Replay Attack

The standardized TOTP operation formalized in Eq. 1 suggests that a smartphone which shares the same secret key with the authentication server, and whose date and time can be arbitrarily modified by an adversary, becomes a perfect "calculator" for any OTP at any past or future date. Notably, knowledge of the secret key is *not needed* if the attacker can perform such calculations using the victim's device!

Using this obvious remark (but apparently not thoroughly investigated in past works), with the term **forward replay**, we define a threat where a malicious opponent is able to:

- access the smartphone at time t_{now}, either manually or using malicious apps (more later on this);
- activate (or access a background running) TOTP authenticator app;
- manipulate the smartphone date/time and set the smartphone time to a sequence of *future* time instants $\{t_1, t_2, \cdots, t_n\}$ (this can also be done by shifting forward the time reference of the smartphone only once, and simply wait for the natural time progression to span a desired target time range);
- for each sampled time instant, read the TOTP generated code, create a log of valid timestamp-code pairs $\{(t_1, \mathrm{OTP}_1), (t_2, \mathrm{OTP}_2), \cdots, (t_n, \mathrm{OTP}_n)\}$, and exfiltrate this set of codes.

In other words, the principle behind the forward-replay attack is trivial: by having the ability to compute and collect future TOTPs (ability granted by just a date/time shift), the attacker can "replay" them to the server at the exact times in which they will be considered valid, i.e. when the server time reaches the sample time of the OTP.

In a classic replay attack, it is necessary to intercept a code to use it while it is valid or convince the server that the current date is actually a past date to trick it into accepting an expired code. The forward-replay attack does not require changing the server clock or eavesdropping the communication channel and shifts the target to the user's device, which is reasonably considered less secure. This offensive should therefore be seen as an additional vulnerability in the use of TOTPs, which can further expand the attack surface.

Practicality of the Attack. In order to carry out this type of attack, a quite powerful attack model appears necessary, as the attacker needs three capabilities:

1. Moving the time forward
2. Capturing the code
3. Extracting the code from the device

These objectives can be accomplished either by obtaining prolonged physical access to the device or by compromising it using malware. Modern devices feature robust protection mechanisms, including facial or fingerprint recognition, which are challenging to bypass without prior knowledge of the victim. Furthermore, as this attack targets a secondary authentication method, user data and accounts remain safeguarded by the primary authentication mechanism. Consequently, adopting strong and secure passwords remains one of the most effective strategies for protecting sensitive data. However, as we will discuss in the next sections, there are many scenarios where such an attack model can be practical and feasible.

3.2   Threat Scenarios

Manual Access. An attacker may have physical access to a victim's device for a given interval of time. This can happen, for instance, when the smartphone is left for repair into a shop, or if the device is temporarily lent to someone else. Within the (eventually short) time interval in which the phone is in someone else's hands, several methodologies can be applied to build a list of future codes, including ways to accelerate the process of sampling dates and scan one day worth of OTP codes in a significantly less time (roughly half an hour using the baseline technique employed in our proof-of-concept discussed in Sect. 4). In the upcoming discussion, we will delve into one of these methodologies: the malicious app. It is worth noting that any application installed to facilitate this process can be uninstalled once the attacker has generated enough codes, restoring the smartphone to an unaltered state. This effectively obscures any trace of the attack and, leaving no visible indication, makes it difficult for the victim to detect that their TOTP codes have been compromised. Note that timestamp-OTP pairs can be maliciously gathered for arbitrary time instants in the future, even years later if the authentication key is never changed (as it happens in practice), and cannot be traced back to the actual date in which they were gathered.

Malicious App. Irrespective of whether it is manually installed or injected through ordinary offensive penetration techniques, the ability to launch and control a malicious app over the victim' smartphone is the most convenient method to perform a forward replay attack. Indeed, a malicious app can be designed, as shown in our proof-of-concept introduced in Sect. 4, to directly manage the date/time changes—hence avoiding the need to rely on external time-travel [10] attacks via NTP or NITZ—and especially generate OTPs valid in the future at a significantly accelerated rate. If manual installation is not viable, the attacker has many classical mechanisms to convict the victim to install an app that carries out the attack covertly. The actual app that performs the attack can be for instance embedded within a legitimate app using well known APK repackaging [24] and obfuscation [5] techniques.

USB Charging Sockets. Public USB charging sockets can be used to carry out attacks such as *juice jacking* [13,16]. In particular, they can pretend to be input-output or network devices [20] or be exploited as a means to use the Android Debug Bridge (ADB). With the use of ADB, one can install applications and execute commands to implement a forward-replay attack. ADB is protected by a security mechanism that requires USB debugging to be enabled and the connected computer to be recognized by the device. Charging at a public outlet poses a security risk. This is why it is recommended to do so only with cables that do not support data transmission.

Each of the above models can be hampered by the device's lock screen protection, which might be absent or easily circumvented. One could argue that the models mentioned earlier are also sufficient for an attacker to capture a single code and use it immediately. However, we strongly believe that a delayed utilization of an access credential, instead of a race condition between the user and attacker which is typical of traditional MITM attacks on TOTP, poses a much more severe and nuanced threat. This is because this sort of attack provides no indication of who is engaging in the attack; it may be someone who had access to our phone many months ago.

4   Proof of Concept

To demonstrate the practical feasibility of an attack, we developed an Android application whose purpose is to trigger the generation of future codes and exfiltrate them. We initially targeted the codes generated by the Google Authenticator app (see Fig. 1), which has more than 100 million downloads in the Google Play Store. Extension to other two TOTP-based apps is discussed in Sect. 4.3. Our app was successfully tested on a completely standard and non-rooted Google Pixel 7 Pro running Android 13 with the March 2023 security update.

Fig. 1. Screenshot (Screenshots are taken from the Android SDK emulator, because the OS prevents screenshots since the app is flagged as secure.) of the Google Authenticator app showing a TOTP code generated for account authentication.

4.1   Overview

The process of the attack is illustrated in Fig. 2. The solution we propose implements the highlighted green elements. Standard solutions are available for the white portions of the diagram. In particular, the malicious app can be embedded within a seemingly harmless app to achieve injection and activation. Communication with remote servers can be accomplished using the standard APIs of the operating system. Acquiring permission is a delicate matter and is highlighted in yellow. The accessibility permission, which is necessary to carry out our attack, must be explicitly granted by the user. Although it is possible to introduce a malicious application into another that already requires the accessibility permission, it may be difficult to convince a user to grant that authorization to an app not downloaded from the Google Play Store. Malicious apps are rarely found on the Play Store due to its rigorous security controls, so the main vectors of infection are third-party app stores. For the above reasons, it is out of the scope of this paper to discuss about these topics. Instead, we will concentrate on the segments that we have implemented.

Very briefly, once injected in the victim's phone and launched (e.g. via some stealth event), our app starts the TOTP app, reads the displayed code, simulates touch inputs to move the clock one minute ahead to capture the next code, and logs the captured codes in a local database. We use the accessibility permission

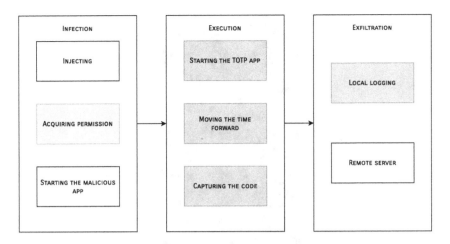

Fig. 2. Scheme of the attack process

to read the code and simulate inputs. The app is a standard Android application written in the Java programming language.

4.2   Implementation Details

Android Accessibility Services. Accessibility services are intended to assist users with disabilities in using Android devices and applications [1]. They run in the background and receive callbacks by the system when accessibility events are triggered. These events indicate a state transition in the user interface. An accessibility service is capable of simulating a gesture on the touch screen as if it had been initiated by the user directly, and provide input as if typed on the keyboard. These services allow individuals with visual, hearing, or physical impairments to interact with their devices through alternative means, but they can also be leveraged by attackers to gain access to sensitive information or perform unauthorized actions on a device. The potential of exploiting accessibility services for malicious purposes has been a known issue for quite some time, and Kraunelis et al. [11] were the first to offer an insightful overview of how such services can be used in the context of malicious applications.

Activating the TOTP Authenticator App. Launching the TOTP app on an Android device is a straightforward task. To launch the app, the package manager can be interacted with to retrieve the launch intent associated with the package name of the OTP generator (e.g., com.google.android.apps.authenticator2). The same package name has to be declared in a `<queries>` element in the malicious app's manifest to comply with package visibility filtering of Android. This intent can then be used to start the corresponding activity, which will bring the TOTP app to the foreground. By following this approach, the attacker can easily trigger the activation of the authenticator app without requiring any user interaction.

Moving the Time Forward. In order to alter the system clock, Android applications necessitate specific permissions, such as those granted to system apps or devices with root access. We overcame this limitation by creating an accessibility service that mimics the touch inputs made by a user who is manually changing the time. As this is done by an application, it enables faster time changes than a human could achieve.

Capturing the Codes. The accessibility service allows us to achieve this capability as well. When the TOTP is shown on the screen, an accessibility event is triggered so that the service can capture the code. Since our accessibility service can capture the TOTP code as soon as it is displayed on the screen, there is no need for any further interaction from the user. Moreover, the application does not require any additional permissions beyond the basic accessibility permission that is granted to it during its setup.

Extracting the Codes from the Device. After obtaining the TOTP codes, extracting them from the device is a straightforward task. However, we have chosen to only make them persistent within a local SQLite database implemented with the Room library [4], as shown in Fig. 3. This serves as an illustration of the use of this data. Alternatively, the information could be saved to a file for later retrieval from the device or transmitted over the network.

4.3 Enhancing the POC to Include Support for Different TOTP Apps

In order to demonstrate that the issue lies at the structural level and not with individual apps, we expanded our proof of concept to capture codes generated by other TOTP apps. Specifically, we targeted the popular apps "Duo Mobile" and "FreeOTP Authenticator", which have over 10 million and 1 million downloads in the Play Store, respectively. To achieve this, we added the package names of these applications, as explained earlier. As a result, our application is capable of activating these apps and receiving their accessibility events. However, it is worth noting that both apps employ different code management approaches compared to Google Authenticator. FreeOTP requires a tap on the code location to display it, while Duo Mobile not only has a button to show the code but also implements a 30-second application-level timer to update it. Consequently, after advancing the clock by one minute, the Duo Mobile app does not display the next code until the timer expires. In order to overcome the limitation posed by the Duo Mobile app's code update mechanism, we devised a solution. After simulating user touches in the settings to force the app to close, we observed that upon restarting the app, the correct code was indeed displayed. This behavior allowed us to capture the subsequent codes generated by the app.

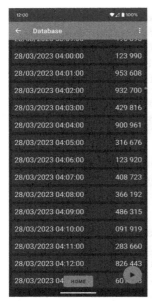

Fig. 3. Screenshot of our app's database showing captured TOTP codes.

Fig. 4. Screenshot of the date and time settings page on a Google Pixel 7 Pro. The image shows the button to be pressed in order to change the time using the keyboard, highlighted in red. (Color figure online)

Fig. 5. Screenshot of the prompt used to modify the time via the keyboard. The areas where touch inputs are simulated are highlighted in red. When selecting the input fields, the virtual keyboard opens, causing the subsequent positions to be clicked to shift vertically. (Color figure online)

4.4   Numerical Results

We conducted a series of experiments to measure the time required to capture a TOTP code using different applications. The data were generated by our custom application, which accurately calculated the time required to capture each code. We performed 70 captures for each application, ensuring a sequential capture process. Results for each of the three apps are summarized in Table 1 in terms of mean value, standard deviation, minimum and maximum.

Our findings indicate that Google Authenticator has the shortest code capture time compared to the other applications we investigated. In contrast, FreeOTP requires an additional touch simulation to display the code, resulting in slightly longer capture times. Notably, Duo Mobile has the longest code capture time, more than double that of the other applications. This is due to

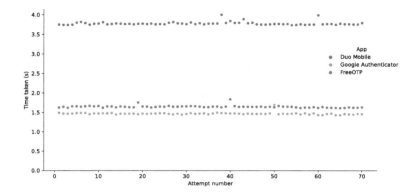

Fig. 6. Time (s) taken to capture one code from different TOTP apps

Table 1. Summary statistics of time (s) required to capture one code on 70 tries

App	Mean	Std. Dev.	Min	Max
Duo Mobile	3.782	0.045	3.740	4.005
Google Authenticator	1.471	0.030	1.434	1.692
FreeOTP	1.648	0.030	1.616	1.840

the procedures involved in the forced shutdown and subsequent restart of the application. The act of restarting introduces a further source of time variance, as its speed is influenced by further factors beyond our direct control. Despite the inherent determinism of the sampling process, where the same actions are repeated, we observed occasional variability in the experiments. This variability is evident in the minimum and maximum reported values, mainly caused by spikes occurring at specific sample times - see Fig. 6 - which correspond to simulating changes not only in the minute but also in the hour.

As of now, our application demonstrates a type of attack that can be performed when an attacker has prolonged access to the victim's phone. Although the attack could be made more covert, we have not pursued this direction due to time constraints. However, it should be noted that such an enhancement constitutes a refinement rather than the main focus of the problem we address in this paper. Based on our experiments, we were able to obtain TOTP codes from Google Authenticator for every minute of an entire day in about 35 min of execution. The one-minute interval for generating TOTP codes is determined by both the granularity allowed by manual time setting and the recommendation in the TOTP RFC [19] to consider both the current and previous OTPs as valid for usability reasons. This effectively creates a time window of valid codes that spans one minute. By leaving the application running overnight or increasing the time interval between one code and the next to be captured, it would be possible to acquire enough TOTPs to cover a much longer period.

5   Discussion

The previously described preliminary proof-of-concept, albeit sufficient to demonstrate the practicality of a forward-replay attack, can be improved in a number of ways. In this section we first discuss some of such improvements, leaving the last section for a brief discussion about possible mitigation techniques.

5.1   Attack Improvements

The current implementation of our application involves simulating touches at specific locations on the screen, as shown in Fig. 4 and Fig. 5. This approach may not be universally effective, as it could encounter issues with particular screen resolutions or customizations of Android implemented by device manufacturers. To increase the compatibility of the app with popular brands of mobile devices, it would be useful to employ additional techniques such as Optical Character Recognition (OCR) on screenshots to locate the necessary touch points for changing the time. Furthermore, an implementation of the same attack could be achieved by exploiting USB communication. It would be worthwhile to create a version based on USB communication tools and compare it with the proposed implementation to assess the differences.

Injection of the threat in the victim's device is a somewhat complementary topic with respect to the goal of this paper. As such, several advanced methods can be used to increase the stealthiness of the attack. For instance, it may be possible to use a repackaging tool such as Repackman [24] to automatically inject a malicious application into a seemingly harmless one. Note that such a repackaging could be performed over a legitimate application that *already utilizes accessibility services*, such as a task automation app or auto-clicker used to cheat in games. This approach could potentially make the attack more covert and less likely to arouse suspicion.

While our study focused on the Android operating system, we recognize the significance of exploring the implications and potential improvements for carrying out similar attacks on iOS. It is important to note that the adaptation of the attack to iOS would likely present its own unique set of challenges and considerations. These could include addressing iOS-specific security mechanisms, potential limitations in terms of background execution and code interception, and the overall feasibility of carrying out the attack in an iOS environment.

Finally, for simplicity of implementation, our Proof-of-Concept utilizes accessibility services and simulates user touch to change the smartphone's date and time. However, it is important to note that there are alternative, more covert methods of carrying out the attack, such as remotely changing the smartphone's date. This can be achieved by exploiting the absence of authentication in the Network Time Protocol (NTP), or by exploiting vulnerabilities in the authentication and/or implementation of the Network Identity and Time Zone (NITZ) protocols employed in wireless cellular systems.

5.2   Possible Mitigations

While an online operation might harden TOTP supplementing it with a crypto-graphic synchronization exchange, mitigation of the described threat is not easy if we wish to retain a standard TOTP operation along with the ability to generate codes offline. As a matter of fact, even if we just demonstrated in Sect. 4 the attack over specific applications, we offline verified that several other apps (including a major one used for an important remote digital signature service) suffer of the same vulnerability, i.e. predictability of future OTPs by changing the device time. This was largely expected, as the issue documented in this paper is not specific of an implementation, but it is a fundamental one for any application that follows the official TOTP specification [19].

Hence, if we assume that time manipulation remains possible, we can only resort to key rotation approaches based on ratcheting techniques which ensure that once the key has been computed for a future time stamp, it cannot be restored back to the past. However, besides requiring great care in their design, these techniques might severely impair usability as potentially legitimate time adjustments (not to mention targeted DoS attacks based on fake time advertisements) might desynchronize the authentication app and mandate for reinstallation - in essence, these techniques might create more problems than the classical HOTP which was also suffering of desynchronization issues.

Rather, solution focusing on application-level mitigation approaches appear more promising and viable. Biometric authentication dialogs, such as those implemented by the Microsoft Authenticator app shown in Fig. 7, can mitigate the threat our implementation of the attack poses. These dialogs should be shown whenever the app switches from background to foreground. However, while it's not mandatory, it's a good practice to allow authentication also with the PIN used to unlock the device or other similar means. This is because authentication devices like fingerprint readers can sometimes fail or be unreliable. Again, if the attacker knows the PIN, it is possible to get past this defense, but the time required to generate codes increases considerably.

Finally, since the attack is enabled by the possibility for an adversary to manipulate back and forth the victim's device clock, hardware solutions which provide a secure time reference obviously thwart the attack. However they are paid in terms of extra complexity and cost, as they need a dedicated design, such as the solution proposed in [26] or trusted execution environments for certifying the time of use - see for instance [6] for a similar problem although in the different context of remote attestation.

Fig. 7. Screenshot of the Microsoft Authenticator app showing a biometric authentication dialog to access the codes.

6   Conclusion

In this paper, we have highlighted an obvious, but perhaps overlooked, vulnerability of the time-based one-time password (TOTP) authentication against what we named as "forward-replay" attacks, i.e., attacks where a malicious opponent having temporary access to a victim' smartphone may compute TOTPs valid at a later time.

Evidence about the feasibility of this threat is provided by implementing an Android malicious application which relies on common accessibility services for manipulating the victim' smartphone date/time, triggering a TOTP-based authenticator, and sampling valid future timestamp-OTP pairs. Despite the lack of any optimization, we could gather about one day of valid TOTPs in roughly half an hour operation.

Even if our assessment was carried out over a small set of authentication apps, the threat described is inherent in any TOTP scheme that adheres to the IETF specification. The main message to take away is that relying solely on a secure server's time reference is not adequate to ensure safe authentication. Therefore, it is important to explore alternative TOTP-based methods to strengthen security and prevent this type of attack.

Acknowledgements. We express our gratitude to the anonymous reviewers for their valuable insights and recommendations, including bringing to our attention the online blog posts [7,9].

This work was partially funded by the project I-Nest (G.A. 101083398 - CUP F63C22000980006) - Italian National hub Enabling and enhancing networked applications and Services for digitally Transforming Small, Medium Enterprises and Public Administration.

References

1. Accessibilityservice. https://developer.android.com/reference/android/accessibili tyservice/AccessibilityService
2. https://github.com/jselvi/delorean
3. Payment services (PSD 2). Directive 2015/2366/EU of the European parliament and of the council (2015)
4. Room. https://developer.android.com/jetpack/androidx/releases/room
5. Aonzo, S., Georgiu, G., Verderame, L., Merlo, A.: Obfuscapk: an open-source black-box obfuscation tool for android apps, vol. 11 (2020). https://doi.org/10.1016/j.softx.2020.100403
6. De Oliveira Nunes, I., Jakkamsetti, S., Rattanavipanon, N., Tsudik, G.: On the toctou problem in remote attestation. In: Proceedings of the 2021 ACM SIGSAC Conference on Computer and Communications Security, pp. 2921–2936 (2021)
7. Deeg, M.: To the future and back: hacking a TOTP hardware token (SYSS-2021-007). https://blog.syss.com/posts/syss-2021-007/
8. Gilsenan, C., Shakir, F., Alomar, N., Egelman, S.: Security and privacy failures in popular 2FA apps. prepublication. In: USENIX Security 2023 (2023)
9. Huseynov, E.: TOTP replay attack - yubikey. https://medium.com/@eminhu seynov_37266/totp-replay-attack-yubikey-et-al-adde8e8c62d3
10. Iovino, V., Vaudenay, S., Vuagnoux, M.: On the effectiveness of time travel to inject COVID-19 alerts. In: Paterson, K.G. (ed.) CT-RSA 2021. LNCS, vol. 12704, pp. 422–443. Springer, Cham (2021). https://doi.org/10.1007/978-3-030-75539-3_18
11. Kraunelis, J., Chen, Y., Ling, Z., Fu, X., Zhao, W.: On malware leveraging the android accessibility framework. In: Stojmenovic, I., Cheng, Z., Guo, S. (eds.) MindCare 2014. LNICST, vol. 131, pp. 512–523. Springer, Cham (2014). https://doi.org/10.1007/978-3-319-11569-6_40
12. Krawczyk, H., Bellare, M., Canetti, R.: RFC2104: HMAC: keyed-hashing for message authentication (1997)
13. Lau, B., Jang, Y., Song, C., Wang, T., Chung, P.H., Royal, P.: Mactans: injecting malware into iOS devices via malicious chargers. Black Hat USA, vol. 92 (2013)
14. Malhotra, A., Cohen, I.E., Brakke, E., Goldberg, S.: Attacking the network time protocol. Cryptology ePrint Archive (2015)
15. Meier, L.C.: On security against time traveling adversaries. Cryptology ePrint Archive (2022)
16. Meng, W., Lee, W.H., Murali, S., Krishnan, S.: Charging me and i know your secrets! Towards juice filming attacks on smartphones. In: Proceedings of the 1st ACM Workshop on Cyber-Physical System Security, pp. 89–98 (2015)
17. M'raihi, D., Bellare, M., Hoornaert, F., Naccache, D., Ranen, O.: RFC 4226: HOTP: an HMAC-based one-time password algorithm (2005)
18. M'Raihi, D., Rydell, J., Bajaj, S., Machani, S., Naccache, D.: RFC 6287: OCRA: oath challenge-response algorithm (2011)

19. M'Raihi, D., Machani, S., Pei, M., Rydell, J.: RFC 6238: TOTP: time-based one-time password algorithm (2011)
20. Nohl, K., Lell, J.: Badusb-on accessories that turn evil. Black Hat USA, vol. 1, no. 9, pp. 1–22 (2014)
21. Ozkan, C., Bicakci, K.: Security analysis of mobile authenticator applications. In: 2020 International Conference on Information Security and Cryptology (ISC-TURKEY), pp. 18–30. IEEE (2020)
22. Park, S., Shaik, A., Borgaonkar, R., Seifert, J.P.: White rabbit in mobile: effect of unsecured clock source in smartphones. In: Proceedings of the 6th Workshop on Security and Privacy in Smartphones and Mobile Devices, pp. 13–21 (2016)
23. Polleit, P., Spreitzenbarth, M.: Defeating the secrets of OTP apps, pp. 76–88. IEEE (2018)
24. Salem, A., Paulus, F.F., Pretschner, A.: Repackman: a tool for automatic repackaging of android apps. In: Proceedings of the 1st International Workshop on Advances in Mobile App Analysis, pp. 25–28 (2018)
25. Selvi, J.: Bypassing http strict transport security. Black Hat Europe, vol. 54 (2014)
26. Sun, H., Sun, K., Wang, Y., Jing, J.: Trustotp: transforming smartphones into secure one-time password tokens. In: Proceedings of the 22nd ACM SIGSAC Conference on Computer and Communications Security, pp. 976–988 (2015)

Social Structure and Community

Cyber Security Researchers on Online Social Networks: From the Lens of the UK's ACEs-CSR on Twitter

Mohamad Imad Mahaini$^{(\boxtimes)}$ (ID) and Shujun Li (ID)

Institute of Cyber Security for Society (iCSS) and School of Computing,
University of Kent, Canterbury, UK
{mim,S.J.Li}@kent.ac.uk

Abstract. Much work in the literature has studied different types of cyber security related users and communities on OSNs, such as activists, hacktivists, hackers, cyber criminals. A few studies also covered no-expert users who discussed cyber security related topics, however, to the best of our knowledge, none has studied activities of cyber security researchers on OSNs. This paper fills this gap using a data-driven analysis of the presence of the UK's Academic Centres of Excellence in Cyber Security Research (ACEs-CSR) on Twitter. We created machine learning classifiers to identify cyber security and research related accounts. Then, starting from 19 seed accounts of the ACEs-CSR, a social network graph of 1,817 research-related accounts that were followers or friends of at least one ACE-CSR was constructed. We conducted a comprehensive analysis of the data we collected: a social structural analysis of the social graph; a topic modelling analysis to identify the main topics discussed publicly by researchers in ACEs-CSR network, and a sentiment analysis of how researchers perceived the ACE-CSR programme and the ACEs-CSR. Our study revealed several findings: 1) graph-based analysis and community detection algorithms are useful in detecting sub-communities of researchers to help understand how they are formed and what they represent; 2) topic modelling can identify topics discussed by cyber security researchers (e.g., cyber security incidents, vulnerabilities, threats, privacy, data protection laws, cryptography, research, education, cyber conflict, and politics); and 3) sentiment analysis showed a generally positive sentiment about the ACE-CSR programme and ACEs-CSR. Our work showed the feasibility and usefulness of large-scale automated analyses of cyber security researchers on Twitter.

Keywords: Cyber Security · Machine Learning · Online Social Network · Community Detection · Natural Language Processing · Topic Modelling · Sentiment Analysis · Twitter

1 Introduction

According to a recent report [36], the active online social network (OSN) users reached 4.76 billion in January 2023, more than half of the world population.

B. Arief et al. (Eds.): SocialSec 2023, LNCS 14097, pp. 129–148, 2023.
https://doi.org/10.1007/978-981-99-5177-2_8

With the popularity of OSNs among people, identifying and finding users who form different online communities has become an interesting research topic for many because studying such communities can reveal useful insights about aspects such as their memberships, people's opinions, intentions and motivations of online users' activities. Such needs have led to a wide range of social network analysis (SNA) applications for different purposes, such as maximising the diffusing of new ideas or technologies, improving recommendations, and increasing the accuracy of expert finding tasks [19].

The application of SNA is also frequently applied to study cyber security related users on OSNs, e.g., cyber criminals [2,15,34], hacktivists [13,14], activists [24], and non-experts [25,30]. However, to the best of our knowledge, no past studies have investigated cyber security researchers on OSNs using a computational data-driven approach, even though many cyber security researchers and organisations are active on OSNs, and their activities can potentially have a significant influence on other users, e.g., how non-experts learn about cyber security. This paper tries to fill this research gap. Studying cyber security researchers and organisations' activities on OSNs could help us to learn more about many aspects, such as their memberships and social structures, their connections with other users, characteristics of their members, topics they often discuss, and their perception and opinions on different cyber security related matters. A better understanding of those aspects can help us better understand how they play a role in the wider online cyber security community.

As a case study, we chose to study the research network around the 19 Academic Centres of Excellence in Cyber Security Research (ACEs-CSR) in the UK on Twitter. ACEs-CSR are UK universities jointly recognised by the National Cyber Security Centre (NCSC, part of GCHQ) and the Engineering and Physical Sciences Research Council (EPSRC, part of UKRI – UK Research and Innovation) [20]. See [20] for a list of all ACEs-CSR. These universities are a good representative subset of cyber security researchers in the UK, allowing us to test how computational data-driven analysis can be done and to have a view of the important part of the UK cyber security research community on Twitter.

The main contributions of this paper can be summarised as follows:

1. We tested the performance of the machine learning (ML) classifiers reported in [18] for detecting cyber security related accounts in a real-world setting.
2. We developed a new ML classifier to detect cyber security research related accounts with good performance.
3. Using graph-based analysis and community detection algorithms, our study showed that such methods can produce useful insights about cyber security researcher communities on Twitter.
4. Using topic modelling, we identified a wide range of topics discussed by cyber security researchers on Twitter, including some less related to cyber security.
5. By applying sentiment analysis, we observed a generally positive sentiment on the ACE-CSR programme and the ACEs-CSR.

The rest of the paper is organised as follows. Some related work is reviewed in Sect. 2. We explain our research questions (RQs) and the methodology we used in Sect. 3. Section 4 describes the data collection process used in our research. The RQ-specific details of the methodology and the corresponding results are given in Sects. 5–8. Further discussions and limitations can be found in Sect. 9. The last section concludes the paper with future work.

2   Related Work

With the enormous content created by OSN users daily, researchers have access to a massive and wide range of individuals [1]. Different types of users can be found on OSNs, such as individuals, businesses, organisations and communities, hacktivists, and cyber criminals [24]. To the best of our knowledge, there has been no previous work on studying cyber security researchers using a data-driven approach based on OSN data. A lot of work has been done on studying cyber criminal groups on OSNs. For example, Aslan et al. [2] studied a list of 100 defacers on Twitter by analysing their activities, social structure, clusters, and public discussions on Twitter. While in [15], a clustering technique based on topic modelling was applied to study the comments of 30,469 users from three carding forums. In another study about cyber criminals [34], Tavabi et al. built and analysed a large corpus of messages across 80 deep and dark web forums to identify the discussion topics and to examine their patterns.

Moreover, several other researchers studied activist and hacktivist groups on OSNs. For instance, Jones et al. [13] analysed the presence of the Anonymous group on Twitter. They built an ML classifier and identified over 20k accounts from the Anonymous group. Then, the key players were identified using SNA and centrality measures. By applying topic modelling, the main topics were found and used to study similarities between the key accounts. Another interesting example is [24], where Nouh & Nurse studied a Facebook Activist group of 274 users with 670 posts. They created several graphs representing the users' friendships and interactions through the replies on the collected posts. Using SNA and different centrality measures, they analysed these graphs and identified the influential users. Also, sub-communities were found and studied. After that, they used sentiment analysis to study how user sentiment affected the group. Finally, they investigated trust relations using link analysis techniques.

A few studies related to analysing non-experts users on OSNs were found. In [25], Pattnaik et al. conducted a large-scale analysis on cyber security and privacy discussions of non-experts on Twitter. The researchers developed two ML classifiers, one for detecting non-expert users and the other for detecting tweets related to cyber security and privacy. Also, they used topic modelling to find the top topics discussed by non-experts. Using sentiment analysis, they discovered a general negative sentiment from non-experts when talking about such topics. Another interesting study was conducted by Saura et al. [30], where they studied cyber security related issues discussed by home users on Twitter using a large dataset of 938k tweets. They used sentiment analysis, topic modelling, and mutual information to find these security issues and studied their effects on user privacy.

Another topic related to our research in this paper is the use of ML classifiers to detect cyber security related accounts and discussions on OSNs. Aslan et al. [3] built a classifier using a small dataset of 424 manually labelled Twitter accounts to detect cyber security related accounts on Twitter and achieved good results using Random Forest and SVM classifiers. Also, in [18], we created a bigger dataset of almost 2k Twitter accounts and built a baseline classifier for cyber security related accounts and several sub-classifiers to detect other sub-groups (academics, hackers, and individuals), all with good results using several ML models.

3 Research Questions and Methodology

We found a gap in the literature about studying cyber security researchers on OSN. Thus, we wanted to explore this area, focusing on the UK ACEs-CSR network on Twitter as a case study. The main research objective is to study the cyber security researchers in the ACEs-CSR network and to see what insights can be obtained from their social structure and sub-communities on Twitter. Also, using quantitative methods (e.g., topic modelling and sentiment analysis), we analysed topics they discussed on Twitter. Thus, our research questions (RQs) for our study are:

– **RQ1**: How to identify cyber security research related accounts on Twitter?
– **RQ2**: What is the social structure of a typical cyber security research community on Twitter, such as the one formed by ACEs-CSR and their followers?
– **RQ3**: What topics do cyber security research related users in the ACEs-CSR network discuss online on Twitter?
– **RQ4**: What is the general sentiment of cyber security research related users when talking about the ACE-CSR program and the ACEs-CSR on Twitter?

RQs 1-3 depend on RQ1. To address RQ1, we used ML classifiers. Developing and evaluating such classifiers required us to collect Twitter data starting from a number of seed accounts of the ACEs-CSR (see Sect. 4 for more details). We studied RQ1 by i) applying two ML classifiers from the literature to detect cyber security related accounts and individual ones, and ii) building a new classifier to detect cyber security research related accounts on Twitter. For RQ2, we constructed the social graph from the connections of friends and followers of the cyber security research related accounts connected to the ACEs-CSR accounts. Then, we studied the graph's social structure and analysed different sub-communities using community detection algorithms. For RQ3, topic modelling analysis was applied using the latent Dirichlet allocation (LDA) algorithm to analyse the timelines of cyber security research related accounts to identify the main topics discussed in the ACEs-CSR network on Twitter. Finally, for RQ4, we used sentiment analysis to analyse all the tweets that mentioned any ACE-CSR account or talked about the ACE-CSR program. Then, we calculated the overall sentiment scores in each detected community from RQ2.

4   Data Collection

To study our RQs, we needed to select the right seed accounts and then crawl their friends and followers to get the needed accounts and connections between them to construct the social graph of the cyber security research related accounts in the ACEs-CSR Twitter network. The data collection for this study was carried out in June 2022. We created a list of 19 Twitter accounts, each corresponding to an ACE-CSR. First, we looked at each ACE-CSR's website and manually searched into Twitter to confirm their official Twitter account. In some cases, when no official account was identified, we chose the ACE-CSR lead's account as the seed account of the corresponding ACE-CSR. However, there was a single case when we found neither an ACE-CSR's official account nor its lead's account. In this case, we chose the account of the most well-known cyber security researcher in that ACE-CSR. Since our RQs are unrelated to the individuals themselves, but about the ACEs-CSR network as a whole, and to eliminate the risk of re-identification of individual researchers, the dataset was anonymised. To this end, this paper does not mention any personal detail related to any account, and our results do not refer to specific individuals or ACEs-CSR. This preserves individual researchers' privacy and avoids comparing individuals and ACE-CSR against each other. Note that such a treatment does not affect the reproducibility of the work presented in this paper.

For each seed account (Level 1, denoted by Lv1), we fetched its friends and followers using the Twitter API at Level 1 (i.e., Lv2). Then, we did the same for the accounts in Lv2, which led to nodes at Level 3 (i.e., Lv3). We fetched only the first 5,000 accounts (determined by the Twitter API) of friends and followers for each Lv2 and Lv3 account, as some accounts had a very large number of followers or friends. After that, we used Lv1, Lv2, and their connections. The retrieval of Lv3, which contained almost 16 million nodes, was necessary to capture all the connections between Lv2 accounts. Finally, we got 42,028 accounts in total for further analysis (19 in Lv1 and 42,009 in Lv2). Lastly, using the Twitter API, we obtained the timelines of these accounts (up to 3,250 tweets per account due to a limit of the API).

5   ML Classifiers

Studying the ACEs-CSR network on Twitter required identifying accounts that are both cyber security and research related. Thus, two classifiers were needed. Additionally, we needed a classifier to detect whether a Twitter account belongs to an individual or non-individual (e.g., group, organisation, government, NGO, news channel). Thus, a third classification task was also needed.

5.1   Cyber Security Related and Individual Classifiers

Regarding the cyber security related and individual classifiers, we used two classifiers we developed in 2021, reported in [18]. Before using these two classifiers, we re-trained and re-evaluated their performances (see Appendix A for more details). We extracted the required feature sets for our data collection as described in [18]. After that, the selected trained classifiers were used to predict the class of each account in the data collection according to each classification task. The prediction statistics are listed in Table 2. The Individual classifier was applied following the Cyber Security (Baseline) classifier to detect cyber security related individuals. Also, we applied the Individual classifier after the Research classifier – described in the next subsection – to detect whether a research related account is for an individual (e.g., researcher) or a non-individual.

5.2   Research Related Classifier

To identify cyber security research related accounts, we needed a new classifier for research related accounts. We considered a data sample as a positive case if it is involved with any research work or activity related to research. This is judged based on the account's description and timeline. This makes any cyber security researcher a positive case even if they does not work in academia or is not associated with any research organisation. This is the significant difference between our **Research** classifier and the **Academia** classifier reported in [18].

Feature Extraction: Besides the features we extracted for the Baseline and Individual classifiers, we introduced new features for this new Research classifier named the Research (**R**) group, which contains the following features. A) **Connections with seeds**, which is a metric of two values. The first is the number of seed accounts that follow this account, while the second is the number of seed accounts that this account follows. B) **Researcher Keywords**, using a compiled list of 27 keywords that can be found in the Twitter "Display Name" and "Description" fields and can refer to an account that is related to research, e.g., "Professor", "Academic", "Lecturer", "Reader", "Scientist", "Research", "Researcher", "Researching", "Research Assistant", "Research Associate", "Research Fellow", "Faculty", "University", and "PHD". These features form a 54-D vector, and each value reflects whether one of the 27 keywords appears at least once in the "Display Name" or "Description" field. C) **Verified**, which is a binary value corresponding to the **Verified** profile attribute in the Twitter account, as indicated by the blue check mark. D) **Website category**, which is derived from the "Website" field of the account's profile. Sometimes a link for a page can tell a lot about the Twitter account owner. We processed the URL found in this field and identified the host of each URL, and then used some regular expressions with manually created lists of hosts, main domains, and top-level domains to assign the parsed URL to one of the following three categories. 1) "Research": this category represents a website more likely related to research, such as a university or a research institute. Some entries used in this category's domain list are ".edu", ".ac.", ".academy", "orcid.org", and "scholar.google%". We noticed that universities do not have a unified domain in some countries. Thus, we used an additional list of university hosts [11] to capture as many cases as possible. 2) "Mixed": here, the website is not specifically related to research, but it might be. Some examples of the hosts and domains in

Table 1. Experimental results of all the machine learning classifiers

Task	Featurs	#F	#S	Decision Tree			Random Forest			Extra Trees		
				F1	Prec	Rec	F1	Prec	Rec	F1	Prec	Rec
Baseline	PBCL	149	1974	0.88	0.88	0.89	0.91	0.90	0.95	0.91	0.91	0.94
Individual	PBCL	149	957	0.84	0.84	0.84	0.89	0.91	0.87	0.88	0.93	0.84
Academia	K:UCIDF	200	245	0.81	0.68	1.00	0.90	0.82	1.00	0.92	0.85	1.00
Research	R	46	1003	0.78	0.94	0.67	0.81	0.94	0.72	0.81	0.94	0.71

Logistic Reg.			XGBoost			SVM (Linear)			SVM (RBF)		
F1	Prec	Rec	F1	Prec	Rec	F1	Prec	Rec	F1	Prec	Rec
0.90	0.91	0.91	0.91	0.90	0.94	0.91	0.91	0.92	0.90	0.91	0.91
0.89	0.90	0.88	0.91	0.92	0.90	0.89	0.91	0.87	0.87	0.91	0.83
0.00	0.00	0.00	0.82	0.69	1.00	0.00	0.00	0.00	0.43	0.71	0.58
0.82	0.97	0.72	0.81	0.94	0.72	0.82	0.97	0.72	0.83	0.96	0.73

this category are "linkedin", "medium", "github", ".info", ".net" and ".com". 3) "Other": any other websites that are less likely related to research and do not fall under the previous two categories.

Classifier Training Dataset & ML Models: The training sub-dataset for this classifier was created as follows. After using the Baseline classifier to predict the labels of the 42k accounts, we kept only the accounts that were predicted as cyber security related accounts. Then, we randomly selected around 1,200 samples from the new group to label them manually. The selection and labelling process was repeated until we got a balanced dataset of 1k data samples. The same seven ML models were used for training and testing, including ET and XGBoost (see Sect. A). Moreover, we experimented with different feature sets to compare their performance scores and report which ones were the best for this new classifier.

Experimental Results: Using the ML Python library Scikit-Learn [26] and the above models, we experimented with the following feature set combinations: R, PR, BR, CR, PBCR, and PBCLR. All models were trained and tested with 5-fold stratified cross-validation. The testing results are shown in Table 1, where we keep only the best-performing feature sets. A colour scale from red to green was used for the F1-scores. The highest F1-score is 83% using the R, BR, CR, PBCR, PBCLR feature sets, and the SVM-R (SVM with RBF kernel), ET, and RF models. Although we wanted to select the best classifier based on the F1-score, we had to consider the **Precision** as well since it corresponds to the accuracy of the positive class (i.e., the research related account). By choosing Precision over Recall, we decided to prioritise false positives (FPs) over false negatives (FNs) since our OSN analysis required working with positive samples and inspecting their profiles, timelines and connections. Moreover, since we were studying the communities resulting from positive samples, we needed the predicted positive samples to be more accurate and the FPs to be as minimum as possible. The

Table 2. The prediction results of the used machine learning classifiers

Task	Features	Model	#(Samples)	Prediction Samples	Positive	Negative
Baseline	PBCL	RF	42,028	42,028	9,377	32,651
Individual	PBCL	RF	42,028	9,377	4,795	4,582
Research	R	SVM-R	42,028	9,377	1,684	7,693

highest Precision score is 97%. Finally, the best-performing models are SVM (RBF and Linear kernel) and LR (Logistic Regression).

Applying the Research Classifier: For the prediction of the research related accounts in our data, we selected the trained Research classifier built using the R feature set and the SVM-R model (F1-score = 83%, Precision = 96%). Since the Research classifier is also a cascaded classifier following the Baseline classifier, we only considered positive samples (9,377) predicted by the Baseline classifier as the input for this classifier. The prediction statistics are listed in Table 2. Finally, we got 1,684 positive samples and 7,693 negative samples.

6 Social Structural Analysis

6.1 Social Graph Construction

To construct the social graph of the ACEs-CSR network, we had to identify the nodes and their edges. For nodes, we used the ML classifiers explained in Sect. 5 to find cyber security and research related accounts. As a result, we got 1,684 nodes, and after manual verification, some false positives were captured. Thus, the selected nodes were 1,817. For edges, we filtered the connections extracted in Sect. 4, where we kept only those where both ends are in selected nodes. As a result, we built a directed graph with 1,817 nodes and 64,826 edges. The constructed OSN graph was visualised using Gephi [4]. Figure 1 shows four example visualisations of the ACEs-CSR graph with different numbers of communities under different parameters. The nodes' sizes are scaled using their in-degree centrality. We can notice a few ACE-CSR nodes that are remarkably bigger than the other ACE-CSR nodes.

6.2 Communities Detection and Analysis

To study the big ACE-CSR graph, we had to break it down into sub-graphs, where each graph represents a community or a group of Twitter accounts that have something in common. A community in a network is defined by [22] as a subset of nodes that are densely connected with each other but at the same time have a few connections to other network nodes. Since the graph nodes had no ground truth labels of any characteristic, using supervised classifiers was impossible. This is normal in such cases as we do not know the number of

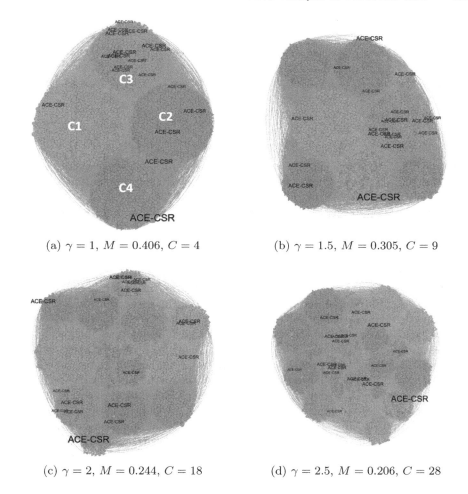

(a) $\gamma = 1$, $M = 0.406$, $C = 4$ (b) $\gamma = 1.5$, $M = 0.305$, $C = 9$

(c) $\gamma = 2$, $M = 0.244$, $C = 18$ (d) $\gamma = 2.5$, $M = 0.206$, $C = 28$

Fig. 1. Four different visualisations of the ACEs-CSR network with different clustering parameters (C: the number of communities, M: modularity)

communities and whether they are roughly equal in size when we want to break a network into communities [22]. As a result, we used unsupervised clustering techniques to divide the graph nodes into clusters (i.e., communities).

We tested several community detection algorithms that are widely adopted in the literature. First, we tried DBSCAN [31], but it did not work with our dataset as the clustering results were not as good as the other methods. Then, we tried the Girvan-Newman algorithm [10]. Despite the long processing time, the results were also not good as it clustered all nodes in one cluster. After that, we examined modularity-optimisation-based algorithms as modularity is a well-known method for community detection [22]. We started to get good results using the Louvain algorithm [7]. However, due to some limitations in this algorithm

Table 3. Statistics of discovered communities ($\gamma = 1$)

Community	Colour	Members	Size	Individual Accounts	Non-individual Accounts
C1	Purple	595	32.75%	72.61%	27.39%
C2	Green	465	25.59%	79.14%	20.86%
C3	Orange	382	21.02%	51.83%	48.17%
C4	Blue	375	20.64%	70.13%	29.87%

(e.g., yielding arbitrarily poorly connected communities), we used the Leiden algorithm [35] instead. These two algorithms use a resolution parameter [16], which controls the size of the detected communities [21].

Increasing the resolution parameter γ in the Leiden algorithm results in more communities while reducing it does the opposite [35]. To illustrate this, we presented four instances of applying the Leiden algorithm in Fig. 1, using the following γ values: 1.0, 1.5, 2.0, and 2.5. The node size and the label are proportionate with its in-degree centrality score. Using the predicted labels from the Individual classifier in Sect. 5.1, the node shape can be either a triangle (individual node) or a circle (non-individual node). Also, we grouped the nodes that belong to the same cluster together using the Circle Pack [8] layout with "hierarchy" set to "cluster" attribute in Gephi. To emphasise the size and members of the clusters, we used a distinctive colour for each cluster. Then, we preserved these colours in the next applications of the Leiden algorithm to understand how these communities split and create new sub-communities when the modularity decreases due to the increase in resolution. Selecting the right resolution depends on how many communities we want to work with. Analysing hundreds of communities manually would be impossible, and analysing 2 or 3 communities would be less indicative. As for the analysis of the detected communities, we could not list all the trials we had with each reasonable resolution and its corresponding communities. Instead, we listed below a few examples of the insights we learned about the ACEs-CSR network and sub-communities we discovered shown in Fig. 1.

A) Initially, we expected each ACE-CSR Twitter account to have a strong community around its node in the graph, but this was not the case for a few of them unless the modularity was significantly reduced. However, that would not reflect a strong and densely connected community. One of the explanations for this is that the seed accounts for some ACE-CSR are not well connected to other cyber security researchers. B) Some ACE-CSR nodes always appear in the same cluster regardless of the chosen resolution. After manual inspection of several cases, one explanation for this might be that these ACEs-CSR are close to each other geographically. We also had some personal observations about this, where we noticed that researchers across these ACEs-CSR have worked together. In two particular cases, some researchers moved from one ACE-CSR to another. C) Using different values for resolution and checking the resulted communities each time, we observed some clusters that do not have any ACE-CSR nodes (see Fig. 1b). We inspected these communities and checked their members' Twitter profiles. We noticed they are also densely connected and represent a mix of national, European, and international research institutions. For simplicity and explainability purposes, we carried out some additional analysis focusing only on the communities corresponding to $\gamma = 1$ (see Fig. 1a and Table 3).

Clusters Analysis – Individual Members: Knowing the percentage of individuals in the ACEs-CSR network is interesting as it might give insights into how many cyber security individual researchers these ACE-CSR accounts attracted on Twitter and how many other non-individuals e.g., research centres, universities, and companies are connected to these ACE-CSR accounts. The overall individual and non-individual percentages in the graph were 69.40%, and 30.60%, respectively. Using the four communities in Fig. 1a as an example, we calculated the individual percentage of each community and the results are shown in Table 3. The individual percentage reached 79.14% for Community C2, which is higher than other communities. Upon inspecting C2, we found that individuals in this community are often well-known researchers and figures in the cyber security research domain.

Clusters Analysis – Location: The account's "Location" field is optional on Twitter, so not all account holders provide such information. The percentage of the accounts with the information provided in the whole data we collected is 61.41%, while it is 77.55% for the ACEs-CSR network. This higher percentage indicates that cyber security research related accounts had a tendency to use this field more often. We analysed the ACE-CSR communities based on their members' declared locations, hoping to gain more insights into how these communities were formed in the first place or what they represent. The "location" field is a free-formatted text where users can write anything they like. We observed names of places (e.g., towns, cities, countries, or even non-existing places), names of affiliations, GPS coordinates, postcodes, country codes (alphabetic such as "GB" and numeric such as "+44"), and Unicode symbols of national flags. Considering the different ways to indicate location information, we had to use a set of methods to extract such information. For some "location" fields representing the location information as GPS coordinates, country codes and national flag symbols, we could extract such information using bespoke Python scripts. For other "location" fields that could not be processed using the previous method, we preprocessed them by removing any email address(es), URL(s), Twitter handle(s), special ASCII character(s), IP address(es)[1] and isolated number(s), and then fed them to the Location Tagger Python library [33] to extract possible location information. The extracted location information was automatically checked against cities' names downloaded from the GeoNames website [9] to resolve the ambiguity that is usually raised when detecting location information from free-formatted texts. For about 10% of "location" fields, the above automated methods could not produce any location information, so we manually inspected them to detect and recover such information. Based on all the

---

[1] IP addresses can sometimes carry location-related information. We considered such information less reliable and too complicated to process, so decided to exclude it.

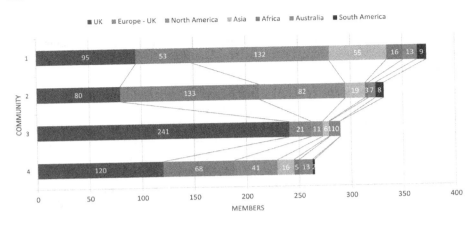

Fig. 2. Continent-specific statistics of the four communities shown in Fig. 1a

extracted location information, we calculated geographical statistics about the nodes in the ACEs-CSR network. Figure 2 shows continent-specific statistics of the four communities shown in Fig. 1a. We split Europe into two sub-groups, UK and Europe excluding UK, in order to know which communities are more national (UK) or international (non-UK) from the perspective of ACEs-CSR.

The location-based analysis revealed interesting insights about the discovered communities. First, for the four communities in Fig. 2, Community C3 seems a more UK-centric one, but the other three are highly international. Communities C1 and C2 are dominated by non-UK accounts – the most accounts were from North America for C1 and from the non-UK part of Europe for C2. Second, across all communities, there are much fewer accounts from Africa, Australia and South America, indicating more biased international connections with Europe, North America and Asia. Third, Community C1 seems to be the most international cluster, where almost an equal number of accounts were from Europe (excluding the UK) and from Asia. The percentage of Asian accounts in C1 is substantially higher than the other three communities, indicating it may be the one representing the UK-Asia links. Finally, when considering UK against non-UK accounts, Community C4 looks like a more balanced cluster with an approximately 1:1 ratio between national and international accounts.

7   Topic Modelling Analysis

We utilised topic modelling to automatically identify topics discussed by the cyber security research related accounts in the ACEs-CSR network. We used the LDA algorithm [6], one of the most widely used topic modelling algorithms in the literature [2,25]. LDA is an unsupervised method for clustering N documents into k categories, i.e., topics. LDA assigns a document to a topic in a probabilistic manner, where each document is assigned to each topic with a probability, and the sum of all these probabilities is 1.0 per document [15]. The LDA algorithm

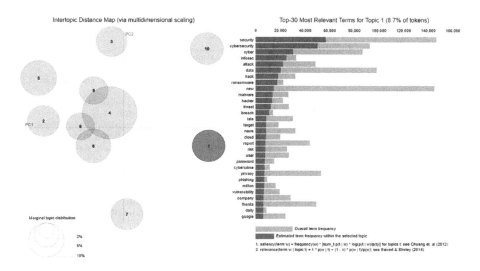

Fig. 3. Visualisation of the estimated topics by the LDA algorithm

works in iterations to do two estimations, the distribution of words (i.e., tokens) into topics, and the distribution of topics over documents [5]. Thus, it requires two essential parameters to work, which are k, the number of topics, and r, the maximum number of iterations.

We used the Scikit-Learn implementation of LDA to process the documents in our dataset, which are timelines of the cyber security research related accounts. Although there are 1,817 accounts, only 1,771 have public timelines. The timelines were preprocessed as follows:

– URLs, emails, Twitter handlers and the beginning word "RT" were removed.
– The text was tokenised using the Gensim library [27].
– Punctuation marks, isolated numbers, and very short tokens were removed.
– Stopwords removal using a list of Gensim and NLTK [23] stopwords.
– Lemmatisation was then applied using the TextBlob library [17].

After that, the tokens were passed to the LDA algorithm. We tried to find the optimum values for the LDA parameters automatically by training the LDA model using a series of values for each parameter. Each time, we used the coherence model from the Gensim library [28] to calculate the UCI coherence score of the created topics [29]. Ultimately, we chose the best value of each parameter that corresponds to the highest coherence score. For k, the tested values were from 2 to 20 with a step size of 1. The potential best values are 5 and 12. For r, the values were from 20 to 300 with a step size of 20. The potential best values are 200 and 220. While several past studies in the literature utilised coherence measures in similar experiments to find the best values for k [13, 25], several other studies agreed that a manual inspection approach for the topics in each cycle is better to find the best values of these parameters [2, 15], which was confirmed in

Table 4. LDA topics with top 15 keywords, ranked in descending order by size

ID	Topic Name	Size (%)	Top Keywords
4	General Terms	24.2	like, people, think, time, good, work, know, need, look, year, thing, day, great, want, way
5	Cyber Security for Students	10.6	student, today, great, day, new, cyber, work, look, event, research, talk, join, team, uk, year
6	Data Protection Laws	10	data, privacy, law, new, right, digital, eu, ai, internet, tech, work, protection, facebook, online, gdpr
10	Vulnerabilities & Threats	8.9	new, security, malware, attack, tool, vulnerability, release, exploit, code, hack, blog, use, android, linux, update
1	Cyber Security Incidents	8.7	security, cybersecurity, cyber, infosec, attack, data, hack, ransomware, new, malware, hacker, threat, breach, late, target
2	Security Research & Education	8.4	research, new, work, security, social, read, join, look, digital, data, online, study, report, project, researcher
7	Cyber Conflict & Politics	8.4	cyber, state, russia, new, russian, china, war, ukraine, government, attack, world, country, intelligence, military, report
3	Cryptography & Research Privacy	7.9	paper, security, work, research, new, privacy, talk, crypto, open, program, phd, bitcoin, student, computer, blockchain
8	Cyber Security Events	6.6	cybersecurity, security, cyber, join, learn, new, register, ic, today, check, day, event, talk, team, course
9	ICT Industry	6.4	ai, iot, technology, data, learn, new, business, tech, future, digital, market, innovation, report, industry, world

our case as well. Considering the coherence model, the manual inspection, and the visualisation-aid analysis (using the pyLDAvis Python library [32]), we set k to 10 and r to 200.

The results in Table 4 demonstrate the topics discussed by cyber security research related accounts in the ACEs-CSR network. Using the inter-topic distance map shown in Fig. 3, we can notice that the correlation between topics is minimum, which was caused mainly by topic T4, a topic with general keywords and non-related to the cyber security domain. This kind of topic is expected to be found in similar textual sources like tweets. The topic distribution is shown in Table 4. Apart from topic T4, all the other topics are relatively balanced in size, ranging from 6.4% to 10.6% with an average of 8.4%. We can spot several topical themes by looking at the generated topics: research, privacy, education, technical, and politics. Ignoring T4, the top discussed topic was T5 ("Cyber Security for Students", 10.6%), followed by T6 ("Data Protection Laws", 10%), T10 ("Cyber Security Vulnerabilities & Threats", 8.9%), T1 ("Cyber Security Incidents", 8.7%), and T2 ("Security Research & Education", 8.4%). Interestingly, politics-related and cyber conflict discussions in T7 also had a good share with 8.4%. Upon checking some tweets, we noticed sub-topics that many researchers discussed within politics, e.g., the Russia-Ukraine cyber conflict and the Trump elections. Finally, by checking the document-topic matrix, we found that the top two main topics across all documents are T5 and T3.

Table 5. Sentiment analysis results for tweets related to ACEs-CSR

Accounts Group	Tweets	Positive		Neutral		Negative	
		Count	%	Count	%	Count	%
Non Research related	13,915	9,306	66.88	3,377	24.27	1,232	8.85
Research related C1	608	406	66.78	134	22.04	68	11.18
Research related C2	1,613	988	61.25	459	28.46	166	10.29
Research related C3	4,485	2,888	64.39	1,205	26.87	392	8.74
Research related C4	753	476	63.21	188	24.97	89	11.82
All accounts	21,374	14,064	65.8	5,363	25.09	1,947	9.11

8 Sentiment Analysis

For RQ4, we utilised sentiment analysis to achieve a better understanding of how the cyber security research community perceive the ACE-CSR programme and the ACEs-CSR. The ACE-CSR programme started almost a decade ago, and such an analysis can provide useful insights about what to do in the future with the ACE-CSR programme. To this end, we created a dataset of tweets by filtering the timelines of the 42,028 accounts in our dataset, searching for tweets related to the ACE-CSR program or any of the ACEs-CSR using a set of selected keywords. Moreover, we added tweets that mentioned any of the 19 seed accounts we used, as such mentions were considered direct or indirect interactions with an ACE-CSR. Finally, we excluded tweets created by the seed accounts as these accounts might be biased when they talked about the ACE-CSR program or themselves. In the end, a total of 21,374 tweets were obtained for the sentiment analysis. The tweets were preprocessed by removing Twitter handlers, URLs, email addresses, and the beginning word "RT" (for retweets).

We examined the two most popular methods for sentiment analysis. The first one we tried is the sentiment analyser in TextBlob [17], a popular Python library for text processing and NLP tasks. TextBlob relies on a lexicon-based sentiment analyser with predefined rules to calculate a "polarity" score between -1 and 1. This score tells whether a text can be considered positive, neutral, or negative. The second method we tried is VADER, a lexicon-based sentiment analyser with a simple rule-based model for general sentiment analysis [12]. The VADER sentiment analyser returns four scores for each piece of input text: "neg", "neu", "pos", and "compound". Each score corresponds to a sentiment type except the last which is a normalised combined value of the first three scores. For the actual implementation of VADER, we used the one in the NLTK library [23]. After applying both sentiment analysers to our data and manually inspecting the results, we concluded that VADER is a better method. Some example tweets wrongly by the TextBlob sentiment analyser can be found in Appendix B.

The results of the VADER sentiment analyser are shown in Table 5. 65.8% of all tweets are classified as positive, 25.09% as neutral, and only 9.11% as negative. These results showed that the cyber security research community perceived the ACE-CSR program and the ACEs-CSR largely positively on Twitter. Following our community analysis discussed earlier, we were also interested in if the sentiment analysis results would vary from one community to another, and between cyber security research related accounts and others in the ACEs-CSR network. To this end, we divided the tweets we selected into sub-datasets, each corresponding to an intended sub-group of accounts.

The sentiment analysis results of each sub-group are largely aligned with the main results for all. However, a few observations were noted, e.g., the percentage of the positive sentiment in Community C2 (the more "European" community) dropped to 61.25% while the negative percentage increased to 10.29%. On the other hand, the more UK-centric Community C3 saw the lowest negative sentiment percentage (8.74%) across the four communities, while the positive sentiment percentage was 64.39%. Comparing the sentiment results of Communities C2 and C3, one may wonder if the accounts' characteristics – e.g., location – can affect the results. One explanation for this observation is that UK-based accounts may be more interested in the ACE-CSR program than those European accounts outside of the UK.

9 Limitations and Future Work

The work presented in this paper has some limitations, but also suggests some future research directions. Our choice of ACEs-CSR in the UK can be seen as a very ad hoc one, but the methods we used can be easily applied to study other OSNs of cyber security researchers, other researcher communities in different research areas and disciplines, or even non-researcher communities. The performance of our Research classifier has an F1-score of 83%, which can be further improved by considering more candidate features and building a bigger dataset so that other hybrid ML models can be used, such as deep learning based ones. Our work is based on a single OSN platform (Twitter), so another future research direction is to consider other data sources to enlarge the diversity and richness of the data, such as LinkedIn and the websites of universities and research organisations. Considering a wider range of data sources will allow covering a more representative subset of the targeted research community and their online activities. Furthermore, we can also consider using scientific data services such as Google Scholar, ResearchGate and DBLP to explore potential correlations between online activities and scientific ones of researchers, e.g., if and how an enhanced level of presence on OSNs can have a positive or negative impact on the dissemination and use of the research work of a researcher or a research organisation, how topics discussed by researchers on OSNs correlate with topics of their research publications and research projects, and how researchers with similar research interests are connected on OSNs and how such connections correlate to their actual scientific or professional collaboration.

10   Conclusion

This paper reports our study on the presence of cyber security experts on OSNs, focusing on the UK's ACEs-CSR network on Twitter as a case study. We used two existing ML classifiers in the literature and developed a new one to help identify cyber security research related accounts for constructing an ACEs-CSR network on Twitter. The results showed that all the classifiers worked well for the case study. Based on the constructed ACEs-CSR network, we conducted a social structure analysis of the ACEs-CSR graph, topic modelling analyses, and sentiment analyses. The social structure analysis revealed some useful insights about the network's structure and sub-communities, e.g., a location-based analysis led to the discovery of a four-community structure: International, European, UK-centric, and balanced. The topic modelling analysis revealed a wide range of topics cyber security researchers of the ACEs-CSR network discussed on Twitter, e.g., cyber security incidents, system vulnerabilities, cyber threats, industry, data protection laws, and even politics and cyber conflicts. The sentiment analysis results showed that the accounts in the ACEs-CSR network talked about the ACE-CSR program and the ACEs-CSR mostly positively. Overall, our study has demonstrated the feasibility and usefulness of a largely automated data-driven approach for analysing cyber security research networks on OSNs.

A   Evaluating Baseline/Individual Classifiers Performance

Classifiers Training: before using the classifiers reported in [18], we re-validated their performance with our ACEs-CSR dataset (i.e. about 42,000 Twitter accounts), which is different from the ones these classifiers were trained with originally. We utilised the same original labelled datasets and followed the same steps for the feature extraction phase from [18]. After that, we selected the best-performing feature sets according to the reported results: C, L, PBC, and PBCL (see the original study for more details on the feature sets). We re-trained the classifiers using the same original models, Decision Tree (DT), Random Forest (RF), Logistic Regression (LR), SVM with linear kernel (SVM-L), and SVM with RBF kernel (SVM-R). To see if we could get better results, we added two more models: Extra Trees (ET) and eXtreme Gradient Boosting (XGBoost). The training process was also done using the Scikit-Learn library with 5-fold stratified cross-validation. The training results are shown in Table 1. We show only the best-performing feature sets.

Our results were similar to the original ones for the first five models. As for the ET models, we noticed a similarity in performance compared to the RF models. This was expected as they are quite similar methods. In some cases, the ET models performed slightly better than the RF models. The XGBoost models performed well for the Baseline classification task with the PBCL feature set, where the F1-score is 91%, similar to the RF and ET models. However, XGBoost was slightly ahead of all the other models (in terms of F1-score) using the PBCL feature set. To summarise the results, we noticed that RF and ET

Table 6. Re-validation results of the Baseline and Individual classifiers

Task	Samples	TP	TN	FP	FN	Acc	F1	Prec	Rec
Baseline	1,154	900	63	87	104	0.83	0.90	0.91	0.90
Individual	1,003	535	281	37	150	0.81	0.85	0.94	0.78

models performed well across all the classification tasks. As for the feature sets, we found that for both Baseline and Individual classification tasks, the PBCL feature set seemed to be a good and stable choice.

Manual Evaluation: to evaluate the performance of the trained classifiers on the prediction dataset, we had to manually verify the results by selecting a subset of Twitter accounts for each classification task and manually labelling them. After that, we compared the actual labels with the predicted labels to calculate the confusion matrix. Next, Accuracy, F1, Precision, and Recall were calculated. The results of the manual verification are shown in Table 6. For the Baseline classifier evaluation, we randomly selected 1,154 samples. The F1-score was 90%, which means a 2% drop in performance compared to the F1-score from the original training/testing results, reported in [18]. For the Individual classifier, we selected 1,003 samples, and the F1-score was 85%, representing a 5% drop in performance. However, considering the significant difference in size between the original training dataset and our prediction dataset (2k vs. 42k accounts) and the relatively small performance drop, we can confidently assert that both the Baseline and Individual classifiers are good enough for our case study.

B   Issue with TextBlob Sentiment Analyser

Below are some example tweets that were wrongly classified by the TextBlob sentiment analyser as negative, while the VADER sentiment analyser classified them correctly as positive.

- *Our Academic Centre of Excellence in Cyber Security Research becomes active this week.*
- *Academic Centre of Excellence in Cyber Security Research Open Day @ucl: @uclisec hosting an open day at the ACE center November 15th #infosec #CyberSecurity.*
- *Congratulations to @UniKent @KingsCollegeLon and @cardiffuni who join @UniofOxford and 13 other UK universities as Academic Centres of Excellence in Cyber Security Research, announced recently by the National Cyber Security Centre @NCSC and @EPSRC.*

References

1. Andreotta, M., et al.: Analyzing social media data: a mixed-methods framework combining computational and qualitative text analysis. Behav. Res. Methods **51**(4), 1766–1781 (2019). https://doi.org/10.3758/s13428-019-01202-8

2. Aslan, C.B., Li, S., Celebi, F.V., Tian, H.: The world of defacers: looking through the lens of their activities on Twitter. IEEE Access **8**, 204132–204143 (2020). https://doi.org/10.1109/ACCESS.2020.3037015

3. Aslan, B., Belen Sağlam, R., Li, S.: Automatic detection of cyber security related accounts on online social networks: Twitter as an example. In: Proceedings of the 9th International Conference on Social Media and Society, pp. 236–240. ACM (2018). https://doi.org/10.1145/3217804.3217919

4. Bastian, M., Heymann, S., Jacomy, M.: Gephi: an open source software for exploring and manipulating networks. Proc. Int. AAAI Conf. Web Soc. Med. **3**(1), 361–362 (2009). https://doi.org/10.1609/icwsm.v3i1.13937

5. Blei, D.M.: Probabilistic topic models. Commun. ACM **55**(4), 77–84 (2012). https://doi.org/10.1145/2133806.2133826

6. Blei, D.M., Ng, A.Y., Jordan, M.I.: Latent Dirichlet allocation. J. Mach. Learn. Res. **3**, 993–1022 (2003). https://www.jmlr.org/papers/v3/blei03a.html

7. Blondel, V.D., Guillaume, J.L., Lambiotte, R., Lefebvre, E.: Fast unfolding of communities in large networks. J. Statist. Mech. Theory Exp. **2008**(10), P10008:1–P10008:12 (2008). https://doi.org/10.1088/1742-5468/2008/10/p10008

8. Bostock, M.: d3-hierarchy: 2D layout algorithms for visualizing hierarchical data (2022). https://github.com/d3/d3-hierarchy

9. GeoNames: Cities (2022). http://www.geonames.org/

10. Girvan, M., Newman, M.E.J.: Community structure in social and biological networks. Proc. Natl. Acad. Sci. (PNAS) **99**(12), 7821–7826 (2002). https://doi.org/10.1073/pnas.122653799

11. Hipo: University domains (2022). github.com/Hipo/university-domains-list

12. Hutto, C.J., Gilbert, E.: VADER: a parsimonious rule-based model for sentiment analysis of social media text. Proc. Int. AAAI Conf. Web Soc. Med. **8**(1), 216–225 (2014). https://doi.org/10.1609/icwsm.v8i1.14550

13. Jones, K., Nurse, J.R.C., Li, S.: Behind the mask: a computational study of Anonymous' presence on Twitter. Proc. Int. AAAI Conf. Web Soc. Med. **14**(1), 327–338 (2020). https://doi.org/10.1609/icwsm.v14i1.7303

14. Jones, K., Nurse, J.R.C., Li, S.: Out of the shadows: analyzing anonymous' Twitter resurgence during the 2020 black lives matter protests. Proc. Int. AAAI Conf. Web Soc. Med. **16**(1), 417–428 (2022). https://doi.org/10.1609/icwsm.v16i1.19303

15. Kigerl, A.: Profiling cybercriminals: topic model clustering of carding forum member comment histories. Soc. Sci. Comput. Rev. **36**(5), 591–609 (2018). https://doi.org/10.1177/0894439317730296

16. Lambiotte, R., Delvenne, J.C., Barahona, M.: Random walks, Markov processes and the multiscale modular organization of complex networks. IEEE Trans. Netw. Sci. Eng. **1**(2), 76–90 (2014). https://doi.org/10.1109/tnse.2015.2391998

17. Loria, S.: TextBlob: Simplified text processing (2022). https://textblob.readthedocs.io/en/dev/

18. Mahaini, M.I., Li, S.: Detecting cyber security related Twitter accounts and different sub-groups: A multi-classifier approach. In: Proceedings of the 2021 IEEE/ACM International Conference on Advances in Social Networks Analysis and Mining, pp. 599–606. ACM (11 2021). https://doi.org/10.1145/3487351.3492716

19. Moscato, V., Sperlì, G.: A survey about community detection over on-line social and heterogeneous information networks. Knowl. Based Syst. **224**, 107112:1–107112:13 (2021). https://doi.org/10.1016/j.knosys.2021.107112

20. National Cyber Security Centre (NCSC), UK: Academic Centres of Excellence in Cyber Security Research (2019). https://www.ncsc.gov.uk/information/academic-centres-excellence-cyber-security-research

21. Newman, M.E.J.: Equivalence between modularity optimization and maximum likelihood methods for community detection. Phys. Rev. E. **94**(5), 052315:1–052315:8 (2016). https://doi.org/10.1103/PhysRevE.94.052315
22. Newman, M.E.J., Girvan, M.: Finding and evaluating community structure in networks. Phys. Rev. E. **69**(2), 026113:1–026113:15 (2004). https://doi.org/10.1103/PhysRevE.69.026113
23. NLTK Team: NLTK: Natural language toolkit (2023). https://www.nltk.org/
24. Nouh, M., Nurse, J.R.C.: Identifying key-players in online activist groups on the Facebook social network. In: Proceedings of the 2015 IEEE International Conference on Data Mining Workshop, pp. 969–978. IEEE (2015). https://doi.org/10.1109/icdmw.2015.88
25. Pattnaik, N., Li, S., Nurse, J.R.C.: Perspectives of non-expert users on cyber security and privacy: an analysis of online discussions on Twitter. Comput. Secur. **125**, 103008:1–103008:15 (2023). https://doi.org/10.1016/j.cose.2022.103008
26. Pedregosa, F., et al.: Scikit-learn: Machine learning in Python. J. Mach. Learn. Res. **12**, 2825–2830 (2011). https://jmlr.org/papers/v12/pedregosa11a.html
27. Řehůřek, R.: Gensim: Topic modelling for humans (2022). https://radimrehurek.com/gensim/index.html
28. Řehůřek, R., Sojka, P.: Software framework for topic modelling with large corpora. In: Proceedings of the LREC 2010 Workshop on New Challenges for NLP Frameworks, pp. 45–50. Elra (2010). http://is.muni.cz/publication/884893/en
29. Röder, M., Both, A., Hinneburg, A.: Exploring the space of topic coherence measures. In: Proceedings of the 8th ACM International Conference on Web Search and Data Mining, pp. 399–408. ACM (2015). https://doi.org/10.1145/2684822.2685324
30. Saura, J.R., Palacios-Marqués, D., Ribeiro-Soriano, D.: Using data mining techniques to explore security issues in smart living environments in Twitter. Comput. Commun. **179**, 285–295 (2021). https://doi.org/10.1016/j.comcom.2021.08.021
31. Schubert, E., Sander, J., Ester, M., Kriegel, H.P., Xu, X.: DBSCAN revisited, revisited: Why and how you should (still) use DBSCAN. ACM Trans. Database Syst. **42**(3), 19:1–19:21 (2017). https://doi.org/10.1145/3068335
32. Sievert, C., Shirley, K.: LDAvis: a method for visualizing and interpreting topics. In: Proceedings of the 2014 Workshop on Interactive Language Learning, Visualization, and Interfaces, pp. 63–70. ACL (2014). https://doi.org/10.3115/v1/W14-3110
33. Soni, K.: locationtagger (2022). https://pypi.org/project/locationtagger/
34. Tavabi, N., Bartley, N., Abeliuk, A., Soni, S., Ferrara, E., Lerman, K.: Characterizing activity on the deep and dark web. In: Companion Proceedings of the 2019 World Wide Web Conference, pp. 206–213. ACM (2019). https://doi.org/10.1145/3308560.3316502
35. Traag, V.A., Waltman, L., van Eck, N.J.: From Louvain to Leiden: guaranteeing well-connected communities. Sci. Rep. **9**(1), 5233:1–5233:12 (2019). https://doi.org/10.1038/s41598-019-41695-z
36. We Are Social: DIGITAL 2023: What we learned. Special report, We Are Social Ltd (2023). https://wearesocial.com/uk/blog/2023/01/digital-2023/

The Social and Technological Incentives for Cybercriminals to Engage in Ransomware Activities

Yichao Wang[1]([✉]) [iD], Sophia Roscoe[1] [iD], Budi Arief[1] [iD], Lena Connolly[2] [iD],
Hervé Borrion[3] [iD], and Sanaa Kaddoura[2] [iD]

[1] University of Kent, Canterbury, UK
{yw300,b.arief}@kent.ac.uk, sophiaroscoe27@gmail.com
[2] Zayed University, Abu Dhabi, United Arab Emirates
{alena.connolly,sanaa.kaddoura}@zu.ac.ae
[3] University College London, London, UK
h.borrion@ucl.ac.uk

Abstract. Ransomware attacks and the use of the dark web forums are two serious contemporary cyber-problems. These two areas have been investigated separately in the past, but there is currently a gap in our understanding with regard to the interactions between them – i.e., dark web forums that can potentially lead to ransomware activities. The rise of Ransomware-as-a-Service (RaaS) exacerbates these problems even further. The aim of this paper is therefore to investigate the social and technological discourse within the dark web forums that may foster or initiate some of the users' pathway towards ransomware-related criminal activities. To this aim, we carried out data collection (crawling) of pertinent posts from the "Dread" dark web forum, based on sixteen keywords commonly associated with ransomware. Our data collection and manual screening processes resulted in the identification of 1,279 posts related to ransomware, with the posting dates between 25 March 2018 and 30 September 2022. Our dataset confirms that ransomware-related posts exist on the Dread dark web forum. We found that these posts can generally be grouped into eight categories: Hacker, Potential Hacker, RaaS Provider, Education, Information, News, Debate and Other. Furthermore, the contents of these posts shed some light on the social and technological incentives that may encourage some actors to get involved in ransomware crimes. In conclusion, such posts pose a threat to cyber security, because they might provide a pathway for wannabe ransomware operators to get in on the act. The findings from our research can serve as a starting point for devising practical countermeasures, for instance by considering how such posts should be handled in the future, or how some follow-up intervention actions can be prepared in anticipation of certain actors getting involved in ransomware as a result of reading posts in such forums.

Keywords: Ransomware · dark web · dark web forum · social interaction · data collection and analysis · crawler

© The Author(s), under exclusive license to Springer Nature Singapore Pte Ltd. 2023
B. Arief et al. (Eds.): SocialSec 2023, LNCS 14097, pp. 149–163, 2023.
https://doi.org/10.1007/978-981-99-5177-2_9

1   Introduction

Ransomware is one of the most harmful cyber threats to individuals and organisations [25]. Ransomware is a type of malware that locks a computer system or prevents users from accessing their data until a ransom is paid. This is in contrast to other types of malware, which are often aimed at replicating, deleting or overburdening system resources [5]. While cyber extortion is at the heart of recently emerged ransomware variants (including threatening to reveal sensitive data), incredible technological advances (e.g., advanced propagation capabilities and virtually unbreakable cryptography) enable criminals to continue these harmful operations and generate rather lucrative returns. Lately, ransomware turned into a transnational organised crime run by so-called "career criminals" who not only initiate attacks but also run Ransomware-as-a-Service (RaaS) operations. Hence, developing measures to combat this threat is of vital importance.

Research on ransomware has focused on several avenues, including an investigation of dark web forums. These sites are commonly used by cybercriminals and other individuals to socialise, exchange information and sell illegal products and services [34]. Scholars believe that dark web forums help sustain cybercrime ecosystems. Several academic papers have investigated various aspects of interactions within these cybercrime ecosystems [1,30,43], even looking in detail into the actors involved [2,33], and specific types of cybercrime ecosystems [17]. However, ransomware research currently receives less attention than spam emails, spam tweets, hate speech detection and other types of cyberattacks. As such, studying ransomware cybercrime ecosystems further is essential in continuing our fight against cybercrime in a more thorough and balanced manner.

This paper examines ransomware-related posts from a dark web forum called "Dread" [10,15]. Dread is a Reddit-like dark web forum that emerged in 2018 and became popular as a result of Reddit's crackdown on several dark web market discussion communities. While one can find posts on illegal drugs and trades of stolen data, Dread also features professional hacking posts and in-depth guides on hacking. Due to its growth, Dread became a target for frequent distributed denial-of-service (DDoS) attacks. After suffering a prolonged downtime in 2022, in late November 2022 Dread went offline for server upgrades [15]. Recently, the forum returned online, and this allowed us to continue our focus on investigating the social interactions of various stakeholders. The collected dataset provides valuable insights into ransomware activities of various actors. Whilst showing a range of behaviours, there is a strong inclination towards the request and sharing of knowledge.

Contributions. The key contributions of our paper are as follows:

- To the best of our knowledge, this is the first academic work that specifically focuses on ransomware posts on a dark web forum;
- The posts were classified into categories, which demonstrated the nature of discussions among individuals who have interest in ransomware. These ranged from educational (e.g., actors who searched/provided advice on various ransomware-related subjects) to malevolent (e.g., actors who were

interested to buy/sell ransomware). These findings confirm that dark web forums such as Dread facilitate cybercrime;
- A quantitative analysis (i.e., counting posts for each category) indicated the overall "tone" and nature of ransomware discussions. While a majority of the observed Dread users demonstrated curiosity towards a ransomware subject and could not be labeled as malicious with certainty, the minority of users clearly asserted their malicious intents;
- A further examination of each post (i.e., a qualitative approach) confirmed the results of the quantitative phase and provided a deeper understanding of intentions of the users (i.e., from potentially non-malicious to clearly malicious). Such understanding can then be used by security researchers and law enforcement agencies to devise more effective intervention measures.

The remainder of this paper is organised as follows: Sect. 2 provides an overview of related work. Section 3 details our methodology, including the implementation of our crawling approach. Section 4 outlines the results obtained, while Sect. 5 discusses the insights gained from our research. Finally, Sect. 6 summarises the main points of the paper and outlines ideas for future work.

2   Related Work

A great deal of research has been conducted to understand the dynamics of dark web forums, including the structures of forum user networks [2,43], the analysis of the key actors [33] as well as their social dynamics such as how users gain or lose trust [1,30], and how these sites might facilitate various forms of cybercrime [17]. This body of research is vital in our attempt to better understand cybercrime and develop more effective measures against the threat of "internet organised crime" [13]. While there are many ongoing investigations in this area, we are currently not aware of any research that specifically focuses on the threat of ransomware and how the dark web forums may influence it.

The development of ransomware has received a lot of (and an increasing) interest within the security community in recent years. Researchers have studied various technical aspects of ransomware, including its detection [3,20,37], recovery from ransomware incident [8,23], as well as other potential mitigation measures [28,36]. In comparison, there are still limited studies that analyse the social aspects of ransomware – some of them are discussed below. Moreover, ransomware attacks nowadays not only rely on technological aspects, but also on human factors, which involve the spread of ransomware and the negotiation process that differ from other attacks. Therefore, there is a need to conduct more detailed investigations into the incentives of ransomware cybercriminals.

With the rise of cryptocurrencies in recent years, several studies have been conducted to track and analyse their economic impact. Huang et al. [19] conducted an end-to-end measurement of ransomware payments, victims and operators over a two-year period based on ransom wallet addresses. They conservatively estimated that approximately 20,000 victims were extorted during the two years of the study and that the criminals earned more than $16 million in illegal revenue in the overall ecosystem. Hernandez-Castro et al. [16] carried out an economic analysis of ransomware, predicting that further ransom increases should be "expected". Moreover, with the increased popularity of RaaS in recent years, criminals from non-technical backgrounds are increasingly getting involved in ransomware attacks [29, 32].

Connolly and Wall [7] conducted an analysis of 26 ransomware attacks by collecting data via interviews with victims and law enforcement representatives, leading to an interdisciplinary data-driven taxonomy of ransomware countermeasures. Connolly et al. [41] utilised data from 55 ransomware cases to assess factors that influence the severity of ransomware attacks. They found that private organisations and/or organisations that had weak security postures may be more vulnerable and that targeted attacks are often more devastating. Yilmaz et al. [39] conducted a survey to examine the relationship between personality characteristics and ransomware victimisation. They found that there is no clear evidence to indicate that personality traits would influence ransomware victimisation. Lang et al. [25] conducted a qualitative comparative analysis of 39 ransomware attacks based on interviews and secondary sources. They aimed to understand how the COVID-19 pandemic affected the tactics of these ransomware attacks. The results showed that working from home increases the risk of being attacked compared to traditional work patterns, while the laissez-faire attitude of organisations towards such attacks may lead to more serious issues.

Interestingly, we found that most of the research on the social aspects of ransomware have been focused on the victims. A closer look at attackers' activities and interactions can offer valuable insights. Dark web forums – as important places for the exchange of information between cybercriminals – are notorious in facilitating cybercriminal activities [27, 34]. They constitute a rich data source to understand the activities and perspectives of cybercriminal actors. By analysing a forum, Pastrana et al. [33] demonstrated how members of this forum, who are interested in technology and games, are gradually transitioning to committing crimes. Yue et al. [40] analysed the discussion of DDoS attacks in forums and discussed the impact of dark web forums on such attacks. Bada and Pete [4] analysed the discussion in the dark web forums around Shodan, which is a search engine that could pose a threat to Internet of Things devices.

The availability of datasets is often a challenge for this type of work. This is usually due to restricted access to dark web forums or technical difficulties [35]. A potential dataset is the CrimeBB [34], collected and maintained by Cambridge Cybercrime Centre. This dataset contains several forums from both dark web and clear web. However, this dataset is not specifically crafted for ransomware-related research (and it was last updated in December 2021). Several other studies [11, 18, 42] have highlighted the need to collect their own data from various dark web or underground forums, such as Dread. These papers have shown that such an approach is possible and can provide valuable insights, because the collected data will be tailored to the specific research questions or aims. As such, we also decided to collect our own pertinent and more recent data from Dread.

3   Methodology

One of the main goals of our research is to understand the pathway, motives and facilitating factors that may lead some people to become a ransomware criminal and decide to prepare or carry out ransomware attacks. To achieve this goal, we analysed ransomware-related posts on the Dread forum. This forum was selected as it contains a comprehensive discussion of general matters and strong reputation [15]. Specifically, we expected discussions on Dread to be less technical than on specialist hacker forums. Therefore, the messages on Dread were likely to have been posted by a more diverse group of users. The rest of this section provides an overview of the methodology we followed for data collection, as well as ethical issues that we had to consider.

3.1   Research Design

We used the search function with a list of keywords related to ransomware to identify the initial list of candidate posts. A researcher then manually screened the results, and labelled all threads and posts that were related to ransomware. The filtered results were manually analysed to determine their purpose and the actors involved. Eight categories (themes) were identified in the posts (n=1,279). These categories were further subdivided (were applicable) into sub-categories to better understand their intent. Each post was then assigned to up to two category groups (e.g., a post could fall into both the "Hacker" and "Information" categories). These categories and sub-categories are:

- **Hacker**. The post indicates that its author has performed a ransomware attack. There are two sub-category labels: "group" and "individual".
- **Potential Hacker**. The post indicates that its author plans to perform a ransomware attack. Sub-category labels: "group" and "individual".
- **RaaS Provider**. The post contains a user offering RaaS for sale. Sub-category labels: "group" and "individual".
- **News**. The post refers to ransomware-related real world events (e.g., actual ransomware attacks). No sub-categories were identified for this category.
- **Education**. The post contains explicit educational information about ransomware related subjects. Sub-category labels: "request" and "provider".
- **Information**. The post requests or provides general information that cannot be classified as "Education" or "News". Sub-category labels: "request", "provider", and "moderator".
- **Debate**. The post presents an opinion, often initiating or contributing to a debate. No sub-categories were identified for this category.
- **Other**. Posts that do not fit any of the previous categories. No sub-categories were identified for this category.

These categories also allowed for a quantitative analysis on the frequency of each category as well as what that entails (i.e., a qualitative approach) as discussed in the Results section. Lastly, statistical analysis regarding the frequency of each keyword was performed within the post and thread respectively.

There are sixteen keywords (case insensitive) used to identify posts related to ransomware activities: *Ransomware, Extortion, Cyber extortion, Cyberextortion, RaaS, REvil, Sodinokibi, LockBit, Avaddon, BlackMatter, Ransomex, DarkSide, BlackCat, ALPHV, Hive,* and *Lockbit Black.* These keywords were provided by two researchers experienced in the field of ransomware. They correspond to terms related to ransomware attacks (e.g., "Ransomware", "Cyberextortion"), or the names of notable ransomware variants and/or groups at the time of the study.

We used a custom crawler to collect ransomware-related posts on 2 November 2022. The initial set of the collected posts (we call them "raw data") contained a sample of 19,109 candidate posts, spanning a period of 1,720 days (16 February 2018 to 1 November 2022). However, there were quite a lot of "false positives" in the raw data, whereby many posts included in this initial dataset were actually not ransomware-related. Therefore, we had to refine the initial dataset to remove any posts that were not ransomware-related. This manual filtering yielded the final dataset of 1,279 posts, covering the period between 25 March 2018 and 30 September 2022. Subsequently, labelling was performed to indicate the purpose and category of each post. The frequencies of the term "ransomware" in the post and thread along with other keywords were also calculated.

To have a better confidence regarding the relevance of the posts, we cross-referenced the ransomware attacks mentioned in some of the posts (e.g., the Colonial Pipeline and the REvil ransomware attacks) to news articles from reliable sources, such as the BBC, Kaspersky, and BleepingComputer.

3.2   Technical Implementation

In this study, we used both The Onion Router (Tor, https://www.torproject. org/) and the Invisible Internet Project (I2P, https://geti2p.net/en/) to access the Dread website. The Tor network experienced widespread DDoS attacks in October 2022, which resulted in reduced accessibility to the Dread forum [9]. Using the I2P network to access and collect data was the only alternative at the time. Technically, both Tor and I2P are decentralisation protocols, and they are just implemented in different ways.

We implemented a customised crawler in Python, based on the Scrapy web-crawling framework [24]. Due to the risk of potential (but unlikely) attacks against us, the crawler run on a virtual machine to avoid compromising the identity of researchers. A VPN tunnel was used to ensure that the geographical location and IP address would not be compromised during data collection. Tor or I2P were employed as a proxy to enable Scrapy to connect to the network. The crawler used the pre-defined keywords to search Dread, and to retrieve relevant posts. It traversed each page to obtain the URLs of all threads, keeping only one URL (if there were duplicates) to minimise the number of requests.

Finally, the crawler accessed each thread's URL and extracted all the necessary data points and features based on the web page structure. We pre-defined

Table 1. The numeric breakdown of the posts among the eight categories

	Hacker		Potential Hacker		RaaS Provider		Education		Information			News	Debate	Other
	Group	Individual	Group	Individual	Group	Individual	Request	Provider	Request	Provider	Moderator	\	\	\
	22	6	22	99	26	44	76	89	216	370	5	\	\	\
Total	28		121		70		165		591			161	265	63
Percentage	2.19%		9.46%		5.47%		12.90%		46.21%			12.59%	20.72%	4.93%

the following features for each post in the raw dataset: post ID, content, creator, whether the post was original or part of a thread, time of post, subdread (like subreddit), thread URL, thread title, number of users involved, number of posts in the thread, the time difference between the previous post in the same thread, the time difference between the last and the original post in the same thread.

3.3   Ethical Considerations

As the dark web is mostly uncensored, there was a risk that the researchers conducting the search could be exposed to detailed information about a wide range of criminal activities. For this reason, data collection was performed automatically and *only textual data* was collected. The data was saved into a comma-separated values (CSV) file on an offline external hard drive to avoid leakage. Access to the file was restricted to the researchers involved in this project.

Due to the anonymous nature of the dark web, we were unable (nor interested) to collect personal information of users, or track their real identities. Nonetheless, we still had to anonymise the usernames of the Dread forum users, because it might be possible to use these usernames to connect back to the their real identities. At the same time, it would still be valuable to be able to link various posts to each entity. As such, when referring to statements from a particular user, we used a pseudonym (e.g., "User 1"), which would still allow some data linking to be performed, while protecting the privacy of the users involved. The ethics of this study has been reviewed and approved by Zayed University Ethics Committee (Ref: ZU22_033_F).

4   Results

In this section, we aim to further examine the reasoning and behaviours of (potential) criminals who engage in ransomware. To achieve this, we have used a combination of figures, tables, and analytical tools to gain insights. This enabled us to find and better understand significant trends and patterns of ransomware activities. In total, eight main categories were identified in the posts (n=1,279), as already outlined in Sect. 3.

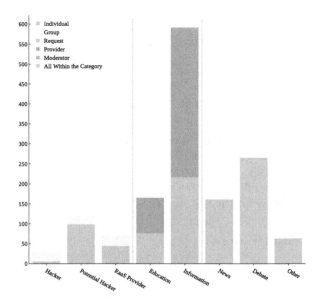

Fig. 1. A stacked bar chart showing the distribution of the eight categories of the ransomware-related posts in the Dread forum

Table 1 provides a detailed breakdown on how the 1,279 posts referencing ransomware topics are being grouped into the eight categories. In order to highlight the popularity of each of the categories more clearly, these 1,279 posts are also represented as a stacked bar chart in Fig. 1. The posts for each category are also colour-coded to indicate their additional sub-groups, in order to provide further distinctions between the types of posts on the site. The goal was to document all our information in one structured location in order to allow easy modification, sharing, and analysis. Due to the large size of the dataset, we cannot show everything in this paper. However, interested readers can view a small snapshot, as well as the full set of the raw data at https://github.com/SocialSec2023-Paper-23/SocialSec-2023-Paper-23-Additional-Information.

5   Analysis and Discussion

Our research has shown that the acquisition and use of large dataset is extremely useful for behavioural science investigations. The diagram shown in Fig. 1 provides us with a clear visual cue regarding the trend and the intents of the discussions around ransomware on the Dread forum, even though there are some variations in the posts collected (e.g., a post can fall into at most two categories).

5.1   Mapping the Posts to Categories

These 1,279 ransomware-related posts were split into the eight categories (as outlined in Sect. 3). In order to better understand their intent, five categories

(Hacker, Potential Hacker, RaaS Provider, Education and Information) were further arranged into up to three sub-categories, as summarised in Table 1. Sub-categories were not identified for the remaining three categories (News, Debate, Other) due to their nature of being too broad.

These sub-categories allow us to better understand the context of an otherwise broad label, and proceed with further analysis regarding the intent of each post. One example of this is "Education" which contains the sub-categories of "request" and "provider", indicating the user's intent to request or provide educational resources respectively. Furthermore, "Hacker" "Potential Hacker", and "RaaS Provider" contain the sub-categories "group" and "individual" to distinguish whether the user is alone or part of a group. This information gives us a deeper understanding of the nature of discussions on the forum.

5.2   Qualitative Analysis of Select Categories

This analysis is useful as it directly allows us to see the most discussed themes during the aforementioned time frame. One immediate insight is the high number of posts where "Information" is requested, with the majority being part of the "provider" sub-category. This is expected, as information is arguably one of the most important tools for those interested in any cybercrime, including ransomware. Posts in this category range from requesting links to leak sites to various ransomware groups (see Quote 1), asking for information on how to access/spread ransomware – RaaS or otherwise (see Quote 2), and discussions around relevant topics at the time (see Quote 3). The quotes are shown below:

> *"anyone happen to have the onion link to the recent babuk ransomware breach?"* [posted by: User 1]   (Quote 1)

> *"can you tell me some gangs that offer raas services and how to contact them, please?"* [posted by: User 2]   (Quote 2)

> *"curious if anyone has any information on if revil was paid by kaseya or if they simply shut down to evade le. read today that kaseya was able to obtain a decryptor key from a third party, any thoughts?"* [posted by: User 1]   (Quote 3)

These posts fit the mindset of a person interested in ransomware – if we can assume that their aim is to become more educated and involved in this environment. This is supported by 22 posts being in both the "Education" and "Information" category. Understanding ransomware (and how to operate it) is not necessarily something that is simple to achieve, and hence people turn to forums such as Dread in order to research this further. In this case, they believe these forums are a place where they can gain this knowledge. Dread is considered easier to access, in comparison to other more specialised forums such as Exploit or Russian Anonymous Marketplace (RAMP). The lack of equivalent information on the clear web only fuels this movement to more specialised channels. This leads to an eager but primarily less knowledgeable group, forming an environment of like-minded individuals that highly encourages a large amount of questions and requests for information.

Notably, a large number of posts requesting information are those asking for RaaS. With RaaS – such as LockBit [12,22] and DarkSide [31] – being on the rise in recent years, it is expected that many conversations would be around such ransomware groups. Since RaaS removed the most technically challenging part in ransomware operation – namely writing the ransomware code – the existence of RaaS increases the accessibility of ransomware software to almost anyone. This ability for RaaS to be used by a large number of people makes it appealing to those who are interested to engage in cybercrime activities. One example of this is a post from a user (known as User 3) who was *"looking for the lockbit2.0 on dread"*. Finally, the user friendly and easy-to-set-up nature of RaaS makes it ideal for newbies to pick up, especially when there are some support communities to learn how to use RaaS via discussion forums such as Dread. This popularity is reinforced by the number of posts occurring even after the soft ban on ransomware discussions following the Colonial Pipeline attack [6].

The category "Debate" also contains a significant number of the posts related to ransomware. One example is discussions regarding best practices; these posts often occur after an information or education request. We consider this category to be significant as it is important for users to share information in order to stay relevant and effective in their aim, especially due to the illegal nature of ransomware. The allure of a supportive community can attract individuals to a forum like Dread where they can connect with others who share common interests, especially on sensitive topics and potentially criminal subjects (in this case, ransomware). This is because these topics are usually not allowed on clear web forums. Regardless of whether a users' post is critical or constructive, it is more likely to be accepted on dark web forums. Furthermore, this debate could contribute to the building of trust between potential criminals and the emergence of more private criminal communities, as well as to encourage further learning. Overall, such debating interactions provide a social incentive to continue being a part of the ransomware community.

A large number of users debate the morality of using ransomware on anyone other then large corporations. This is shown in the forum with users calling those who disagree with this principle as "thieves" (and using other expletives). These companies concisely fit the criteria for being justifiable to become a target of ransomware, as described by the idea of Routine Activity Theory [26] (sensitive information, ability to pay high ransom etc.) in addition to being viewed as immoral or corrupt by many in the community. Because of this, many see it as their "duty" to attack these companies as a form of vigilante justice. This drives them to increase their skills and continue attacks. It is important to note that some in Dread disagree with this viewpoint. During the COVID-19 pandemic, many condemned the attacks on healthcare facilities, citing the "impact of it on people's lives" (posted by User 4) despite the valuable information that could be gained.

Posts related to "News" were also prevalent with 161 posts fitting this category. A majority of these messages (54.66%) were posted by a single user, showing a consistent news-like outlet. This access to real world events (which

Table 2. The frequencies and percentages of the keywords being found in ransomware-related posts

Keywords	Ransomware	RaaS	REvil	Extortion	DarkSide	LockBit	Sodinokibi	BlackCat	Hive	Avaddon	BlackMatter
Frequency	618	58	44	39	32	10	7	3	2	1	1
Percentage	75.83%	7.12%	5.40%	4.79%	3.93%	1.23%	0.86%	0.37%	0.25%	0.12%	0.12%

may not be presented as prominently on mainstream news sites) can embolden others, especially if attacks were successful. One prominent example of this is the Colonial Pipeline attack by DarkSide [14, 31].

Finally, we would like to note that information sharing in Dread predominately follows the "horizontal communication" model [38]. Horizontal communication is when information is shared between people of the same level in a group. This system of communication works well in a public forum dedicated to similar topics. In addition, due to the illegal nature of ransomware and Dread as a forum, the necessity of protecting it from law enforcement (referred to as "le" in some posts) is paramount. Because of this "us vs. them" mentality, there is an incentive to share knowledge while trying to elude law enforcement and prevent exposure. Vertical communication does exist in the forum too. It involves a communication between "superiors" and "subordinates" and provides the forum with structure. Vertical communication was found within a small group of respected and knowledgeable individuals, with one example being a user who runs an extensive education course called "Hacktown" with many being "very impressed" with its contents. One considers the inspiration and specialised knowledge they and other notable users provide.

5.3   Analysis on the Keywords

Table 2 presents descriptive statistics and frequencies of the keywords in the posts. The term "Ransomware" is the most frequent with 618 total hits (75.83% of the total keywords found). This was expected due to the purpose of this investigation. The same applies to the keywords "RaaS" and "Extortion" which were found 58 (7.12%) and 39 (4.79%) times respectively.

Keywords related to notable ransomware groups were also reasonably prevalent with "REvil" having 44 hits (5.40%) and "DarkSide" 32 hits (3.93%). These figures indicate these groups are being discussed more frequently. This lines up with notable attacks from these groups [21, 31], which would encourage this discussion. In comparison, groups with less prominence – such as "Avaadon" (1 reference), "BlackMatter" (1) and "BlackCat" (3) – appeared less often.

Other keywords did not receive any references including "Cyberextortion" and "Cyber extortion". One reason for this may be that this term is more closely associated with DDoS attacks, and thus is preferred not to be used in the context of ransomware. Another keyword ("Lockbit Black") should have already been covered by "LockBit". In addition, the keyword "Hive" (2 hits) – despite being linked to the name of a notable ransomware group – has strong connections to the drug market and "hive-mind" conspiracies. However, this is not confirmed. Refining our keywords will provide us with more accurate information.

5.4   Challenges and Limitations

The number of posts analysed is rather limited and future research should focus on collecting a greater amount of data and from a wider range of forums. One immediate limitation was due to the Dread forum being unavailable from 30 November 2022, caused by DDoS attacks against it. This made extraction of new posts through our web crawler impossible. The reduced time-frame led to a smaller dataset. Nonetheless, we managed to collect more than four years' worth of data, providing a good starting point to reveal some interesting insights into ransomware discussions on the dark web.

Because Dread is not a ransomware-specific forum, it does not attract many ransomware-experienced users, leading to the collection of a relatively small number of ransomware-related posts. This results in a loss of insights from those with more knowledge on the subject. Subsequently, we could use more specialised forums – e.g., RAMP – to further analyse why people engage in ransomware activities in the long term, allowing us to compare these "experts" against those less experienced users. For instance, User 6 mentioned that "*most of the active ransomware gangs now, conti, avos, pysa, grief, lockbit, sugar you can contact only on ramp*", which suggests potentially more revealing insights from RAMP. However, due to the secrecy of these forums, gaining access to them may be difficult. Furthermore, exploring other forums will bring its own challenges. Several forums (e.g., XSS, Exploit and RAID) have banned ransomware topics due to the increased surveillance from law enforcement after certain notable events, such as the Colonial Pipeline attack [6]. Whilst not fully enforceable, this ban may decrease the number of conversations related to ransomware in the future, limiting our dataset. This makes Dread one of the best options at this time.

Finally, despite using a wide range of techniques to achieve the large batch of information we have, this approach is still prone to potential faults. The ad-hoc crawler built for this project is in its early stages of development and therefore requires some refinement. For example, the crawler found 32 instances of the keyword "Darkside" whilst Microsoft Excel formulas found 44. As such, accuracy will need to be improved. Furthermore, the manual filtering of a large number of ransomware posts and categories by a single person did leave room for human errors and biases. This makes categories which have similarities – such as "Education" and "Information" – difficult to objectively separate. To deal with this issue, each category has been given a clear definition to ensure its consistent meaning and help with separation. Nonetheless, further improvement will be beneficiary, for example by employing automation.

6   Conclusion

We present the findings from a study in which ransomware-related discussions posted on a dark web forum called Dread were collected and analysed. Sixteen keywords were used to search for the pertinent ransomware-related posts, leading to eight main themes being identified in these posts: Hacker, Potential Hacker, RaaS Provider, Education, Information, News, Debate and Other.

Our analysis contributed to the growing body of evidence showing that ransomware is a topic of discussion on dark web forums. Our dataset covers a period of more than four years, providing useful social and technological insights into the prevalence and trends of ransomware-related discussions over time. On top of the quantitative indicators, the classification of the posts into four categories (Education, Information, News, and Debate) sheds further light into the nature of the interactions between dark web forum users. Further analysis could be conducted to infer the possible roles, status and influence of their authors.

For future work, the dataset can be expanded by including more keywords and more variations of ransomware terms, such as misspelling. Moreover, both clear web and other dark web forums – such as Russian Anonymous Marketplace (RAMP) and XSS – could be crawled to generate more data. In addition to the descriptive analysis done in this work, machine learning techniques can be employed to carry out predictive analysis. This dataset will be utilised as input for a machine learning-based system to create a model for classifying ransomware posts. This will contribute to automatic detection of such posts and could be used to prevent them from being posted on (legitimate) social networks.

References

1. Afroz, S., Garg, V., McCoy, D., Greenstadt, R.: Honor among thieves: a common's analysis of cybercrime economies. In: 2013 APWG eCrime Researchers Summit, pp. 1–11. IEEE (2013)
2. Afroz, S., Islam, A.C., Stolerman, A., Greenstadt, R., McCoy, D.: Doppelgänger Finder: taking stylometry to the underground. In: 2014 IEEE Symposium on Security and Privacy, pp. 212–226. IEEE (2014)
3. Aslan, Ö.A., Samet, R.: A comprehensive review on malware detection approaches. IEEE Access **8**, 6249–6271 (2020)
4. Bada, M., Pete, I.: An exploration of the cybercrime ecosystem around Shodan. In: 2020 7th International Conference on Internet of things: Systems, Management and Security (IOTSMS), pp. 1–8. IEEE (2020)
5. Bekkers, L., van't Hoff-de Goede, S., Misana-ter Huurne, E., et al.: Protecting your business against ransomware attacks? explaining the motivations of entrepreneurs to take future protective measures against cybercrimes using an extended protection motivation theory model. Comput. Secur. **127**, 103099 (2023)
6. Cimpanu, C.: Three major hacking forums ban ransomware ads as some ransomware gangs shut down (2021). https://therecord.media/three-major-hacking-forums-ban-ransomware-ads-as-some-ransomware-gangs-shut-down
7. Connolly, L.Y., Wall, D.S.: The rise of crypto-ransomware in a changing cybercrime landscape: taxonomising countermeasures. Comput. Secur. **87**, 101568 (2019)
8. Continella, A., et al.: ShieldFS: a self-healing, ransomware-aware filesystem. In: Proceedings of 32nd Annual Conference on Computer Security Applications, pp. 336–347 (2016)
9. DarknetOnions: dread DDOS attack continues, onion site goes offline (2022). https://darknetone.com/dread-ddos-attack-continues-onion-site-goes-offline/

10. Dread: dread (2023). http://dreadytofatroptsdj6io7l3xptbet6onoyno2yv7jicoxknya zubrad.onion/
11. Du, P.Y., Zhang, N., Ebrahimi, M., et al.: Identifying, collecting, and presenting hacker community data: forums, IRC, carding shops, and DNMs. In: 2018 IEEE International Conference on Intelligence and Security Informatics (ISI), pp. 70–75. IEEE (2018)
12. Eliando, E., Purnomo, Y.: LockBit 2.0 ransomware: analysis of infection, persistence, prevention mechanism. CogITo Smart J. **8**(1), 232–243 (2022)
13. Europol: internet organised crime threat assessment (IOCTA) (2021). https://www.europol.europa.eu/cms/sites/default/files/documents/internet_organised_crime_threat_assessment_iocta_2021.pdf
14. FBI press: FBI statement on network disruption at colonial pipeline (2021). https://www.fbi.gov/news/press-releases/fbi-statement-on-network-disruption-at-colonial-pipeline
15. Flashpoint: give me libre or give me dread: the fleeting promise of centralized illicit communities (2023). https://flashpoint.io/blog/libre-forum-centralized-illicit-communities/
16. Hernandez-Castro, J., Cartwright, A., Cartwright, E.: An economic analysis of ransomware and its welfare consequences. R. Soc. Open Sci. **7**(3), 190023 (2020)
17. Holz, T., Engelberth, M., Freiling, F.: Learning more about the underground economy: a case-study of keyloggers and Dropzones. In: Backes, M., Ning, P. (eds.) ESORICS 2009. LNCS, vol. 5789, pp. 1–18. Springer, Heidelberg (2009). https://doi.org/10.1007/978-3-642-04444-1_1
18. Huang, C., Guo, Y., Guo, W., Li, Y.: HackerRank: identifying key hackers in underground forums. Int. J. Distrib. Sens. Netw. **17**(5), 15501477211015144 (2021)
19. Huang, D.Y., Aliapoulios, M.M., Li, V.G., et al.: Tracking ransomware end-to-end. In: 2018 IEEE Symposium on Security and Privacy (SP), pp. 618–631 (2018). https://doi.org/10.1109/SP.2018.00047
20. Hull, G., John, H., Arief, B.: Ransomware deployment methods and analysis: views from a predictive model and human responses. Crime Sci. **8**, 1–22 (2019)
21. Kaseya press: Kaseya responds swiftly to sophisticated cyberattack (2022). https://www.kaseya.com/press-release/kaseya-responds-swiftly-to-sophisticated-cyberattack-mitigating-global-disruption-to-customers/
22. Kaspersky: LockBit ransomware - what you need to know (2022). https://www.kaspersky.com/resource-center/threats/lockbit-ransomware
23. Kolodenker, E., Koch, W., Stringhini, G., Egele, M.: PayBreak: defense against cryptographic ransomware. In: Proceedings of the 2017 ACM on Asia Conference on Computer and Communications Security, pp. 599–611 (2017)
24. Kouzis-Loukas, D.: Learning Scrapy. Packt Publishing Ltd, Birmingham (2016)
25. Lang, M., Connolly, L.Y., Taylor, P., Corner, P.J.: The evolving menace of ransomware: a comparative analysis of pre-pandemic and mid-pandemic attacks. Research and Practice, ACM Digital Threats (2022)
26. Leukfeldt, E.R., Yar, M.: Applying routine activity theory to cybercrime: a theoretical and empirical analysis. Deviant Behav. **37**(3), 263–280 (2016)
27. McAlaney, J., Hambidge, S., Kimpton, E., Thackray, H.: Knowledge is power: an analysis of discussions on hacking forums. In: 2020 IEEE European Symposium on Security and Privacy Workshops (EuroS&PW), pp. 477–483. IEEE (2020)
28. McIntosh, T., Kayes, A., Chen, Y.P.P., Ng, A., Watters, P.: Ransomware mitigation in the modern era: a comprehensive review, research challenges, and future directions. ACM Comput. Surv. (CSUR) **54**(9), 1–36 (2021)

29. Meland, P.H., Bayoumy, Y.F.F., Sindre, G.: The ransomware-as-a-service economy within the darknet. Comput. Secur. **92**, 101762 (2020). https://doi.org/10.1016/j. cose.2020.101762
30. Motoyama, M., McCoy, D., Levchenko, K., Savage, S., Voelker, G.M.: An analysis of underground forums. In: Proceedings of the 2011 ACM SIGCOMM Conference on Internet Measurement Conference, pp. 71–80 (2011)
31. Nuce, J., Kennelly, J., Goody, K., et al.: Shining a light on darkside ransomware operations. Technical Report, Mandiant (2021). https://www.mandiant. com/resources/blog/shining-a-light-on-darkside-ransomware-operations
32. O'Kane, P., Sezer, S., Carlin, D.: Evolution of ransomware. Iet Netw. **7**(5), 321–327 (2018)
33. Pastrana, S., Hutchings, A., Caines, A., Buttery, P.: Characterizing eve: analysing cybercrime actors in a large underground forum. In: Bailey, M., Holz, T., Stamatogiannakis, M., Ioannidis, S. (eds.) RAID 2018. LNCS, vol. 11050, pp. 207–227. Springer, Cham (2018). https://doi.org/10.1007/978-3-030-00470-5_10
34. Pastrana, S., Thomas, D.R., Hutchings, A., Clayton, R.: CrimeBB: enabling cybercrime research on underground forums at scale. In: Proceedings of the 2018 World Wide Web Conference, pp. 1845–1854 (2018)
35. Pete, I., et al.: POSTCOG: a tool for interdisciplinary research into underground forums at scale. In: 2022 IEEE European Symposium on Security and Privacy Workshops (EuroS&PW), pp. 93–104. IEEE (2022)
36. Pont, J., Abu Oun, O., Brierley, C., Arief, B., Hernandez-Castro, J.: A roadmap for improving the impact of anti-ransomware research. In: Askarov, A., Hansen, R.R., Rafnsson, W. (eds.) NordSec 2019. LNCS, vol. 11875, pp. 137–154. Springer, Cham (2019). https://doi.org/10.1007/978-3-030-35055-0_9
37. Pont, J., Arief, B., Hernandez-Castro, J.: Why current statistical approaches to ransomware detection fail. In: Susilo, W., Deng, R.H., Guo, F., Li, Y., Intan, R. (eds.) ISC 2020. LNCS, vol. 12472, pp. 199–216. Springer, Cham (2020). https:// doi.org/10.1007/978-3-030-62974-8_12
38. Ratten, V.: The effect of cybercrime on open innovation policies in technology firms. Information Technology & People (2019)
39. Yilmaz, Y., Cetin, O., Grigore, C., Arief, B., Hernandez-Castro, J.: Personality Types and Ransomware Victimisation. Research and Practice, ACM Digital Threats (2022)
40. Yue, W.T., Wang, Q.H., Hui, K.L.: See no evil, hear no evil? Dissecting the impact of online hacker forums. Mis Q. **43**(1), 73 (2019)
41. Yuryna Connolly, L., Wall, D.S., Lang, M., Oddson, B.: An empirical study of ransomware attacks on organizations: an assessment of severity and salient factors affecting vulnerability. J. Cybersecur. **6**(1), tyaa023 (2020)
42. Zhang, Y., Fan, Y., Hou, S., Liu, J., Ye, Y., Bourlai, T.: iDetector: automate underground forum analysis based on heterogeneous information network. In: 2018 IEEE/ACM International Conference on Advances in Social Networks Analysis and Mining (ASONAM), pp. 1071–1078. IEEE (2018)
43. Zhao, Z., Ahn, G.-J., Hu, H., Mahi, D.: SOCIALIMPACT: systematic analysis of underground social dynamics. In: Foresti, S., Yung, M., Martinelli, F. (eds.) ESORICS 2012. LNCS, vol. 7459, pp. 877–894. Springer, Heidelberg (2012). https://doi.org/10.1007/978-3-642-33167-1_50

Security and Privacy Matters

Graph Analysis of Blockchain P2P Overlays and Their Security Implications

Aristodemos Paphitis[1]([envelope]), Nicolas Kourtellis[2], and Michael Sirivianos[1]

[1] Cyprus University of Technology, Limassol, Cyprus
am.paphitis@edu.cut.ac.cy, michael.sirivianos@cut.ac.cy
[2] Telefonica Research, Barcelona, Spain
nicolas.kourtellis@telefonica.com

Abstract. In blockchain systems, similar to any distributed system, the underlying network plays a crucial role and provides the infrastructure for communication and coordination among the participating peers. As a result, the properties of the network define the level of security, availability, and fault tolerance within a blockchain system. This study aims to improve our understanding of the structural properties of peer-to-peer overlay networks that underpin blockchain applications. Our objective is to gain insights into the security and resilience of these systems. By analyzing seven distinct blockchain overlay networks and evaluating a comprehensive set of graph characteristics, we draw important conclusions about their overall robustness. Our findings reveal that major blockchain networks have vulnerabilities that make them susceptible to exploitation by malicious actors. Furthermore, despite relying on similar protocols for node discovery and network formation, we observe dissimilar characteristics among these blockchains.

Keywords: Blockchain · P2P Networks · Resilience

1 Introduction

Blockchain (BC) technology has garnered significant attention in recent years for its potential to revolutionize various industries and enhance trust in digital transactions [5,12,13,66]. The decentralized and immutable nature of blockchain systems has introduced novel solutions to long-standing problems, such as secure and transparent transactions, efficient supply chain management, and decentralized finance. However, while the benefits of blockchain technology have been widely discussed, the underlying peer-to-peer (P2P) networks that power these systems have received comparatively little scrutiny [25,27].

The P2P networks that support blockchain systems serve as the backbone of their operation, facilitating consensus, data propagation, and transaction validation. Understanding the structural properties, topological characteristics, and vulnerabilities of these networks is crucial for realizing the full potential of blockchain technology and ensuring its robustness against emerging threats [17,30]. Yet, the research community's attention has predominantly

B. Arief et al. (Eds.): SocialSec 2023, LNCS 14097, pp. 167–186, 2023.
https://doi.org/10.1007/978-981-99-5177-2_10

focused on the cryptographic and consensus aspects of blockchain systems, leaving the underlying P2P networks relatively unexplored.

This research paper aims to bridge this gap by delving into the largely uncharted territory of blockchain's P2P networks. By investigating the structure and behavior of these networks, we can gain valuable insights into their limitations, vulnerabilities, and potential improvements. This exploration is critical for devising effective strategies to enhance network resilience, scalability, and security in blockchain systems.

1.1 Research Question and Objectives

In this work, we aim to analyze the graph properties of underlying P2P overlays in blockchain networks to gain insights into their network robustness. Our goal is two-fold: First, we would like to understand the resilience properties of blockchain overlay networks, by uncovering potential vulnerabilities that might be exploited by adversaries to compromise the security of blockchain systems. Second, we would like to look into their structural properties to examine whether they are structured in a similar fashion and whether they exhibit properties similar to other well-known networks like the Web, the Internet, or Social Networks.

To address these questions, we conducted a study on the most important structural properties of seven distinct BC networks. Specifically, we continuously probed and crawled these BC networks over a period of 28 days to gather information about all available peers. We analyzed 335 network snapshots per BC network, resulting in a total of 2345 snapshots. At regular intervals, we constructed connectivity graphs for each BC network, consisting all potential connections between peers. We then analyzed the structural graph properties of these networks and compared them across the seven BC networks.

2 Background and Related Work

The following seven networks are included in our study: Bitcoin, Bitcoin Cash, Dash, Dogecoin, Ethereum, Litecoin, and ZCash. These networks were chosen based on their importance and high market capitalization as indicated by [15]. All networks use similar overlay implementations [19]. Two exceptions are Dash and Ethereum. Dash uses similar network messages as Bitcoin but employs a two-tier network consisting of mining nodes (peers) and master nodes that facilitate network discovery and message dissemination. Ethereum uses a different set of protocols based on the Kademlia [44] P2P architecture for network discovery.

2.1 Bitcoin Overlay Network

In the Bitcoin overlay network, nodes communicate through unencrypted TCP connections to create a random P2P network. The security of Bitcoin is achieved through its Proof-of-Work consensus protocol, ensuring that all nodes see the same version of the blockchain. The protocol is outlined in the Bitcoin developer guide [24]. To better understand its intricacies, we alse studied previous research papers [7,34,48] and analyzed the source code of Bitcoin's reference client [23].

When a node joins the network, it queries a set of hardcoded DNS seeds in the Bitcoin Core client to obtain the IP addresses of full nodes that accept new connections. Once connected, a node receives unsolicited `addr` messages from its peers, containing IP addresses of other nodes in the network. The client can also proactively request additional addresses using `getaddr` messages. The response to a `getaddr` message can include up to 1000 peer addresses. All known addresses are stored in-memory by the address manager (`ADDRMAN`) and periodically saved to disk in the `peers.dat` file. This allows the client to directly connect to these peers on future launches without relying on DNS seeds.

In terms of connections, when Alice initiates a connection to Bob, it is considered an outbound connection from Alice's perspective and an inbound connection for Bob. Each peer is permitted to establish up to eight outbound connections to active Bitcoin nodes and maintain a maximum of 125 active connections in total.

2.2   Ethereum Overlay Network

Ethereum's network protocols utilize both UDP for node discovery and TCP TLS channels for other communication, as described in the Ethereum Developer's Guide to the P2P network [26]. Node discovery in Ethereum is based on the Kademlia routing algorithm, which employs a distributed hash table (DHT) [44]. Each peer in Ethereum has a unique 512-bit node ID, and the XOR operation is used to compute the distance between two node IDs.

Ethereum nodes maintain internally 256 buckets, with each bucket containing a number of Etehreum-peers node IDs. Peers assign known nodes to specific buckets based on their XOR distance from themselves. To find peers, a new node initially adds a pre-defined set of bootstrap node IDs to its routing table. It then sends a `FIND_NODE` message to these bootstrap nodes, specifying a random target node ID. In response, each peer provides a list of 16 nodes from its routing table that are closest to the target. The node subsequently attempts to establish a certain number of connections (typically 25 or 50) with other peers.

2.3   Related Work

Delgado-Segura *et al.* [19] emphasize that blockchain P2P networks present unique characteristics and challenges compared to previously known P2P networks. Similarly, Dotan *et al.* [25] recognize the distinct requirements of blockchain overlay networks and highlight the lack of understanding of their fundamental design aspects. Their work identifies differences and commonalities between blockchains and traditional networks, emphasizing open research challenges in network design for distributed decentralized systems.

Miller *et al.* [45] were the first to successfully infer Bitcoin's public network topology. They discovered links between nodes using the timestamps included in `addr` messages. In their work, they found indications that the Bitcoin network is not purely random, having a skewed degree distribution. Biryukov *et al.* [8], proposed sending fake addresses to reachable nodes and then monitor their propagation to the network to infer connections among peers. Delgado-Segura *et al.* [18] inferred Bitcoin's network topology using orphaned transactions. Their method relies on subtleties of Bitcoin's transaction propagation behavior. Their results also indicate that Bitcoin's testnet does not resemble a random graph. Neudecker *et al.* [49] used timing analysis of transaction propagation delays, as observed by a monitoring node, to infer the topology. Their approach requires a highly connected monitoring node and the creation of transactions. Grundmann *et al.* [34], proposed mechanisms for Bitcoin topology inference based on double–spending transactions. However, this method was not intended to perform a complete network topology inference due to the high incurred cost of fabricated transactions. Taking advantage of block-relay mechanisms, Daniel *et al.* [16] presented a passive method to infer the connections of mining nodes and their direct neighbors in the ZCash network. Neudecker and Hartenstein [50] surveyed the network layer of permissionless BCs, simulated a passive method to infer the network topology with substantial accuracy, and highlighted that keeping the network topology hidden is an intermediate security requirement.

To hinder attacks that utilize topology inference, Bitcoin Core developers implemented a series of changes to the network protocol. To mitigate the methods described in [8], the Bitcoin client now rejects `getaddr` requests from inbound connections [22]. To address adversarial methods proposed by Miller et al. [45], nodes stopped updating the timestamp field in the address manager, making it impossible to infer active connections [52]. Neudecker's timing analysis is also rendered impractical due to code changes [21].

Works like [31,61] shed light on the unreachable side of Bitcoin. More recently, Grundmann *et al.* calculated the degree distribution of reachable peers in the Bitcoin network, by leveraging a spam wave of IP addresses [32].

Despite previous efforts, little is known regarding the structure and topological properties of BC overlay networks. Past studies have mainly focused on methods for inferring the well-hidden topology of Bitcoin, either against the whole network or a specific peer. With the exception of [45], these studies were validated against the Bitcoin testnet [18], or against selected nodes [34,49].

Graph Analysis and Its Applicability to Blockchain Networks. Graph analysis is a powerful tool for understanding network resilience. It has been widely used to characterize complex networks and investigate resilience in various fields and applications in a variety of network types, such as technological, social, infrastructure, transportation, and biological. A recent survey highlights the prevalence of graph analysis with respect to network resilience research [29]. Graph analysis has also been used extensively to study the transaction graphs of major BCs, namely Bitcoin and Ethereum [4,11,37,41,53,64,65]. Using similar methods, Lee *et al.* analyze Bitcoin's Lightning Network [39]. In their work, they found that it exhibits strong scale-free network characteristics, implying that the

Lightning Network can be vulnerable to DDoS attacks targeting some central nodes in the network.

Although it is an indispensable tool for assessing network robustness, graph analysis has not been applied to BC networks. We believe that a contributing factor to this omission in the literature is mainly the lack of topological information on the underlying networks.

A recent work by Paphitis et al. [55], examines the partition resistance of these networks against random failures and targeted attacks, as well as the potential for malicious attacks facilitated by the presence of common entities across different networks and their placement in Autonomous Systems.

To our knowledge, this is the first study to focus on the structural properties of P2P networks of multiple blockchains. By crawling the reachable nodes in the network, we circumvent the challenges of topology inference and build a simple network monitor that can probe seven different BC networks in parallel to uncover all potential connections. Our implementation does not require high connectivity in each network and is free of transaction processing costs, allowing greater scalability. Finally, we analyze the graph properties of BC overlay networks to compare their structure and investigate how their characteristics affect their security properties.

3   Methodology

To analyze a graph, information is needed about the graph topology, i.e., how the vertices are connected to each other. Acquiring exact topological information on a dynamic P2P network is a challenge. More so in blockchain overlays, where this information is considered paramount for the security of the network, and, as previously discussed, a variety of topology hiding techniques are used [34,45,50].

3.1   Data Collection Process

To mitigate the challenges associated with acquiring a precise snapshot of the overlay network, as discussed in Sect. 2.3, we employ the same approach that the authors introduced in a related research study conducted by Paphitis et al. [55]. In more detail, we collect all known peers for each reachable node in the P2P network. We achieve this by repeatedly sending getaddr messages to each connected node. Nodes receiving the message respond with an addr message that contains a number of IP addresses known to the replying peer. Each BC is assigned to a process that creates hundreds of user-level threads. Intermediate data collected during crawling are stored in an in-memory key-value store, each process having its own instance. Following the protocols of each BC, each process connects to its assigned network and recursively asks each discovered node for its known peers. Each new discovered node is stored in a pending set. Threads constantly poll their pending set for a new node, initiate a connection, and retrieve a list of its known peers.

Upon successful connection to a peer, its entry is removed from the `pending` set. On each response received to a `getaddr` message, the process makes an entry, mapping the originating node (N_{or}) to the peer list it knows of: $N_{or} \rightarrow \{P_0, P_1, ..., P_n\}$, where P_{0-n} are the peers included in the reply of N_{or}. In effect we draw an outgoing edge from N_{or} to each peer in the reply. This entry is stored in the `edges` set. When the `pending` set becomes empty, the crawler starts over. The `edges` set remains intact and is updated in subsequent rounds. Replies from nodes that are already mapped in the `edge` set are appended to the respective entry. After a period of approximately two hours, all processes synchronize and dump their `edge` set to storage.[1] After the dump, all sets are emptied and each process restarts and repeats the same procedure.

In this fashion, we construct *connectivity graphs*, i.e., graphs that contain all possible connections that could be made in the network. Our methodology is presented in more detail in [55], where we also show that this method is capable of reconstructing the contents of the address manager (`ADDRMAN`). In the same work, the accuracy of the collected data is validated against a controlled monitoring node, as well as against external data sources. The collected data set is available at [54]. The observed graphs were analyzed using the SNAP [40] and NetworkX [35] packages.

Ethical Considerations. We emphasize that we only collected and processed publicly available data, with no intention of deanonymizing users or establishing connections between individuals or organizations and their IP addresses. No personally identifiable information was collected during the study. We have gathered IP addresses known to each node using the node discovery mechanism of the protocol. We only established short-lived connections with discovered peers and responded only to the expected initial handshake. Finally, we have refrained from frequent retransmissions and requests to avoid exhausting a peer's network resources.

3.2   Limitations

Arguably, the observed connectivity graphs contain a number of false edges in the graph, i.e., they contain edges that do not exist in the real network. To understand how much the network properties are affected by these errors, we turn to an area of research that deals with measurement errors in network data. Wang *et al.* [60] studied the effect of measurement errors on node-level network measures and found that networks are relatively robust to false positive edges. Similarly, Booker described the effects of measurement errors on the attack vulnerability of networks [9]. Booker also finds that false positive edges have the least impact on the effectiveness of random and targeted attacks.

To investigate the accuracy of the observed graphs compared to real networks, we adapt the methods used by Booker and Wang [9, 60]. In particular, we

---

[1] Two-hour periods were chosen, to allow future analysis of longitudinal evolution of the networks. We believe that a larger window would not capture enough of the evolution dynamics.

construct a random graph G_{real} consisting of $N = 1000$ vertices, assigning to each vertex k outgoing links, so that k is drawn from the real Bitcoin degree distribution, as calculated by Grundmann *et al.* in [32]. Then, starting with G_{real}, we add random edges with the constraint that the resulting observable graph, G_{obs}, has a degree sequence drawn from the observed degree distribution we obtain using the methodology described above (see Sect. 3.1), by probing peers for their known addresses. Since Grundman's calculated degree distribution applies only to reachable peers, we also use the degree sequence of reachable peers, ignoring any unreachable nodes. In this way, the resulting *observable* graph G_{obs} contains a number of real links plus an additional number of edges that correspond to the known peers of each node (false positive edges in [9]). To inspect the effects of false edges on the observed network characteristics, we calculated a set of graph metrics for both graphs G_{real} and G_{obs} and compared them.

The average values calculated from 20 simulations are presented in Table 1. G_{obs} exhibits more robust characteristics, evident by a higher clustering and a lower average betweenness. This is expected as it contains much more edges than G_{real}. On the other hand, the average shortest-path values are very close in both sets of graphs. The results of this simulation show that the differences in the calculated metrics are consistent and almost constant. Thus, the calculated properties of the observed graphs can serve as a bound to the properties of the real graphs. The Chebyshev distance in the last row indicates the maximum absolute distance between the corresponding values.

Table 1. Measurement error simulation results. *Betweenness not normalized.

Metric→	Avg. Shortest Path	Average Degree	Clustering	Assortativity	Avg Betweenness*
G_{real}	1.89	114.6	0.21	-0.02	447,893
G_{obs}	1.56	437.7	0.63	0.07	280,648
Chebyshev Distance	0.34	333.9	0.43	0.12	172,904

4   Analysis of P2P Overlays

We aim to answer the following questions about BC overlay networks: a) What are their structural properties and network characteristics? b) Are they all structured similarly? c) Do they share common properties? d) Do their properties relate to other networks such as the Internet topology, Web or social networks, or are they random? e) How do their characteristics affect security? This section presents metrics, adapted from previous research [1,2,29,36,56,62], to assess the resilience of a blockchain network. These metrics are considered standard for analyzing networks and understanding non-obvious properties [62], and can be used to evaluate network resilience to errors and attacks. In this section, we use the following notation for clarity and conciseness: each set of edges corresponds to a graph, denoted S_c^t, representing a snapshot of the BC network c, on date t.

Other Online Networks. Online social networks, the Web and the Internet/AS topology are the most studied online networks [10, 42, 46, 58]. This section shares much of the methodology used in such studies. It is reasonable to compare the structure of blockchain networks with the structure of other known technological and information networks. Nevertheless, we are aware that: a) the studied graphs do not represent the actual network topology, and b) the P2P structure of blockchain networks is fundamentally different from the aforementioned networks. The comparisons made throughout this section serve as a reference point for the results collected. However, we note that useful conclusions can be drawn about blockchain overlays, especially when comparing the different networks between them, since they implement similar protocols [19] and we follow the same measurement methodology.

4.1   Fundamental Graph Properties

The most important properties of the derived graphs are summarized in Table 2. The metrics were individually calculated on each graph S_c^t and then averaged. The values extracted from the collected data sets match the values reported in related measurement work [16, 20, 38]. Specifically, each day, the monitoring node was able to discover 120081 nodes in Bitcoin, 19543 in Ethereum, and 4132 in Zcash (reporting median values). On average, the monitoring node made more than 1.3 M requests per day, covering all networks.

The diameter of a connected graph is defined as the longest shortest path between all pairs of nodes. A smaller diameter usually indicates better robustness, as adding edges would shorten the longest shortest path between distant nodes, making the network more tightly coupled. The Average Shortest Path (ASP) is closely related to network connectivity. Smaller average shortest paths imply increased robustness, since the distance between any pair of nodes is reduced. All networks appear to be well connected, given the size of their largest connected component, their low diameters, and short ASP. Moreover, we observe that Dash is markedly the most dense network and is almost fully connected. It has a strongly connected component (SCC), i.e., a subgraph in which all nodes are reachable from all other nodes. The SCC comprises 75% of the total network nodes. Larger blockchain networks have a smaller SCC compared to smaller ones. Networks differ mainly in size, but this is independent of their protocols; in a free market, user perception of value determines a network's popularity.

4.2   Degree Distribution

The degree (number of links with other nodes) distribution affects many network phenomena, such as network robustness and efficiency in information dissemination [6]. In addition, random networks have binomial degree distributions, while in real systems, we usually encounter highly connected nodes that the random network model cannot account for. In Fig. 1, we plot the complementary cumulative distribution (CCDF) of the out-degree of all snapshots collected for all networks in our study.

Table 2. Basic network graph metrics per BC network (average values across all collected snapshots) For each metric we highlight the value that indicates less resilience. * Normalized Betweenness using the min-max method.

Network:	Bitcoin	Bitcoin Cash	Dash	Dogecoin	Ethereum	Litecoin	Zcash
Nodes	120k	33k	9k	2.1k	17.5k	11.7k	4.1k
Edges	37M	748k	29M	330k	556k	3.7M	231k
Connected Component	1	1	1	1	0.99	1	1
Strongly Connected Component	0.06	**0.03**	0.75	0.2	0.13	0.14	0.06
Diameter	4	4	3	3	**5**	3	4
Density	0.004	**0.001**	0.5	0.11	0.004	0.047	0.024
Avg. Degree	254.16	**20.22**	2370.88	126.45	31.14	278.85	48.84
Assortativity	-0.2	**−0.64**	−0.06	−0.13	−0.02	−0.01	−0.22
Reciprocity	0.32	0.21	0.49	0.34	0.02	0.27	0.25
Global Clustering Coefficient	0.049	0.011	0.166	0.28685	**0.0022**	0.0735	0.3094
Avg. Shortest Path	2.55	2.82	1.93	1.77	**3.78**	1.96	1.72
Average Betweenness	**2.40e+07**	1.95e+06	2.74e+06	1.62e+04	1.12e+06	5.35e+05	1.43e+04
Normalized Betweenness*	**49727**	23018	8666	1257	8871	8160	1462

We color the snapshots according to their timestamp. Our first observation is that networks such as Bitcoin and Ethereum manifest considerable variability in degree distribution between snapshots. In contrast, the degree distributions in Dash and Dogecoin have less variability (seen by the distance between snapshots). Another interesting observation is that in most networks we have a high fraction of unreachable nodes, either because they are offline or behind NATs. This observation confirms the findings of Wang and Pustogarov [61] who studied the prevalence and deanonymization of unreachable peers. The presence of unreachable peers is discussed in a following paragraph.

Our results also suggest that these blockchain networks have heavy-tailed degree distributions. We further discuss their best distribution fit and their scale-free property in a following paragraph. Finally, we observe significant deviations from the network protocols. In Bitcoin, for instance, one would expect that reachable nodes would have at least 1K out-degree, since Bitcoin clients with the default parameters are set to respond with 1K known peers. In contrast, we observe a number of nodes with an out-degree less than 100, i.e., nodes reply with fewer addresses than the default parameter. We note that this behavior along with network churn could be leveraged to amplify eclipsing or network attacks similar to the SyncAttack [57].

Comparing the network densities, we observe that DASH has a very tight network, while Bitcoin, BitcoinCash, and Etherum are much less dense. This result indicates that DASH and Dogecoin have a more resilient structure than other networks.

4.3 Degree Assortativity

In general, a network shows degree correlations if the number of links between the high- and low-degree nodes is systematically different from what is expected

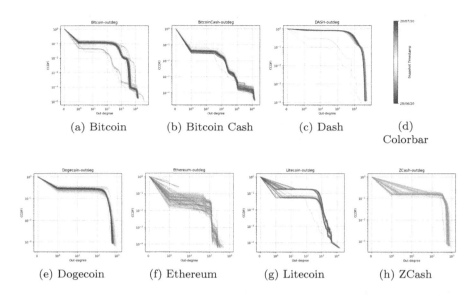

Fig. 1. Out-degree complementary cumulative distribution function of collected graphs. Snapshots are colored according to the colorbar.

by chance. In some types of networks, high-degree nodes (or hubs) tend to link to other such hubs, while in other types, hubs tend to link to low-degree nodes, i.e., what is known as a hub-and-spoke pattern. Assortativity, or assortative mixing, is a preference for nodes in a network to attach to others that are similar in some property; usually a node's degree.

The assortativity coefficient, ρ, is the Pearson's correlation coefficient of degree between pairs of linked nodes and lies in the range $-1 \leq \rho \leq 1$. A network is said to be assortative (ρ tends to 1) when the high-degree nodes tend to link to each other and avoid linking to the low-degree nodes, while the low-degree nodes tend to connect to other low-degree nodes. A network is said to be disassortative (ρ tends to -1) when the opposite happens. A random network has ρ close to zero and can be characterized as neutral. Incorporating this feature into network models improves the accuracy of the model in simulating the behavior of real-world networks. Disassortative networks tend to exhibit greater vulnerability to targeted attacks [36,43,51].

Correlations between nodes of similar degree are common in various observable networks. Social networks tend to exhibit assortative mixing, while technological and biological networks often show disassortative mixing, with high-degree nodes connecting to low-degree nodes. In disassortative networks, low-degree nodes, particularly those that have recently joined the network, can be discovered more quickly when connected to hubs. Removing these hubs can impact node discovery, graph connectivity, and potentially facilitate attacks such as eclipsing. Adversaries with high connectivity can exploit this knowledge to advertise malicious peer addresses, compromising the ADDRMAN of benign peers. We compute the assortativity coefficient for each snapshot, reporting the average values in Table 2. The networks analyzed exhibit negative assortativity, with DASH, Dogecoin, and Litecoin being closer to neutral (assortativity close to 0). Conversely, Bitcoin Cash, Zcash, and Bitcoin display more pronounced disassortativity. The negative assortativity indicates a hub-and-spoke structure in these networks, suggesting the presence of central peers that are crucial to the network and susceptible to targeted DDoS attacks.

4.4 Clustering Coefficient

The global clustering coefficient C is based on the number of triplets of nodes in the graph and provides an indication of how well the nodes tend to cluster together. A triplet is defined as three nodes connected by two edges. A triangle is a closed triple, i.e., three nodes connected by three edges. The global clustering coefficient is the number of closed triplets (or 3 x triangles) over the total number of triplets (both open and closed). A higher clustering coefficient indicates the presence of redundant pathways between nodes (due to the higher number of triangles), increasing the overall robustness of the network. The global clustering values are presented in Table 2. We observe that larger networks, tend to have lower clustering than smaller networks with Ethereum having the lowest value. This indicates that larger networks exhibit less robust characteristics. We suspect that this is closely related with the presence of unreachable peers, which is addressed in a following paragraph.

Unlike global clustering, the local clustering coefficient CC_i measures the density of links in the immediate neighborhood of node i: $CC_i = 0$ means that there are no links between i's neighbors, while $CC_i = 1$ implies that each of i neighbors also links to each other. In a random network, the local CC is independent of the node's degree, and average CC, i.e., $< CC >$, depends on the size of the system with respect to the number of nodes, N. On the contrary, measurements indicate that for real networks, e.g., the Internet, the Web, science collaboration networks, CC decreases with the degree of the node and is largely independent of the size of the system [6]. The local CC in a random network (CC_{rand}) is calculated as the average degree $< k >$ over N, i.e., $CC_{rand} = \frac{<k>}{N}$. The average degree of a network is $\frac{2L}{N}$, where L is the number of links. The average CC of a real network is expected to be much higher than that of a random graph.

In Fig. 2(a), we compare the average CC of the collected graphs with the expected CC for random networks of similar size. As in other real networks, we observe a higher CC than expected for a random network, indicating that the synthesized graphs deviate significantly from random networks. In Fig. 2(b), we plot the dependence of CC on the degree of the node for two of the networks studied, where we make some remarkable observations. Although the empirical rule of Barabasi [6] states that higher-degree nodes have lower CC, in Bitcoin we observe a significant fraction of high-degree nodes with high CC. The same finding was observed in the Ethereum and Zcash graphs. Another deviation

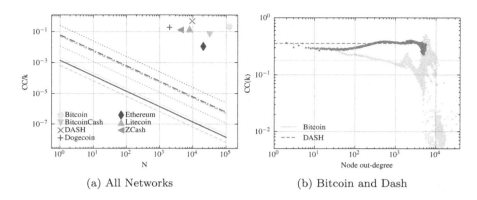

(a) All Networks   (b) Bitcoin and Dash

Fig. 2. Analysis of Clustering Coefficient (CC) results. (a) $\frac{<CC>}{<k>}$ vs. network size; Size and CC averaged across snapshots $S_c^t \forall t \in T$. Markers correspond to the networks of Table 2. Lines correspond to the prediction for random networks, $CC = \frac{<k>}{N}$, with constant $< k >$ and varying size N. Similar to other known networks, the average CC appears to be independent of the network size N. (b) The dependence of the local CC on the node's degree for each network. $CC(k)$ is measured by averaging the local CC of all nodes with the same degree k (showing results of aggregating all snapshots of a given network). Horizontal lines correspond to the average CC of the network.

from the same empirical rule is observed in Dash, where all nodes appear to have an almost constant CC, independent of the node degree. We attribute this behavior to its temporal characteristics, previously discussed in the results related to Fig. 1. Further inspection reveals that Dash has very low churn and that most nodes are always online. The observed CC distributions indicate that the collected graphs are governed by rules that are rarely encountered in other known network systems. Note that the actual networks represented by these synthesized graphs are likely to have lower CCs, since we would expect fewer edges (see also Table 1).

As explained in Sect. 3, synthesized graphs are constructed by node advertisements. From Fig. 2 we can say that almost all nodes in the Dash network know and advertise almost all other peers. This is not surprising given the size of the network and the strongly connected component being very high. In contrast, the Bitcoin network exhibits variations in the clustering coefficient, indicating that not all nodes know and advertise all other peers. This is partly explained by the size of the network and the high presence of unreachable peers (see also Sect. 4.8). The temporal dynamics of the network could also affect peer announcements.

4.5   Average Betweenness Centrality

Average betweenness centrality measures how many short paths between vertices in the network pass through a given vertex. The betweenness centrality of a node v is given by the expression: $g(v) = \sum_{s \neq v \neq t} \frac{\sigma_{st}(v)}{\sigma_{st}}$ where σ_{st} is the total number of shortest paths from node s to node t and $\sigma_{st}(v)$ is the number of those paths that pass through v. Nodes with high betweenness centrality act as bridges between parts of the network and therefore have a great control in the connectivity and information propagation of the network. It has been demonstrated that attacking or removing highly central nodes is one of the most effective strategies to partition a network or diminish its largest connected component.

The average node betweenness is the sum of node betweenness centrality for all nodes in a graph. Betweenness centrality of a node v is the sum of the fraction of the shortest paths of all pairs that pass through v [28]. A smaller average betweenness indicates that shortest paths are more evenly distributed among nodes; thus, it implies greater robustness. Nodes with high betweenness centrality tend to play a prominent role in networks, as they act as a bridge between groups of other nodes. Nodes with fewer connections than others may still have high betweenness, allowing them to fulfill a broker role and facilitate communication and information flow throughout the network. In effect, high average betweenness implies that network connectivity relies on a few central nodes, and such networks are more susceptible to targeted attacks. High variance in the betweenness centrality distribution is also an indication of lower robustness, as observed in [1,63]. Bitcoin and BitcoinCash have very high values of average betweenness, which further suggests that these networks are less resilient.

4.6   Scale-Free Property

One network property, tightly related with the degree distribution of a network, is the scale-free property. A scale-free network is defined as a network whose degree distribution follows a power law, i.e., having a probability distribution $p(k) \propto k^{-\alpha}$. The exponent α is known as the scaling parameter and typically lies in the range $2 < \alpha < 3$. The scale-free property strongly correlates with the network's robustness to random failures and has received tremendous attention in the scientific literature (e.g., see [6]). Many real-world networks have been reported to be scale-free, although their prevalence is questioned [14]. To test how well the degree distribution of each network snapshot can be modeled by a *power-law (PL)*, *log-normal (LN)*, *power-law with exponential cutoff (PLEC)* or *stretched exponential (SE)*, we calculate the best fit using the *powerlaw* package available by Alstott *et al.* [3].

In Table 3, we report the number of times each type of distribution was the best fit, for all snapshots of the same network The calculated results indicate the dynamic nature of blockchain networks. Such networks that change over time may fit different distributions depending on the snapshot collected, something that is also visible in Fig. 1. These results suggest that blockchain overlays are not structured in the same way. However, in general, the degree distributions of the collected graphs belong to the exponential family of distributions. According to sources [17,18,25] Bitcoin's network formation procedure is intended to induce a random graph. Previous research [18,45] showed that the Bitcoin network does not resemble a random graph. Our results indicate that the synthesized graphs are also substantially different from random networks.

Table 3. Degree distributions of graphs best-fit for different types of exponential distributions. PL:power-law; LN: log-normal; $PLEC$: power-law with exponential cutoff; SE: stretched exponential.

Disrtibution	Bitcoin	Bitcoin Cash	Dash	Dogecoin	Ethereum	Litecoin	Zcash
LN	6.29%	76.90%	–	49.40%	21.90%	40.10%	0.60%
PL	0.60%	16.20%	1.80%	4.80%	24.60%	12.60%	18.90%
PLEC	93.11%	6.90%	57.20%	–	18.30%	46.40%	–
SE	–	–	41%	45.80%	35.30%	0.90%	80.50%

4.7   Small-World Property

The small-world phenomenon states that if you choose any two individual nodes in a small-world graph, the distance between them will be relatively short and definitely orders of magnitude smaller than the size of the network. We examined all collected snapshots to see if they satisfy the small-world property, by calculating the ω metric proposed in [59]. The metric is defined as $\omega = \frac{L_r}{L} - \frac{C}{C_l}$ where L and C are the average shortest path and the average clustering coefficient of the snapshot, respectively. L_r is the average shortest path for an equivalent random network, and C_l is the average clustering coefficient of an equivalent lattice network. The value of ω ranges between -1, when the network has lattice characteristics, to $+1$ when the network has random graph characteristics, with values near 0 interpreted as evidence of small worldliness. The average shortest path of a random network, L_r, is given by $\frac{ln(n)}{ln(k)}$ [6]. The Clustering Coefficient of the lattice, C_l is calculated as $\frac{3}{4}\frac{k-1}{k-2}$ [47]. The parameter k is the average degree.

We did not find evidence that the networks under study satisfy this property. Although we observe low average distances in all graphs, they do not have high enough clustering coefficients to be considered as small-world. Indicatively, the ω values we calculated are greater than 0.5 for Dash and Zcash. The rest of the networks have values greater than 0.8. According to Table 1 we would expect the real networks to exhibit lower clustering coefficients but similar average shortest path length, therefore driving ω even higher. Thus, we do not expect that the real BC networks would satisfy the small-world property.

4.8   Presence of Unreachable Nodes

It is well known that the vast majority of nodes on the Bitcoin overlay network are unreachable [33,61]. Our collected data verify this and also suggest that unreachable peers are present in all blockchain overlays. In Table 4 we list our findings. The in-degree indicates how many reachable peers advertise an unreachable address. Notably, a high percentage of unreachable nodes appears in all networks, leading to the observation that blockchain networks have a strongly connected core and a high number of unreachable nodes that lie on the fringe of the network. DASH stands out for having much less unreachable peers.

Table 4. Presence and median in-degree of unreachable peers in each overlay.

Network	% of unreachable nodes	Median in-degree
Ethereum	98%	4
BitcoinCash	96%	3
Bitcoin	88%	3
Litecoin	86%	**75**
ZCash	84%	4
Dogecoin	73%	**68**
DASH	18%	**984**

Unreachable nodes were previously known to exist in the Bitcoin and Ethereum networks. Our results indicate that they are also present in all blockchain networks, although at different percentages. The existence of unreachable peers is long known, but this class of peers has received little attention from the research community. It has been demonstrated that they play an important role in blockchain systems [61].

The presence of unreachable peers, which can affect the properties of a network, is not related to the network protocols used. Their presence is more likely influenced by socioeconomic factors such as the popularity of a cryptocurrency, its value, and the availability of compatible wallet software. Many blockchain clients, such as cryptocurrency wallets, appear as unreachable peers in a network, and the number of these peers depends on the factors mentioned above. However, we observe that networks with a high percentage of unreachable nodes exhibit rather less robust properties (see Table 2) such as high average betweenness, lower density, and lower clustering.

5   Discussion

In this study, we analyze the structure of seven blockchain networks and evaluate their resilience based on the computed graph properties. Our results are summarized below:

- Major blockchain networks have characteristics that indicate towards a less resilient structure. In particular, Bitcoin, BitcoinCash, and Ethereum display lower density and higher average betweenness than other networks, suggesting increased vulnerability to targeted attacks.
- Among the networks studied, BitcoinCash appears to be the most vulnerable, demonstrating lower density, a dissassortative nature, and high average betweenness.
- Despite utilizing similar protocols (excluding Ethereum), the networks exhibit distinct structural properties and resilience traits. Possible explanations for these differences include variations in network size, temporal characteristics, and the presence of unreachable peers.

- The networks' degree distribution per snapshot demonstrates significant variation. While some snapshots align with power-law distributions, others exhibit better fits with log-normal, power-law with exponential cut-off, or stretched exponential distributions.
- Their clustering coefficient distributions are similar to other real networks, and differ from random networks with similar size and average degree. They have low diameters and short average shortest path lengths, but we did not observe evidence of satisfying the small-world property.

It is important to note that our results are derived from connectivity graphs constructed using P2P address propagation, rather than representing the real topology of the networks. As a result, the networks studied may not accurately reflect precise network properties. Table 1 illustrates how these results can establish limits for the properties of real networks. Our simulations in Sect. 3 indicate that real networks are likely to exhibit lower clustering and higher betweenness, rendering them less resilient than our observations suggest.

6   Conclusions

To conclude, we have presented a comprehensive examination and analysis of the structural properties of seven distinct blockchains, focusing on their resilience. By leveraging selected graph metrics, we extract valuable insights into the resilience properties of these overlay networks. To achieve this, we employ custom crawlers to probe 32 million blockchain peers, capturing each node's list of known peers and extracting their potential connections. Our dataset is made available for future research purposes.

Through graph analysis, we have discovered that blockchain networks exhibit a distinct structure compared to traditional networks such as the Web. Surprisingly, we have observed significant variations in the graph characteristics among the studied blockchain networks, despite their similar protocols. Our findings highlight a concerning vulnerability in major blockchains: they heavily rely on a limited number of central nodes for connectivity, making them susceptible to targeted denial-of-service (DoS) attacks. While blockchains are renowned for their decentralized nature, it is crucial to acknowledge that vulnerabilities at the network layer can introduce significant risks. These vulnerabilities may lead to network partitioning, leaving the blockchain exposed to various attacks, including user deanonymization, node eclipsing, consensus breaches, and double spending [27].

Acknowledgements. This project has received funding from the European Union's Horizon 2020 Research and Innovation program under the Marie Skłodowska-Curie INCOGNITO project (Grant Agreement No. 824015), CONCORDIA project (Grant Agreement No. 830927), SPATIAL project (Grant Agreement No. 101021808) and the Cyprus's Research and Innovation Foundation (Grant Agreement: COMPLEMENTARY/0916/0031). The authors bear the sole responsibility for the content presented in this paper, and any interpretations or conclusions drawn from it do not reflect the official position of the European Union nor the Research Innovation Foundation.

References

1. Alenazi, M.J.F., Sterbenz, J.P.G.: Comprehensive comparison and accuracy of graph metrics in predicting network resilience. In: 2015 11th International Conference on the Design of Reliable Communication Networks (DRCN), pp. 157–164 (2015)
2. Alenazi, M.J.F., Sterbenz, J.P.G.: Evaluation and comparison of several graph robustness metrics to improve network resilience. In: 2015 7th International Workshop on Reliable Networks Design and Modeling (RNDM), pp. 7–13 (2015)
3. Alstott, J., Bullmore, E., Plenz, D.: powerlaw: a python package for analysis of heavy-tailed distributions. PLoS ONE **9**(1) (2014). https://doi.org/10.1371/journal.pone.0085777
4. Atish Kulkarni, M.: Leeuwen: graph pattern mining for blockchain networks (2021)
5. Azaria, A., Ekblaw, A., Vieira, T., Lippman, A.: Medrec: using blockchain for medical data access and permission management. In: OBD. IEEE Computer Society (2016)
6. Barabási, A.L., et al.: Network Science. Cambridge University Press, Cambridge (2016)
7. Biryukov, A., Tikhomirov, S.: Deanonymization and linkability of cryptocurrency transactions based on network analysis. In: IEEE European Symposium on Security and Privacy (EuroS&P) (2019). https://doi.org/10.1109/EuroSP.2019.00022
8. Biryukov, A., Khovratovich, D., Pustogarov, I.: Deanonymisation of clients in bitcoin P2P network. In: CCS, ACM (2014)
9. Booker, L.B.: The effects of observation errors on the attack vulnerability of complex networks: technical report, defense technical information center, Fort Belvoir, VA, November 2012. https://doi.org/10.21236/ADA576235, http://www.dtic.mil/docs/citations/ADA576235
10. Broder, A.Z., et al.: Graph structure in the web. Comput. Networks **33**(1–6), 309–320 (2000)
11. Casale-Brunet, S., Ribeca, P., Doyle, P., Mattavelli, M.: Networks of ethereum non-fungible tokens: a graph-based analysis of the ERC-721 ecosystem. In: 2021 IEEE International Conference on Blockchain (Blockchain), IEEE, December 2021. https://doi.org/10.1109/Blockchain53845.2021.00033
12. Chen, W., Xu, Z., Shi, S., Zhao, Y., Zhao, J.: A survey of blockchain applications in different domains. In: ICBTA, ACM (2018)
13. Christidis, K., Devetsikiotis, M.: Blockchains and smart contracts for the internet of things. IEEE Access **4**, 2292–2303 (2016)
14. Clauset, A., Shalizi, C.R., Newman, M.E.J.: Power-law distributions in empirical data. SIAM Rev. **51**(4), 661–703 (2009)
15. CoinMarketCap: Coinmarketcap (2021). https://coinmarketcap.com
16. Daniel, E., Rohrer, E., Tschorsch, F.: Map-z: exposing the zcash network in times of transition. In: LCN, IEEE (2019)
17. Decker, C., Wattenhofer, R.: Information propagation in the bitcoin network. In: 13th IEEE International Conference on Peer-to-Peer Computing, IEEE P2P 2013, IEEE (2013). https://doi.org/10.1109/P2P.2013.6688704
18. Delgado-Segura, S., et al.: TxProbe: discovering bitcoin's network topology using orphan transactions. In: Goldberg, I., Moore, T. (eds.) FC 2019. LNCS, vol. 11598, pp. 550–566. Springer, Cham (2019). https://doi.org/10.1007/978-3-030-32101-7_32

19. Delgado-Segura, S., Pérez-Solà, C., Herrera-Joancomartí, J., Navarro-Arribas, G., Borrell, J.: Cryptocurrency networks: A new P2P paradigm. Mob. Inf. Syst. **2018**, 2159082:1–2159082:16 (2018)
20. Deshpande, V., Badis, H., George, L.: Btcmap: mapping bitcoin peer-to-peer network topology. In: 2018 IFIP/IEEE International Conference on Performance Evaluation and Modeling in Wired and Wireless Networks (PEMWN), IEEE (2018)
21. Developers, B.C.: Replace global trickle node with random delays (2015). https://github.com/bitcoin/bitcoin/pull/7125
22. Developers, B.C.: Ignore getaddr msg from inbound connections (2020). https://github.com/bitcoin/bitcoin/blob/37e9f07996d3a7504ea54180d188ca91fdf0c884/src/net_processing.cpp#L3567
23. Developers, B.C.: Bitcoin core integration/staging tree (2021). https://github.com/bitcoin/bitcoin
24. Developers, B.C.: Bitcoin p2p network (2021). https://developer.bitcoin.org/devguide/p2p_network.html
25. Dotan, M., Pignolet, Y.A., Schmid, S., Tochner, S., Zohar, A.: Sok: cryptocurrency networking context, state-of-the-art, challenges. In: Proceedings of the 15th International Conference on Availability, Reliability and Security, ARES 2020, ACM (2020). https://doi.org/10.1145/3407023.3407043
26. Ethereum: Ethereum peer-to-peer networking specifications (2014). https://github.com/ethereum/devp2p
27. Franzoni, F., Daza, V.: Sok: network-level attacks on the bitcoin p2p network. IEEE Access **10**, 94924–94962 (2022). https://doi.org/10.1109/ACCESS.2022.3204387
28. Freeman, L.C.: A set of measures of centrality based on betweenness. Sociometry **40**(1), 35–41 (1977). http://www.jstor.org/stable/3033543
29. Freitas, S., Yang, D., Kumar, S., Tong, H., Chau, D.H.: Graph vulnerability and robustness: a survey. IEEE Trans. Knowl. Data Eng. 1 (2022). https://doi.org/10.1109/TKDE.2022.3163672
30. Gervais, A., Karame, G.O., Wüst, K., Glykantzis, V., Ritzdorf, H., Capkun, S.: On the security and performance of proof of work blockchains. In: CCS, pp. 3–16. ACM (2016)
31. Grundmann, M., Amberg, H., Hartenstein, H.: On the estimation of the number of unreachable peers in the bitcoin P2P network by observation of peer announcements. CoRR abs/2102.12774 (2021)
32. Grundmann, M., Baumstark, M., Hartenstein, H.: On the peer degree distribution of the bitcoin p2p network. In: 2022 IEEE International Conference on Blockchain and Cryptocurrency (ICBC), pp. 1–5 (2022)
33. Grundmann, M., Baumstark, M., Hartenstein, H.: On the peer degree distribution of the bitcoin P2P network. In: ICBC, pp. 1–5. IEEE (2022)
34. Grundmann, M., Neudecker, T., Hartenstein, H.: Exploiting transaction accumulation and double spends for topology inference in bitcoin. In: Zohar, A., et al. (eds.) FC 2018. LNCS, vol. 10958, pp. 113–126. Springer, Heidelberg (2019). https://doi.org/10.1007/978-3-662-58820-8_9
35. Hagberg, A.A., Schult, D.A., Swart, P.J.: Exploring network structure, dynamics, and function using networkx. In: Varoquaux, G., Vaught, T., Millman, J. (eds.) Proceedings of the 7th Python in Science Conference (2008)
36. Iyer, S., Killingback, T., Sundaram, B., Wang, Z.: Attack robustness and centrality of complex networks. PLoS ONE **8**, e59613 (2013)

37. D Khan, A.: Graph analysis of the ethereum blockchain data: a survey of datasets, methods, and future work. In: 2022 IEEE International Conference on Blockchain (Blockchain), IEEE, August 2022. https://doi.org/10.1109/Blockchain55522.2022. 00042

38. Kim, S.K., Ma, Z., Murali, S., Mason, J., Miller, A., Bailey, M.: Measuring Ethereum network peers. In: IMC, ACM (2018)

39. Lee, S., Kim, H.: On the robustness of lightning network in bitcoin. Pervasive Mob. Comput. **61**, 101108 (2020)

40. Leskovec, J., Sosič, R.: Snap: a general-purpose network analysis and graph-mining library. ACM Trans. Intell. Syst. Technol. (TIST) **8**(1), 1–20 (2016)

41. Li, Y., Islambekov, U., Akcora, C., Smirnova, E., Gel, Y.R., Kantarcioglu, M.: Dissecting Ethereum blockchain analytics: what we learn from topology and geometry of the ethereum graph?, pp. 523–531. Society for Industrial and Applied Mathematics, January 2020. https://doi.org/10.1137/1.9781611976236.59

42. Magoni, D.: Tearing down the internet. IEEE J. Sel. Areas Commun. **21**(6), 949–960 (2003)

43. Mahadevan, P., Krioukov, D., Fomenkov, M., Dimitropoulos, X., Claffy, K.C., Vahdat, A.: The internet as-level topology: three data sources and one definitive metric. SIGCOMM Comput. Commun. Rev. **36**(1), 17–26 (2006). https://doi.org/10. 1145/1111322.1111328

44. Maymounkov, P., Mazières, D.: Kademlia: a peer-to-peer information system based on the XOR metric. In: Druschel, P., Kaashoek, F., Rowstron, A. (eds.) IPTPS 2002. LNCS, vol. 2429, pp. 53–65. Springer, Heidelberg (2002). https://doi.org/10. 1007/3-540-45748-8_5

45. Miller, A., Litton, J., Pachulski, A., Gupta, N., Levin, D., Spring, N., Bhattacharjee, B.: Discovering bitcoin's network topology and influential nodes. University of Maryland, Technical Report (2015)

46. Mislove, A., Marcon, M., Gummadi, K.P., Druschel, P., Bhattacharjee, B.: Measurement and analysis of online social networks. In: Proceedings of the 7th ACM SIGCOMM Conference on Internet Measurement. IMC 2007, Association for Computing Machinery (2007). https://doi.org/10.1145/1298306.1298311

47. Montana, C.H.S., Huerta-Quintanilla, R.: Generalization of clustering coefficient on lattice networks applied to criminal networks. Int. J. Math. Comput. Sci. **4** (2017)

48. Neudecker, T.: Characterization of the bitcoin peer-to-peer network (2015–2018). Technical Report, 1, Karlsruher Institut für Technologie (KIT) (2019). https:// doi.org/10.5445/IR/1000091933

49. Neudecker, T., Andelfinger, P., Hartenstein, H.: Timing analysis for inferring the topology of the bitcoin peer-to-peer network. In: UIC/ATC/ScalCom/CBDCom/ IoP/SmartWorld. IEEE Computer Society (2016)

50. Neudecker, T., Hartenstein, H.: Network layer aspects of permissionless blockchains. IEEE Commun. Surv. Tutorials **21**(1) (2019). https://doi.org/10. 1109/COMST.2018.2852480

51. Newman, M.E.J.: Mixing patterns in networks. Phys. Rev. E, Stat. Nonlinear Soft Matter Phys. **67**2 Pt 2, 026126 (2002)

52. Nick, J.: Guessing bitcoin's p2p connections (2015). https://jonasnick.github.io/ blog/2015/03/06/guessing-bitcoins-p2p-connections/

53. Ozisik, A.P., Andresen, G., Levine, B.N., Tapp, D., Bissias, G., Katkuri, S.: Graphene. In: Proceedings of the ACM Special Interest Group on Data Communication. ACM, August 19 2019. https://doi.org/10.1145/3341302.3342082

54. Paphitis, A., Kourtellis, N., Sirivianos, M.: A first look into the structural properties of blockchain P2P overlays. https://doi.org/10.6084/m9.figshare.23522919
55. Paphitis, A., Kourtellis, N., Sirivianos, M.: Resilience of blockchain overlay networks. In: LNCS. Lecture Notes in Computer Science, vol. 17th International Conference on Network and System Security (NSS 2023). Springer, Cham (2023)
56. Rueda, D.F., Calle, E., Marzo, J.L.: Robustness comparison of 15 real telecommu-
nication networks: structural and centrality measurements. J. Netw. Syst. Manage.
25(2), 269–289 (2016). https://doi.org/10.1007/s10922-016-9391-y
57. Saad, M., Chen, S., Mohaisen, D.: Syncattack: Double-spending in bitcoin without
mining power. In: Proceedings of the 2021 ACM SIGSAC Conference on Computer
and Communications Security, CCS 2021, pp. 1668–1685. ACM, New York, NY,
USA (2021). https://doi.org/10.1145/3460120.3484568
58. Siganos, G., Tauro, S.L., Faloutsos, M.: Jellyfish: a conceptual model for the as
internet topology. J. Commun. Networks **8**(3), 339–350 (2006)
59. Telesford, Q.K., Joyce, K.E., Hayasaka, S., Burdette, J.H., Laurienti, P.J.: The
ubiquity of small-world networks. Brain Connectivity **1**(5) (2011)
60. Wang, D.J., Shi, X., McFarland, D.A., Leskovec, J.: Measurement error in network
data: a re-classification. Soc. Networks **34**, 396–409 (2012)
61. Wang, L., Pustogarov, I.: Towards better understanding of bitcoin unreachable
peers. CoRR abs/1709.06837 (2017)
62. Wasserman, S., Faust, K.: Social Network Analysis: Methods and Applications.
Structural Analysis in the Social Sciences, Cambridge University Press, Cambridge
(1994). https://doi.org/10.1017/CBO9780511815478
63. Xia, Y., Fan, J., Hill, D.: Cascading failure in watts-strogatz small-world networks.
Phys. A Stat. Mech. Appl. **389**(6), 1281–1285 (2010). https://doi.org/10.1016/j.
physa.2009.11.037
64. Yap, T.T.V., Ho, T.F., Ng, H., Goh, V.T.: Exploratory graph analysis of the network data of the Ethereum blockchain. F1000Research **10**, 908 (2021). http://dx.
doi.org/10.12688/f1000research.73141.1
65. Zhao, C., Guan, Y.: A graph-based investigation of bitcoin transactions. In: Peter-
son, G., Shenoi, S. (eds.) DigitalForensics 2015. IAICT, vol. 462, pp. 79–95.
Springer, Cham (2015). https://doi.org/10.1007/978-3-319-24123-4_5
66. Zyskind, G., Nathan, O., Pentland, A.S.: Decentralizing privacy: using blockchain
to protect personal data. In: 2015 IEEE Security and Privacy Workshops (2015)

Secure and Efficient Data Processing for Cloud Computing with Fine-Grained Access Control

Jingjing Wang[1], Hao Feng[1], Zheng Yu[1], Rongtao Liao[1], Shi Chen[1], and Ting Liang[2(✉)]

[1] State Grid Hubei Electric Power Co., Ltd. Information Communication Company, Shiyan, China
[2] School of Computer Science and Artificial Intelligence, Wuhan University of Technology, Wuhan, China
liangting@whut.edu.cn

Abstract. Nowadays, with rapid development of cloud computing, many information systems are running on the cloud platform. However, the cloud servers are not fully trustworthy, for the purpose of privacy preserving, the users need to encrypt their data before uploading it to the cloud. However, this also brings challenges in utilizing the data. Generally speaking, several desirable properties should be achieved for data processing on the cloud platform. First, the cloud servers should be able to perform computations on the encrypted data without learning users' sensitive information. Second, fine-grained access control should be enforced on the computed results. Third, flexibility requires that the identities who can access the computed results should be unknown when these results are generated. Fourth, the scheme should have low overheads on computation and communication. To the best of our knowledge, most of the existing schemes cannot satisfy these requirements simultaneously. In order to address this issue, we propose a secure and efficient privacy preserving data processing scheme for cloud computing with fine-grained access control, using a homomorphic proxy re-encryption scheme and an efficient attribute-based encryption scheme. Security analyses prove that it satisfies all the desirable security properties, and performance evaluation demonstrates that it is more efficient than the state-of-the-art schemes targeting similar problems. In particular, the size of ciphertexts and the decryption time for the computed results are constant in our scheme, regardless the access structure. Therefore, our scheme contributes to a more practical data processing scheme for the cloud platform with fine-grained access control.

1 Introduction

Thanks to the appealing properties, such as reliability, mobility and cost saving, cloud computing has attracted great attentions nowadays and many information systems are running on the cloud platform. For example, wearable devices

B. Arief et al. (Eds.): SocialSec 2023, LNCS 14097, pp. 187–202, 2023.
https://doi.org/10.1007/978-981-99-5177-2_11

and smart medical services are widely deployed, providing great convenience for healthcare. In this application, cloud computing can help to reduce the heavy burden of edge devices [16]. In the era of big data, the storage and processing of data in the smart grid also need the assistance of cloud computing [17].

However, privacy preserving is a crucial requirement for most cloud-based applications, as the cloud servers are not fully trustworthy in many circumstances [11]. If users' sensitive information is leaked, their privacy will be violated, and sometimes it can cause catastrophic consequences. Recently, many countries have issued laws and regulations for data protection. One feasible solution is that the users encrypt their data before uploading it to the cloud platform, but this also brings challenges in utilizing the data. To address this issue, many research efforts have been devoted in privacy preserving computations, where homomorphic encryption and multiparty computation are two popular cryptographic techniques. In both approaches, the encrypted data can be processed or analyzed without leaking its underneath plaintexts [8,18,20].

In some scenarios, not only users' sensitive information but also the processing results should be protected. In the literature, a few researchers have also investigated this issue and some solutions have been proposed with fine-grained access control on the computed results. However, most of these schemes are either inflexible or inefficient. For example, some schemes [23] require that the identities who can access the computed results are known by the time these results are generated, making them less versatile in real-world applications. For example in smart grid, the staffs responsible for data management need to rotate frequently, hence some staffs will take this position after the computed results are generated. In some other schemes [5,21], the computational complexity in decrypting the computed results is relatively high, i.e. the size of ciphertexts and the decryption time are proportional to the number of attributes.

To the best of our knowledge, very few schemes can satisfy the above desirable features simultaneously. In order to fulfil these requirements, we propose a secure and efficient data processing scheme for cloud computing with fine-grained access control, using a homomorphic proxy re-encryption scheme and an efficient attribute-based encryption scheme as the main building blocks. Our contributions can be summarized as follows:

- Our scheme not only allows users' encrypted data to be processed without leaking their sensitive information, but also achieves fine-grained access control for the computed results in a flexible way, i.e. the identities who can access the computed results can be configured after these results are generated.
- Our scheme is more efficient than the state-of-the-art schemes that satisfy similar properties. In particular, the size of ciphertexts and the decryption time for the computed results can be made constant in our scheme, regardless the access structure.

2   Related Works

Cloud computing provides sufficient storage space and computing power, and it has become an important infrastructure for information systems. Privacy preserving and access control are two security issues that need to be considered for processing and utilizing the data in the cloud platform. In this section, we review some existing works on privacy preserving data processing and fine-grained access control.

Multiparty computation allows several participants to jointly generate the outputs for some function without leaking each individual input, and it has already been demonstrated that any Turing computable function can be evaluated by MPC [15]. For example, it has already been designed for various different tasks, such as federated learning [2], computation of biomedical data [12], and avoidance for satellite collision [13]. Therefore, this technique can be used for privacy preserving data processing in cloud computing. However, for general purpose MPC, it is still impractical for large scale applications due to the heavy overheads in computation and communication.

Homomorphic encryption enables to perform computations on the encrypted data, and the same effect applies as if the operations are performed on the corresponding plaintexts. This technique can be further divided into two categories: fully homomorphic encryption [9] and partial homomorphic encryption [4]. The first type is more versatile, i.e. it supports both addition and multiplication. However, its performance still cannot meet the demands in real-world applications due to the large key size and high storage overheads. The second type only supports either addition or multiplication. But it is more efficient and many schemes have already been deployed in large scale applications. For example, it has been used to design secure e-voting, privacy preserving data aggregation and federated learning.

Fine-grained access control requires that the information can only be accessed by the designated recipient whose attributes satisfy the access control policy. In cryptography, there are two approaches to guarantee this property: proxy re-encryption (PRE) and attribute-based encryption (ABE). The first type allows the ciphertext encrypted under one entity's public key to be transformed into a different ciphertext encrypted under another entity's public key. In [23], Zhang et al. used PRE to propose a privacy preserving data aggregation scheme for smart grid with fine-grained access control. However, it requires that the identities who can access the computed results are known in advance before these results being generated. The second type also solves this issue, and it is more flexible [1, 10], but it suffers some limitations. First, most existing ABE schemes do not have the additive homomorphic property that is required for privacy preserving computations. And second, their computational overheads are relatively high when the access structure is complex, because the size of ciphertexts and the decryption time are proportional to the number of attributes [5,21].

Recall that our purpose is to design a secure and efficient data processing scheme with privacy preserving and fine-grained access control. Based on the above analyses, it is non-trivial to achieve the purpose just using either PRE or ABE. Instead, our design integrates a homomorphic PRE scheme and a novel ABE scheme. The advantage is that it not only satisfies the desirable security features, but also is more efficient than the state-of-the-art schemes with similar properties.

3   Preliminaries

In this section, we briefly review some cryptographic primitives that will be used to design our proposed scheme.

3.1   A Homomorphic Re-encryption Scheme

In [4], Bresson, Catalano and Pointcheval have proposed an encryption scheme, called the BCP scheme, with the additive homomorphic property. Compared with Paillier encryption, the BCP scheme has two unique features. First, it contains two trapdoors: the master trapdoor can decrypt any ciphertext, while a user's trapdoor can only decrypt the ciphertexts under her public key. Second, its mathematical structure contains a finite cyclic group of quadratic residues in which the discrete logarithm assumption holds, and this feature enables it to be extended into a proxy re-encryption scheme. The BCP scheme works as follows:

- **Initialization.** Given the security parameter κ, one chooses two large safe primes p, q, such that $p = 2p' + 1, q = 2q' + 1$ where p', q' are also primes. Denote $n = pq$ and $\lambda = p'q'$. Let $\mathbb{G} = \mathsf{QR}_{n^2}$ be the cyclic group of quadratic residues modulo n^2. We have $\mathsf{ord}(\mathbb{G}) = n\lambda$. Then, one randomly chooses a value $\alpha \in \mathbb{Z}_{n^2}^*$ and compute $g = \alpha^2 \bmod n^2$. Now, g is a random element in $\mathbb{G}$ and it has maximal order with overwhelming probability. Finally, the system parameters (n, g) are made public.
- **Key generation.** The user randomly chooses a value $a \in [1, \mathsf{ord}(\mathbb{G})]$ and sets $h = g^a \bmod n^2$. Her public key is h and her private key is a.
- **Encryption.** Given a message $m \in \mathbb{Z}_n$, one randomly chooses a value $r \in [1, \mathsf{ord}(\mathbb{G})]$ and computes the ciphertext $C = (A, B)$ as:

$$A = g^r \bmod n^2 \quad B = h^r(1 + n)^m \bmod n^2$$

- **Decryption.** The user can decrypt the ciphertext using her private key as:

$$m = \frac{B/A^a - 1 \bmod n^2}{n}$$

Some Remarks. Note that the value $\mathsf{ord}(\mathbb{G})$ should be unknown in the key generation and encryption algorithms, because this value reveals the master trapdoor and it enables one to decrypt any ciphertext. Instead, one can randomly select a value in $[1, n^2/4)$ instead of $[1, \mathsf{ord}(\mathbb{G})]$. The statistical distance between these two sets is $O(n^{-1/2})$, which is indistinguishable for any probabilistic polynomial time (PPT) adversary. In the rest of the paper, we will ignore this issue and simply use $\mathsf{ord}(\mathbb{G})$ in the description. Besides, we assume that all computations are modular n^2 unless otherwise stated.

In [7], Ding et al. have extended the BCP scheme into a proxy re-encryption scheme, such that a ciphertext can not only be decrypted, but also be transformed into a different ciphertext under another public key. The proxy re-encryption process is implemented by two proxies, but it also can be done in the distributed fashion by arbitrary number of proxies as shown in [22]. Ding's scheme works as follows:

- **Initialization.** Same as in the BCP scheme.
- **Key generation.** Two proxies generate their key pairs separately. The first proxy randomly selects $a \in [1, \text{ord}(\mathbb{G})]$ and sets $h_a = g^a$. The second proxy randomly selects $b \in [1, \text{ord}(\mathbb{G})]$ and sets $h_b = g^b$. The public keys (h_a, h_b) are published. Moreover, they negotiate a Diffie-Hellman key as $h = h_a{}^b = h_b{}^a = g^{ab}$, and publish h.
- **Encryption.** Same as in the BCP scheme. We assume that the message is encrypted under the public key h.
- **Proxy re-encryption.** Denote $\mathsf{H} : \{0,1\}^* \rightarrow [1, \text{ord}(\mathbb{G})]$ as some cryptographic hash function. To re-encrypt a ciphertext $(A, B) = (g^r, h^r(1+n)^m)$ under the public key $h = g^{ab}$ to a different ciphertext under another public key $\hat{h} = g^x$, the first proxy computes $\sigma_1 = \mathsf{H}(\hat{h}^a)$ and $(A', B') = (A^a g^{\sigma_1}, B)$, and sends the result to the other proxy. Then, the second proxy computes $\sigma_2 = \mathsf{H}(\hat{h}^b)$ and $(A'', B'') = (A'^b g^{\sigma_2}, B')$, and sends the result to the designated recipient with public key $\hat{h}$.
- **Decryption.** This recipient can decrypt the ciphertext (A'', B'') by computing $\sigma_1 = \mathsf{H}(h_a{}^x)$, $\sigma_2 = \mathsf{H}(h_b{}^x)$ and

$$m = \frac{B'' \cdot h_b{}^{\sigma_1} \cdot g^{\sigma_2}/A'' - 1 \bmod n^2}{n}$$

3.2 An Efficient ABE Scheme

In [14], Li et al. have introduced a novel ABE scheme with AND-gate access structure. Compared with the traditional ABE schemes in which the decryption costs increase linearly with the number of attributes, the size of ciphertext and the number of bilinear pairing operations in Li's scheme remain constant in the decryption process. This scheme consists of four algorithms: *Setup*, *Encrypt*, *KeyGen*, and *Decrypt*, and it works as follows.

Setup. It takes as input the security parameter κ, and outputs the public parameters and system keys. The key generation center (KGC) first chooses two finite cyclic groups G_1, G_2, both with order p. g is denoted as the generator of G_1 and e is a bilinear map: $G_1 \times G_1 \rightarrow G_2$. The system parameters (e, g, p, G_1, G_2) are made public. Then, the KGC randomly picks $3n$ elements $h_1, h_2, \cdots, h_{3n}$ in G_1, where $n = |U|$ is denoted as the number of attributes in the system. h_i, h_{n+i} and h_{2n+i} denote three types of attributes: positive, negative and wildcard. Finally, the KGC randomly picks $\alpha, a \in \mathbb{Z}_p$ and calculates $Y = e(g, g)^\alpha$ and g^a. Now, the public key is $PK = (e, g, Y, g^a, h_1, h_2, \cdots, h_{3n})$, and the master private key is $MK = (g^\alpha, a)$.

KeyGen. It takes as input the user's attribute set S, and outputs the private key for this user. For each $i \in U \wedge i \in S$, the KGC sets the tag $i' = +i$. For each $i \in U \wedge i \notin S$, the KGC sets the tag $i' = -i$. Note that the attributes not in S are considered as negative states. The KGC randomly chooses $r, c \in \mathbb{Z}_p$ and sets $L' = c$. It then computes $D = g^{-r}, L = g^{-ar}$. For each attribute $i \in U$, it sets $D_i = h_i^r$ if $i' = +i$; and it sets $D_i = h_{n+i}^r$ if $i' = -i$. For each $i \in U$, it computes $F_i = h_{2n+i}^r$. The KGC chooses a random value $j \in U$ and computes $D_j' = g^{\alpha/(a+c)} \cdot D_j$, $F_j' = g^{\alpha/(a+c)} \cdot F_j$. As follows, the values D_j, F_j are replaced by D_j', F_j'. Note that for any PPT adversary, such a substitution is indistinguishable. Finally, the KGC outputs $SK = (D, L, L', \langle D_i, F_i \rangle \mid i \in U)$.

Encrypt. It takes as input the access structure $W = \Lambda_{i \in I} i'$ and a message, and outputs a ciphertext. Note that AND-gate is employed in the access structure, while I denotes the attribute set of access policy and i' denotes the state of the attribute i. Each attribute has three different states: positive $(+i)$, negative $(-i)$, and wildcard. The last type means that the attribute is not mentioned in the access structure. To encrypt a message M, one first randomly picks $s \in \mathbb{Z}_p$ and calculates $C = M \cdot Y^s, C_1 = g^s$, and $C_2 = g^{as}$. Then, for each $i \in I \wedge i' = +i$, it sets $H_i = h_i$. For each $i \in I \wedge i' = -i$, it sets $H_i = h_{n+i}$. For each $i \in U \wedge i \notin I$, it sets $H_i = h_{2n+i}$. Finally, it computes $C_3 = (\prod_{i \in U} H_i)^s$. The ciphertext is $CT = (W, C, C_1, C_2, C_3)$.

Decrypt. It takes as input a ciphertext and the user's secret key, and outputs $\perp$ or a plaintext. If the set S does not satisfy W, it outputs the symbol $\perp$. Otherwise, for each $i \in I$: if $i' = +i \wedge i \in S$, it computes $A_1 = \prod D_i$; if $i' = -i \wedge i \notin S$, it computes $A_2 = \prod D_i$. For each $i \notin I$, it computes $A_3 = \prod_{i \in U \setminus I} F_i$. Then, it calculates

$$K = e(A_1 \cdot A_2 \cdot A_3, C_1^{L'} \cdot C_2) \cdot e(D^{L'} \cdot L, C_3) = e(g, g)^{\alpha s}$$

Finally, the plaintext M can be derived by computing $M = C/K$.

4   Models and Definitions

In this section, we outline the models and definitions, including the system model, the communication model, the adversary model, the security requirements, and the security assumptions.

4.1   System Model

There are five types of entities in our proposed scheme: authority, data service provider (DSP), computation party (CP), data provider (DP), and data requester (DR). The system model is shown in Fig. 1:

- **Authority**: Its main responsibility is to initialize the system parameters and generate secret keys for the users.

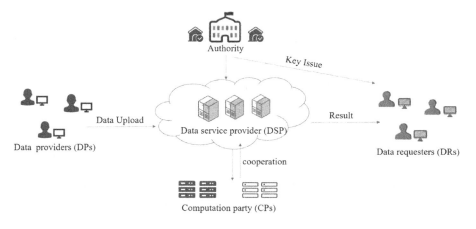

Fig. 1. The System Architecture

- **DSP**: It takes in charge of data storage, data sharing and data processing. For example, it stores the encrypted data uploaded by the DPs, performs data processing, collaborates with the CP for proxy re-encryption, and outputs the computed results to the DRs. The DSP is normally run by some cloud platform.
- **CP**: It is responsible for enforcing fine-grained access control on the computed results, collaborating with the DSP to perform proxy re-encryption.
- **DP**: The data providers are the data owners. They encrypt their data before uploading it to the cloud platform, where the uploaded data can be used for data analysis.
- **DR**: The data requester is a consumer of the computed results, subject to proper access control. In other words, if its attributes satisfy the access structure, it can decrypt the computed results. Otherwise, it learns no information of the computed results.

4.2 Communication Model

We assume that secure channels exist between the authority and the DRs as well as between the DSP and the CP. All other communications are assumed to be exchanged through authenticated channels. The adversary can neither intercept nor tamper with the messages transmitted through the secure channels. And in authenticated channels, the authenticity and integrity of the received messages can be verified. Note that the assumption of these channels enables us to focus on the protocol design without digging into low-level technical details, and these channels can be implemented by standard cryptographic primitives, such as encryption and digital signature.

4.3   Adversary Model

In our proposed scheme, the authority is assumed to be fully trustworthy. All other entities are assumed to be semi-honest, i.e. they will follow the protocol but be curious to learn information beyond their authorization. Besides, we assume that the DSP and the CP will not collude, e.g. parties with conflicting interests can be chosen. And an adversary $\mathcal{A}$ with the following capabilities is considered.

- $\mathcal{A}$ can eavesdrop the exchanged messages on the authenticated channels, but it cannot eavesdrop on the secure channels.
- $\mathcal{A}$ may compromise the DSP or the CP, but not both, with the purpose of learning DP's sensitive information or the computed results.
- $\mathcal{A}$ may compromise some DRs, trying to combine their attributes to form a larger set so that it can access the computed results that none of these DRs is authorized.

To prevent trivial break of our proposed scheme, we assume that $\mathcal{A}$ will not compromise a DP to learn its uploaded data, and $\mathcal{A}$ will not compromise a DR to obtain its decryption privilege.

Some Remarks. Note that in real-world applications, the authority's power can be distributed among multiple parties and the behavior of all entities can be verified by zero-knowledge proofs. Hence, there is no need to assume that the authority is fully trustworthy and all entities are semi-honest. The assumption here is only to simplify the description of our proposed protocol.

4.4   Security Requirements

The following security requirements are considered in our proposed scheme.

- **Correctness.** If all participants honestly follow the protocol, the uploaded encrypted data can be processed in the privacy preserving way and the computed results can only be decrypted by the designated recipient.
- **Privacy.** $\mathcal{A}$ can neither learn the data stored in the cloud platform nor the computed results output by the CP.
- **Fine-grained access control.** Only the designated recipient whose attributes satisfy the access structure can decrypt the computed results.
- **Flexibility.** The identities who can access the computed results should be unknown when these results are generated, i.e. some parties can register after the computed results are generated and still be able to decrypt them.
- **Collusion resistance.** The DRs cannot collude to gain more decryption privilege by combining their attributes.

4.5   Security Assumptions

DDH Assumption over $Z_{n^2}^*$ [4]: Given two large safe primes p, q, and $n = pq$. $\mathbb{G}$ is denoted as the cyclic group of quadratic residues modulo n^2, and g is the generator of $\mathbb{G}$. $x, y \in [1, \mathsf{ord}(\mathbb{G})]$ are randomly selected and $X = g^x$, $Y = g^y$.

For every PPT adversary $\mathcal{A}$, it cannot distinguish the two elements $Z_0 = g^z$, $Z_1 = g^{xy}$ with non-negligible advantage. This statement can be expressed as:

$$\Pr[\mathcal{A}(g, X, Y, Z_0) = 1] - \Pr[\mathcal{A}(g, X, Y, Z_1) = 1] \leq \varepsilon$$

where the probability is taken over the random choice of g in $\mathbb{G}$, the random choice of $z \in [1, \mathsf{ord}(\mathbb{G})]$, and the random bits used by $\mathcal{A}$.

l-**BDHE Assumption** [3]: Given a bilinear map $e : G \times G \rightarrow G_1$, where both G and G_1 are finite cyclic groups with prime order p. g, h are two generators of G. Given a vector of $2l + 1$ elements $(h, g, g^\alpha, g^{(\alpha^2)}, ..., g^{(\alpha^l)}, g^{(\alpha^{l+2})}, ..., g^{(\alpha^{2l})})$, for every PPT adversary $\mathcal{A}$, it cannot compute the value $e(g, h)^{\alpha^{l+1}} \in G_1$ with non-negligible probability. This statement can be expressed as:

$$\Pr[\mathcal{A}(h, g, g^\alpha, g^{(\alpha^2)}, ..., g^{(\alpha^l)}, g^{(\alpha^{l+2})}, ..., g^{(\alpha^{2l})}) = e(g^{(\alpha^{l+1})}, h)] \leq \varepsilon$$

where the probability is taken over the random choice of generators g, h in G, the random choice of $\alpha \in Z_p$, and the random bits used by $\mathcal{A}$.

5 The Proposed Scheme

In this section, we describe our proposed privacy-preserving data processing scheme with fine-grained access control. We first give a high-level overview of the scheme and then present its technical details.

5.1 An Overview

Our proposed scheme consists of the following seven algorithms:

- **System setup.** Given the security parameter, the authority initializes both the PRE scheme and the ABE scheme. Moreover, it selects a cryptographic hash function that maps from the plaintext space of ABE scheme to the plaintext space of the PRE scheme. Note that this step is crucial as the plaintext spaces for these two encryption schemes are not compatible.
- **Key generation.** The DSP and the CP each generates a key pair in the PRE scheme. They also negotiate a Diffie-Hellman key as the system-wide public key. Moreover, each DR registers with the authority, and receives her private key.
- **Encryption.** Each DP can encrypt her data using the BCP scheme, and uploads it to the cloud platform.
- **Data processing.** The DSP can perform data analysis and data mining using the stored data. Note that all operations are done on encrypted data without disclosing DPs' privacy.
- **Proxy re-encryption I.** Once the computed results are generated, the DSP first performs partial decryption as well as re-encryption on the computed results.

- **Proxy re-encryption II.** The CP continues to perform partial decryption and re-encryption on the computed results. In the output, the computed result have been transformed from a ciphertext in the BCP scheme into a ciphertext in the ABE scheme.
- **Decryption.** Finally, only the designated recipients whose attributes satisfy the access structure can decrypt the computed results

5.2   The Details Scheme

System Setup. In this phase, the authority initializes the protocol and generates the public parameters. First, given the security parameter κ, the authority chooses two large safe primes p', q' and computes $n = p'q'$. $\mathbb{G}$ is denoted as the cyclic group of quadratic residues modulo n^2 and $\bar{g}$ is the generator of $\mathbb{G}$. Next, the authority chooses two finite cyclic groups G_1, G_2, both with prime order p. g is denoted as the generator of G_1 and e is a bilinear map $e : G_1 \times G_1 \rightarrow G_2$. Then, the authority randomly picks $3k$ elements $h_1, h_2, \ldots, h_{3k}$ in G_1, where $k = |U|$ is denoted as the number of attributes in the system. h_i, h_{k+i} and h_{2k+i} denote three types of attributes: positive, negative and wildcard. As follows, the authority randomly picks $\alpha, a \in \mathbb{Z}_p$, and computes $Y = e(g, g)^\alpha$ and g^a. Finally, two cryptographic hash functions are selected: $\mathsf{H} : \{0,1\}^* \rightarrow [1, \mathsf{ord}(\mathbb{G})]$, $\mathsf{H}' : G_2 \rightarrow \mathbb{Z}_n$. It publishes the public parameters $PK = (\bar{g}, n, \mathbb{G}, e, g, G_1, G_2, Y, g^a, h_1, h_2, \ldots, h_{3k}, \mathsf{H}, \mathsf{H}')$ and keeps the master secret key $MK = (g^\alpha, a)$ private.

Key Generation. Each entity generates its key pairs. For example, the DSP randomly chooses a value $x \in [1, \mathsf{ord}(\mathbb{G})]$ as its secret key and computes the public key $pk_{DSP} = \bar{g}^x$. The CP randomly chooses a value $y \in [1, \mathsf{ord}(\mathbb{G})]$ as its secret key and computes the public key $pk_{CP} = \bar{g}^y$. Afterwards, they negotiate a Diffie-Hellman key $\bar{h} = pk_{DSP}{}^{sk_{CP}} = pk_{CP}{}^{sk_{DSP}} = \bar{g}^{xy}$. Each DR registers with the authority to obtain her private key. Suppose a particular DR is with the attribute set S. For each $i \in U \wedge i \in S$ the authority sets the tag $i' = +i$; for each $i \in U \wedge i \notin S$ the authority sets the tag $i' = -i$. Then, the authority randomly chooses $r, c \in \mathbb{Z}_p$ and sets $L' = c$. It then computes $D = g^{-r}$ and $L = g^{-ar}$. For each $i \in U$, it sets $D_i = h_i{}^r$ if $i' = +i$, and it sets $D_i = h_{k+i}{}^r$ if $i' = -i$. For each $i \in U$, it computes $F_i = h_{2k+i}{}^r$. The authority then randomly chooses a value $j \in U$ and computes $D_j{}' = g^{\alpha/(a+c)} \cdot D_j$ and $F_j{}' = g^{\alpha/(a+c)} \cdot F_j$. As follows, the values D_j, F_j are replaced by $D_j{}', F_j{}'$. Finally, the authority publishes the public keys $pk_{DSP}, pk_{CP}, \bar{h}$, and sends the private key SK to each DR through secure channels.

$$SK = (D = g^{-r}, L = g^{-ar}, L' = c, \langle D_i, F_i \rangle \mid i \in U)$$

Encryption. Each DP encrypts its data $m_i \in \mathbb{Z}_n$ and uploads the ciphertext $(\bar{g}^r, \bar{h}^r(1+n)^{m_i})$ to the cloud platform.

Data Processing. The DSP can process the encrypted data according to the specific requirement. Note that the BCP scheme already enjoys the additive homomorphic encryption, and Ding et al. [7] have also introduced a toolkit of basic operations over ciphertexts. Suppose that the computed result is a ciphertext $(A, B) = (\bar{g}^r, \bar{h}^r(1+n)^m)$.

Proxy Re-encryption I. The DSP randomly selects $w_1 \in G_2$ and encrypts it as $CT_1 = (W, C, C_1, C_2, C_3)$, where $W = \Lambda_{i \in I} i'$ is the access structure for the designated recipients, $C = w_1 \cdot Y^{s_1}$, $C_1 = g^{s_1}$ and $C_2 = g^{as_1}$. For each $i \in I \wedge i' = +i$, it sets $H_i = h_i$. For each $i \in I \wedge i' = -i$, it sets $H_i = h_{k+i}$. For each $i \in U \wedge i \notin I$, it sets $H_i = h_{2k+i}$. And $C_3 = (\prod_{i \in U} H_i)^{s_1}$. The DSP then transforms the ciphertext (A, B) into $(A', B') = (\bar{g}^{xr}, \bar{h}^r(1+n)^{m+\sigma_1})$, where $\sigma_1 = \mathsf{H}'(w_1)$, and sends (A', B') and CT_1 to the CP through a secure channel.

Proxy Re-encryption II. The CP randomly selects $w_2 \in G_2$ and encrypts it as $CT_2 = (W, C', C_1', C_2', C_3')$, where $C' = w_2 \cdot Y^{s_2}$, $C_1' = g^{s_2}$, $C_2' = g^{as_2}$ and $C_3' = (\prod_{i \in U} H_i)^{s_2}$. The CP then transforms the ciphertext (A', B') into $(A'', B'') = (\bar{g}^{xyr}, \bar{h}^r(1+n)^{m+\sigma_1+\sigma_2})$, where $\sigma_2 = \mathsf{H}'(w_2)$, and sends (A'', B''), CT_1 and CT_2 to the designated DR.

Decryption. The DR first computes $m' = m + \sigma_1 + \sigma_2$ by

$$m' = \frac{B''/A'' - 1 \bmod n^2}{n}$$

Then, it decrypts CT_1 and CT_2, obtaining w_1 and w_2, respectively. For example, to decrypt CT_1, the DR computes

$$w_1 = \frac{C}{e(A_1 \cdot A_2 \cdot A_3, C_1^{L'} \cdot C_2) \cdot e(D^{L'} \cdot L, C_3)}$$

where $A_1 = \prod D_i$ for each $i \in I$ where $i' = +i \wedge i \in S$, $A_2 = \prod D_i$ for each $i \in I$ where $i' = -i \wedge i \notin S$, and $A_3 = \prod_{i \in U \setminus I} F_i$. The ciphertext CT_2 can be decrypted similarly. Finally, The plaintext m can be derived by computing

$$m = m' - \mathsf{H}'(w_1) - \mathsf{H}'(w_2) \bmod n$$

6   Security Analyses

In this section, we prove that the proposed scheme achieves the desirable security properties, such as correctness, privacy, fine-grained access control, flexibility and collusion resistance.

Theorem 1. *The proposed scheme satisfies the correctness property.*

Proof. First, we prove that if the DSP and the CP are honest, the computed result can be correctly transformed into a ciphertext under some access structure. Second, we prove that the party whose attributes satisfy the access structure can decrypt the computed result. To see the first point, once receiving a ciphertext

$(A, B) = (\bar{g}^r, \bar{h}^r(1 + n)^m)$, the DSP first partially decrypt it, and then uses a random value $\sigma_1 \in \mathbb{Z}_n$ to blind the plaintext as

$$(A', B') = (A^x, B \cdot (1 + n)^{\sigma_1}) = (\bar{g}^{xr}, \bar{h}^r(1 + n)^{m+\sigma_1})$$

Similarly, once the CP receives (A', B'), it will partially decrypt it, and uses another random value $\sigma_2 \in \mathbb{Z}_n$ to further blind the plaintext as

$$(A'', B'') = (A'^y, B' \cdot (1 + n)^{\sigma_2}) = (\bar{g}^{xyr}, \bar{h}^r(1 + n)^{m+\sigma_1+\sigma_2})$$

At this moment, anyone can derive $m' = m + \sigma_1 + \sigma_2$ as

$$m' = \frac{B''/A'' - 1 \bmod n^2}{n}$$

where $\sigma_1 = \mathsf{H}'(w_1), \sigma_2 = \mathsf{H}'(w_2)$, and w_1, w_2 are randomly chosen in G_2. Therefore, if a party can decrypt the ciphertexts for w_1, w_2, she can decrypt the computed result. Recall that w_1, w_2 are both encrypted using an ABE scheme according to some access structure. Therefore, the party whose attributes satisfy this access structure can decrypt these values. Therefore, our proposed scheme satisfies the correctness property.

Theorem 2. *The proposed scheme satisfies the privacy property.*

Proof. To prove that the adversary $\mathcal{A}$ cannot learn any information in our proposed scheme. We need to prove that neither $\mathcal{A}$ can learn information from DP's uploaded encrypted data, nor $\mathcal{A}$ can learn information from the transformed ciphertext. Recall that DP's uploaded data is encrypted using the BCP scheme, and this scheme is semantic secure under the DDH assumption over $\mathbb{Z}_{n^2}^*$ [4]. Hence, $\mathcal{A}$ cannot learn the stored data on the cloud platform. During the proxy re-encryption phase, the DSP and the CP each just performs a partial decryption and then uses some random value to blind the plaintext. Hence, even if $\mathcal{A}$ can collude with either DSP or CP, it cannot learn any information of the plaintext during this phase. Finally, the transformed ciphertexts are encrypted using an ABE scheme that is semantic secure under the l-BDHE assumption [14]. Hence, $\mathcal{A}$ cannot learn any information from the transformed ciphertext. Therefore, based on the DDH assumption over $\mathbb{Z}_{n^2}^*$ and the l-BDHE assumption, the proposed scheme satisfies the privacy property.

Theorem 3. *The proposed scheme satisfies the fine-grained access control property.*

Proof. After the proxy re-encryption, the computed result is blinded by two random values σ_1, σ_2, and these two values are encrypted by an ABE scheme. Hence, only the parties whose attribute satisfy the access structure can decrypt them and derive the computed result. This proves that fine-grained access control has been enforced on the computed results.

Theorem 4. *The proposed scheme satisfies the flexibility property.*

Proof. In theory, fine-grained access control also can be achieved through proxy re-encryption, i.e. the information can be re-encrypted so that only the designated recipients can decrypt it. However, this requires the re-encryption to be performed in real-time when the recipients' identities are known. In our proposed scheme, although proxy re-encryption is also used, it is only used to transform a ciphertext into an ABE ciphertext. In this way, the identities do not need to be known by the time these results are generated, and users can join afterwards. Hence, it is more versatile than the proxy re-encryption approach.

Theorem 5. *The proposed scheme satisfies the collusion resistance property.*

Proof. In our proposed scheme, when generating private keys for the DRs, the authority will assign a unique value r for each DR. Therefore, the private keys for different DRs will be associated with different values. Hence, they cannot put their attributes together to form a larger attribute sets. And this implies that multiple DRs cannot collude to gain more decryption privilege.

7   Efficiency Analyses

In this section, we analyze the performance of our scheme and compare it with two related works: called the PYS scheme [19] and the DTD scheme [21]. In the PYS scheme, a CP-ABE scheme is proposed based on the AND-Gate with wildcard access policy. In the DYD scheme, a privacy-preserving data processing scheme with flexible access control is proposed, using the KP-ABE scheme [10] for access control.

7.1   Communication Costs

As shown in Table 1, we compare the communication costs considering three aspects: size of public parameters, size of the secret key, and size of ciphertext. Let n be the number of attributes in the system. Let $|G_1|$ be the size of an element in the group G_1, and let $|G_2|$ be the size of an element in the group G_2. $|W|$ is the size of the access policy and λ is the number of attributes in W.

Although the size of public parameters and the size of secret key are larger in our proposed scheme. This information only generates once, and the size of ciphertext will dominates the communication costs. The size of ciphertext can remain constant in our proposed scheme, while it is proportional to the number of attributes in the DYD scheme. Hence, our scheme is more efficient in communication, compared with the DYD scheme. The PYS scheme just introduced an en efficient ABE scheme. Although it is more efficient than ours, it has not considered the privacy preserving data processing requirement and it cannot be used to solve the research problems in this paper.

Table 1. Comparison of communication costs

	Public parameters	Ciphertext	Secret Key
PYS Scheme	$(n+4)|G_1|+2|G_2|$	$3|G_1|+|G_2|+|W|$	$(n+6)|G_1|$
DYD Scheme	$(n+1)|G_1|+|G_2|$	$\lambda|G_1|+|G_2|+|W|$	$\lambda|G_1|$
Our scheme	$(3n+2)|G_1|+|G_2|$	$3|G_1|+|G_2|+|W|$	$(2n+2)|G_1|+|G_2|$

7.2   Computation Costs

To compare the computation costs, we have performed some experiments on the Windows platform with an Intel(R) Core(TM) i7-8550U CPU at 1.80 GHz and 8.00 GB RAM. Since the exponentiation operation and the bilinear pairing operation dominate the costs in computation, only these two operations are considered. In the experiment, we have used a Type A elliptic curve with 512 bits in the JPBC library [6]. The comparison of computation costs between these three schemes is shown in Fig. 2. In our proposed scheme, the computation costs are constant, while in the PYS and DYD schemes, they are linear to the system parameters, i.e. the number of attributes. Therefore, our proposed scheme is more practical, especially in large scale applications.

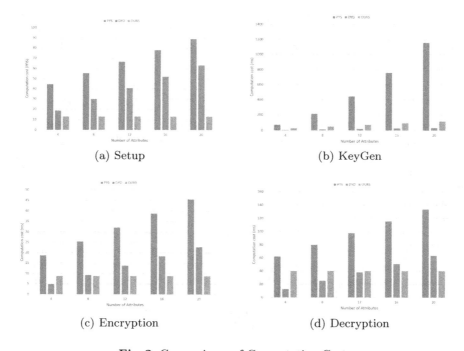

(a) Setup

(b) KeyGen

(c) Encryption

(d) Decryption

Fig. 2. Comparisons of Computation Cost

8   Conclusion

In this paper, we proposed a secure and efficient data processing scheme for cloud computing with fine-grained access control, using a homomorphic proxy re-encryption scheme and an efficient ABE scheme as the main building blocks. Our scheme supports privacy preserving computations on encrypted data, and fine-grained access control can be enforced on the computed results. Moreover, it is more efficient than the related schemes that satisfy similar properties. In particular, the size of ciphertexts and the decryption time for the computed results can be made constant. Therefore, our scheme contributes to a more practical data processing scheme for the cloud platform with fine-grained access control. For example, when it is used in smart grid, users' power consumption data can be stored and processed by the cloud platform and the results can only be utilized by the designated recipients, harmonizing security, scalability and usability.

Acknowledgement. We thank the anonymous reviewers for some helpful comments to improve the paper.

References

1. Bethencourt, J., Sahai, A., Waters, B.: Ciphertext-policy attribute-based encryption. In: 2007 IEEE Symposium on Security and Privacy (SP 2007), pp. 321–334. IEEE (2007)
2. Bogdanov, D., Kamm, L., Laur, S., Pruulmann-Vengerfeldt, P., Talviste, R., Willemson, J.: Privacy-preserving statistical data analysis on federated databases. In: Preneel, B., Ikonomou, D. (eds.) APF 2014. LNCS, vol. 8450, pp. 30–55. Springer, Cham (2014). https://doi.org/10.1007/978-3-319-06749-0_3
3. Boneh, D., Gentry, C., Waters, B.: Collusion resistant broadcast encryption with short ciphertexts and private keys. In: Shoup, V. (ed.) CRYPTO 2005. LNCS, vol. 3621, pp. 258–275. Springer, Heidelberg (2005). https://doi.org/10.1007/11535218_16
4. Bresson, E., Catalano, D., Pointcheval, D.: A simple public-key cryptosystem with a double trapdoor decryption mechanism and its applications. In: Laih, C.-S. (ed.) ASIACRYPT 2003. LNCS, vol. 2894, pp. 37–54. Springer, Heidelberg (2003). https://doi.org/10.1007/978-3-540-40061-5_3
5. Chen, S., Wang, J., Yu, Z., Xu, H., Dong, C.: A cloud-assisted data processing scheme for smart grid with flexible access control. In: Proceedings of the 2022 5th International Conference on Algorithms, Computing and Artificial Intelligence, pp. 1–6 (2022)
6. De Caro, A., Iovino, V.: jPBC: Java pairing based cryptography. In: 2011 IEEE Symposium on Computers and Communications (ISCC), pp. 850–855. IEEE (2011)
7. Ding, W., Yan, Z., Deng, R.H.: Encrypted data processing with homomorphic re-encryption. Inf. Sci. **409**, 35–55 (2017)
8. Ge, C., Susilo, W., Liu, Z., Xia, J., Szalachowski, P., Fang, L.: Secure keyword search and data sharing mechanism for cloud computing. IEEE Trans. Dependable Secure Comput. **18**(6), 2787–2800 (2020)
9. Gentry, C.: Fully homomorphic encryption using ideal lattices. In: Proceedings of the Forty-First Annual ACM Symposium on Theory of Computing, pp. 169–178 (2009)

10. Goyal, V., Pandey, O., Sahai, A., Waters, B.: Attribute-based encryption for fine-grained access control of encrypted data. In: Proceedings of the 13th ACM Conference on Computer and Communications Security, pp. 89–98 (2006)

11. Hamza, R., Yan, Z., Muhammad, K., Bellavista, P., Titouna, F.: A privacy-preserving cryptosystem for IoT e-healthcare. Inf. Sci. **527**, 493–510 (2020)

12. Jagadeesh, K.A., Wu, D.J., Birgmeier, J.A., Boneh, D., Bejerano, G.: Deriving genomic diagnoses without revealing patient genomes. Science **357**(6352), 692–695 (2017)

13. Kamm, L., Willemson, J.: Secure floating point arithmetic and private satellite collision analysis. Int. J. Inf. Secur. **14**(6), 531–548 (2015)

14. Li, Q., Xia, B., Huang, H., Zhang, Y., Zhang, T.: TRAC: traceable and revocable access control scheme for mhealth in 5G-enabled IIoT. IEEE Trans. Industr. Inf. **18**(5), 3437–3448 (2021)

15. Lindell, Y.: Secure multiparty computation. Commun. ACM **64**(1), 86–96 (2020)

16. Liu, D., Yan, Z., Ding, W., Atiquzzaman, M.: A survey on secure data analytics in edge computing. IEEE Internet Things J. **6**(3), 4946–4967 (2019)

17. Lyu, L., Chau, S.C.-K., Wang, N., Zheng, Y.: Cloud-based privacy-preserving collaborative consumption for sharing economy. IEEE Trans. Cloud Comput. **10**(3), 1647–1660 (2020)

18. Nasiraee, H., Ashouri-Talouki, M.: Privacy-preserving distributed data access control for cloudiot. IEEE Trans. Dependable Secure Comput. **19**(4), 2476–2487 (2021)

19. Phuong, T.V.X., Yang, G., Susilo, W.: Hidden ciphertext policy attribute-based encryption under standard assumptions. IEEE Trans. Inf. Forensics Secur. **11**(1), 35–45 (2015)

20. Shen, J., Yang, H., Vijayakumar, P., Kumar, N.: A privacy-preserving and untraceable group data sharing scheme in cloud computing. IEEE Trans. Dependable Secure Comput. **19**(4), 2198–2210 (2021)

21. Ding, W., Yan, Z., Deng, R.H.: Privacy-preserving data processing with flexible access control. IEEE Trans. Dependable Secure Comput. **17**(2), 363–376 (2020)

22. Xia, Z., Yang, Q., Qiao, Z., Feng, F.: Quorum controlled homomorphic re-encryption for privacy preserving computations in the cloud. Inf. Sci. **621**, 58–73 (2023)

23. Zhang, W., Liu, S., Xia, Z.: A distributed privacy-preserving data aggregation scheme for smart grid with fine-grained access control. J. Inf. Secur. Appl. 103–118 (2022)

Detection of Privacy-Harming Social Media Posts in Italian

Federico Peiretti and Ruggero G. Pensa$^{(\boxtimes)}$ ⬤

Department of Computer Science, University of Turin, 10149 Turin, Italy
{federico.peiretti,ruggero.pensa}@unito.it

Abstract. As many psychological and sociological study reveal, many people disclose too much privacy-harming information in social media in the form of text and multimedia posts, thus exposing themselves and other persons to several security risks. Consequently, many researchers have addressed this problem by investigating on the detection and analysis of the so-called self-disclosure behavior in social media and blogging platforms. Among the others, content sensitivity analysis has emerged as a promising research direction, but, so far, it has only focused on English text posts, although it is well-known that people tend to disclose mostly in their own native languages. Therefore, in this paper, we address this limitation by proposing a new text corpus of Italian posts that we have annotated following to the anonymity assumption. We then apply several language models based on transformers to classify them according to their sensitivity. Moreover, since Italian is a lower-resource language compared to English, we also apply some multilingual zero-shot transfer learning architectures trained on a rich and manually annotated English corpus and tested on the Italian one. We show experimentally that the approaches trained directly on the Italian corpus, still outperform multilingual ones trained on the English data and tested on Italian, although some of them exhibit promising prediction performances.

Keywords: Privacy · Neural language models · Social media

1 Introduction

Online social media are valuable and somehow irreplaceable content sharing and networking platforms, but are often subject of criticism, for many reasons. Sometimes such reasons are unjustified and the results of prejudices or lack of knowledge about social media and their enabling technologies (e.g., smartphones), but those regarding privacy are real, as proven by the many studies [2, 7, 18, 30, 39, 42, 66, 68]. The concerns about the risks of privacy violation in social media also inspired documentaries and movies, including several episodes of the award-winning TV show "Black Mirror" [13]. However, when referring to personal data in social media platforms, there are two complementary aspects that should be considered. The first one concerns the usage social media companies do with personal data, which is often the object of their terms of service and can be partly customized by

B. Arief et al. (Eds.): SocialSec 2023, LNCS 14097, pp. 203–223, 2023.
https://doi.org/10.1007/978-981-99-5177-2_12

registered users (e.g., the users may decide not to allow the access to their geolocation data). The second aspect regards the way people communicate and interact with other users and how much personal information they expose about themselves, a phenomenon that, in psychology, is referred to as self-disclosure [32]. Self-disclosure has been studied in relation to different contexts, including online forums [5], online support groups [65] and social media [39], although it has often been investigated for discussion boards dealing with intrinsically sensitive topics, such as health issues, intimate relationships or sex life, and where the identity of the users is masked by pseudonyms or entirely anonymous. Instead, in most social media platforms, social profiles usually carry the real identities of their owners, and yet this does not prevent their users from disclosing very private information [7,18,48] thus harming their own security.

In a very recent work [12], the authors have addressed the analysis of what they call "content sensitivity" (a more general problem than self-disclosure) of social media posts, and has drawn interesting insights about the possibility of automatically detecting the sensitivity of short texts by using natural language processing (NLP) techniques and also proposing a new annotated text corpus. However, as in most previous closely-related works, their study was focused on contents written in English only, although it is a well-known fact that most people mainly interact on social media using their own native language and, consequently, they tend to self-disclose more in their native language, than in English [56]. Unfortunately, with the exception of English, Chinese, Japanese and some European languages, the majority of national or regional idioms are considered low-resource languages, due to the lack of large monolingual or parallel corpora and/or manually crafted linguistic resources sufficient for building statistical NLP applications. As a result, all major existing works on the automated characterization or recognition of sensitive contents focus on English texts only [12,31,45,46,65,67].

In this work, we address this limitation by presenting a new annotated corpus of Italian posts and applying several monolingual and multilingual approaches for classifying them according to their privacy-sensitivity. We compare several pre-trained language models including the main transformer-based models and two alternative approaches, LASER [3] and MultiFiT [26], in two different experimental settings: in the first one the models are trained on the Italian corpus only; in the second one, the models are trained on the English corpus and the knowledge is transferred on the Italian one. Our experiments show that, although promising, multi-lingual approaches can not replace fully monolingual models in such task, where short social media posts are considered.

2   Related Work

Since modern online social networking platforms have gained popularity and success, the characterization and measurement of the exposure of user privacy in the Web has attracted the scientific interest of many research groups [41,42]. To assess the risk of privacy disclosure in social networks, many different approaches have been proposed [2,60], mostly focusing on measures based on the privacy settings of the users [36,47], or on their position within the network [48]. On the other hand, very few studies have investigated the problem of detecting the sensitivity of the contents posted by social network users, also because there is no consensus on how to define privacy-sensitivity [28,57].

A common solution to this problem is to consider all contents posted anonymously as sensitive, thus simplifying the construction of specifically annotated corpora. According to this assumption (called "anonymity assumption" [12]), if some content is posted anonymously, it is deemed sensitive, otherwise it is considered as non sensitive. This strategy is adopted, for instance, to apply some machine learning model and analyze anonymous and non anonymous posting behavior in question-and-answer platforms [45], or to compare content posted on anonymous and non-anonymous social media, according to their topics and linguistic features [11,22]. The largest available corpus supporting this category of studies consists of nearly 90 million posts downloaded from Whisper, an anonymous social media platforms [40]. Another solution is to consider the privacy settings associated to shared items as a proxy for measuring sensitivity: contents posted with more restricting visibility are deemed sensitive, as done by Yu *et al.* to measure the sensitivity of photos and to identify categories of privacy-sensitive objects according to a deep multi-task learning model [67].

The concept of content sensitivity is closely related to the one of self-disclosure, defined as the act of revealing personal information to others. It has been extensively investigated well before the advent of the Internet and social media [32]. In more recent years, self-disclosure has been studied to show that people behave differently in online support groups and discussion forums [5]. Other studies analyze the differences in the degree of positive and negative disclosure according to the visibility (private or public) of discussion channels in online support groups for cancer patients and their relatives. They apply support vector machines on lexical, linguistic, topic-related and word-vector features extracted from a small annotated corpus [65]. In [63], machine learning has been used to detect the degree of self-disclosure of social media posts and to replicate patterns from other empirical and theoretical work using a feature engineering approach. The experiments, conducted on a relatively small and proprietary corpus, identify post length, emotional valence, the presence of certain topics, social distance and social normality, among the most distinctive features for self-disclosure. Instead, in [31], Jaidka *et al.* report the results of a challenge concerning a relatively large corpus consisting of posts collected from Reddit, all annotated according to their degree of informational and emotional self-disclosure. Finally, in [12] the task of *content sensitivity analysis* is defined and different classification models are applied on three different text corpora of short social media posts, including a specifically annotated corpus of Facebook posts. The authors show the results for different lexical-based models as well as several classifiers based on CNNs, RNNs and language models in predicting content sensitivity of short posts.

All the works mentioned so far focus on English text, making it a high-resource language even for content sensitivity analysis. In fact, the few existing works on self-disclosure on non-English languages are psychological studies based on surveys [4,23,27,35]. To bypass the lack of linguistic resources when dealing with languages other than English, one may consider cross-lingual or multilingual models, which have been applied with success to many problems, including sentiment analysis [25], emotion detection [1] and information retrieval [59]. Multilingual language models have gained popularity thanks to their success in zero-shot transfer learning. The idea behind cross-lingual or multi-lingual models is to learn a shared embedding space for two or more languages to improve their ability for machine translation. One of the early models is XLM [21], which defines a new cross-lingual objective trained on two different languages. Another early approach is CMLM [51], which computes cross-lingual n-gram embeddings and infers an n-gram translation table from them. Both the models are cross-lingual, while, more recently, multilingual approaches have emerged, which are pre-trained once for all languages. Notable examples are mBART [37] and mT5 [64]: the former consists in a sequence-to-sequence denoising auto-encoder pre-trained on large-scale monolingual corpora in many languages using the BART objective [34]; the latter is a multilingual variant of a text-to-text transfer transformer trained on a dataset covering 101 languages. Other multilingual representations are based on contrastive learning that samples sentences from the document and constructs positive and negative pairs based on their saliency [62], or computing a contrastive loss on the representations of aligned pairs of sentences (considered as positive examples) and randomly selected non-aligned pairs (considered as negative examples) [43].

3   Identifying Privacy-Sensitive Content

In this section, we describe the task of content sensitivity analysis, introduced in [8,12]. However, since there is no agreement in the definition of privacy-sensitive content, we first precise what we mean by it in this paper.

3.1   Privacy-Sensitive Content

User-generated content, in the form of text and/or multimedia items (photos, videos), may carry sensitive information concerning the private life of the author or any other identifiable person and its explicit or implicit disclosure could potentially cause harm or embarrassment to them. In fact, such content could involve financial or medical information, sexual orientation and preferences, religious or political beliefs, or any other kind of personal data that, if posted online, could be exploited by third parties for malicious purposes, such as identity theft, frauds, discrimination, cyberbullying or stalking. A social media post with all these characteristics is defined as *privacy-sensitive* by Battaglia *et al.* [8]. This concept is a generalization of *self-disclosure* since, unlike it, revealing privacy-sensitive information could not only concern the author himself, but also other individuals mentioned (explicitly or implicitly) in the content item. Another important key point is how information is disclosed: sometimes sensitive information is clearly, directly and voluntarily disclosed. However, often it can be inferred from the context or by using some background knowledge. Some examples of sensitive and non sensitive posts are showed below.

1. *Guys, I'm taking some days off! On my way to Barcelona with my friend Alice. See you in two weeks.*
2. *How would you react if your doctor told you that they diagnosed you with cancer and that you need to start chemotherapy?*
3. *A 5th person is likely cured of HIV, and another is in long-term remission.*

The first text discloses information about the author and their friend *Alice* explicitly, despite neither does it have any sensitive term, nor deals with any sensitive topic. From the text, it is clear that they will be far from their respective homes for two weeks. It also contains hidden spatiotemporal references that are clear from the context.

The second post is a general question that does not disclose any sensitive information apparently, but this assumption might not be true. Is very likely, indeed, that the author themself was diagnosed with cancer and will have to start chemotherapy. It is an implicit way to reveal very sensitive medical information.

Finally, despite the third text item deals with a sensitive topic, it does not really disclose any private information that could put in danger the privacy of any people, since there is not any direct or indirect reference to a specific identifiable person. This sentence could be a citation from a newspaper or scientific article.

3.2   Content Sensitivity Analysis

Content sensitivity analysis is a data mining task aimed at recognizing whether a given user-generated content item is privacy-sensitive or not, according to the definition given above [8]. This particular task has been extensively investigated for the analysis of text posts written in English [12]. Instead, in this paper, we focus on user-generated content written in different languages, with a special focus on Italian, as it has been shown that most users mainly use their own native language in social media and, consequently, they tend to self-disclose more in their mother tongue(s), than in a different vehicular language, such as English [56]. The original definition of content sensitivity analysis is as follows.

Definition 1 (Content sensitivity analysis). *Given a user-generated content item $c_i \in \mathcal{C}$, where $\mathcal{C}$ is user-generated content domain,* content sensitivity analysis *is a task aimed at defining a function $f_s : \mathcal{C} \rightarrow \{sensitive, non - sensitive\}$, such that:*

$$f(c_i) = \begin{cases} sensitive & \textit{if } c_i \textit{ is privacy-sensitive} \\ non\text{-}sensitive & \textit{otherwise.} \end{cases}$$

In the following, without loss of generality, we will limit the scope of this definition to text posts only. Examples of privacy-sensitive posts are those containing information that violates a person's privacy (not necessarily of the author of the post), for instance: information about current or future travels; physical or mental well-being; lifestyle habits that may reveal the writer's location or that of others mentioned; romantic relationship status; opinions that may suggest political or religious belief.

According to Definition 1, a simple way to implement an inductive content sensitivity analysis task is by defining it as a binary classification task, where the parameters of the classification function are learned by training the classifier from an annotated corpus of sensitive and non sensitive posts.

On the other hand, the definition does not take into account the possible different nuances of sensitivity, i.e., how much privacy-sensitive a content is. The degree of sensitivity of a post may vary according, for instance, to its topic, its lexical features, or its context. For instance: a post revealing health information is much more sensitive than one about holidays, although both are considered privacy-sensitive. A more precise definition taking into account different degrees of sensitivity has been given in [8], but, for simplicity, in this paper we refer to this task as a binary classification, as it has been done in [12] for English posts.

4   Text Corpora for Content Sensitivity Analysis

Training a classifier to make it capable of solving a content sensitivity analysis task, requires to feed it with a huge amount of user-generated text content also including privacy-harming information and, additionally, annotated by experts according to its actual sensitivity. However, finding and collecting such type of information on the Web is very hard and the reason is, mainly, the privacy itself. Indeed, social networks, such as Facebook, Instagram and Twitter, would be very rich sources to accomplish this goal as posts and tweets with sensitive information are very likely published in users' personal profiles, but, although visible to their contacts and friends, they cannot be download using the API made available by those platforms. After the Cambridge Analytica scandal in 2018, Facebook introduced restrictions on data access by developers [54], followed by other social media companies. Currently, albeit with some limitation, they only allow to download public posts or posts published on public pages, which, however, are less relevant to our purposes. Fortunately, there exists some corpora of social media posts collected and released publicly for research purposes before these restrictions were introduced, or downloaded from anonymous blogging platforms. For instance, the *myPersonality* [16] corpus is made up of around 10 000 posts downloaded from Facebook, collected by Cambridge University between 2009 and 2012 for a psychological study [33]. Another example is *CL-Aff #OffMyChest* [31], a corpus containing discussions on family and intimate relationships downloaded from Reddit. All posts of the two corpora, with few exceptions, are in English. In the remainder of this section, we will first introduce a new corpus in Italian for content sensitivity analysis; then, we will briefly describe the existing English corpora already used in similar tasks, that we will employ to train cross-linguals models.

4.1   An Italian Corpus for Content Sensitivity Analysis: ITA-SENS

Most of the (annotated) corpora extracted from social networks are mainly in English, due to the huge amount of natural language processing resources available and to the necessity of making the research findings universally accessible. There exists also corpora in other languages (including Italian), but most of them focus on very specific topics and tasks, such as the detection of racial stereotypes [14] or hate speech [53]. To train a content sensitivity classifier, instead, we need posts dealing with various generic topics. Therefore, we construct a new dataset, called *ITA-SENS*, consisting of more than 15 000 social media posts written in Italian. In this work, we rely on the anonymity assumption, i.e., we consider as sensitive all posts that have been shared anonymously, while posts shared publicly are considered non-sensitive. Hence, we focus on Italian and identify two sources of non-anonymous and anonymous posts: Twitter and Insegreto[1]. Regarding the first source, we take into account *Feel-IT* [10] and *SENTIPOLC* [6], two corpora of Italian tweets covering a wide range of generic topics. *FEEL-IT*[2] is a corpus of tweets written in Italian and annotated according to four base emotions: anger, fear, joy and sadness [10]. The curators of this dataset have downloaded tweets at a daily basis, by monitoring trend topic in a three-month period. The dataset consists of 1000 tweets per day covering different topics, including health, sports, societal problems and TV programs. Topics have different time-spans, from hours (e.g., tweets related to TV programs) or days (e.g., major sports events) to the entire observation period (general topics such as COVID-19). *SENTIPOLC*[3], instead, is a dataset consisting of tweets written in Italian and constructed to solve sentiment polarity classification [6]. It has been presented during EVALITA 2016, a periodic evaluation campaign of Natural Language Processing (NLP) and speech tools for the Italian language[4]. Each tweet is annotated according to its topic; however, since most of them are related to a very specific political topic, we only retain 295 tweets addressing more different and general subjects. Additionally, to broaden the variety and quantity of tweets, we downloaded further tweets directly from Twitter, by filtering them according to popular general hashtags or by retrieving them from news accounts, using the official Twitter API.

As anonymous source, we take into consideration posts from Insegreto, an Italian social network that allows people to share their lives, secrets and opinions on different topics, in a totally anonymous way (the Italian locution "in segreto" means "secretly" in English). The posts are organized into several categories ranging from school to health, from politics to religion, from love to sexuality. As such, this is a valuable source of sensitive posts.

The statistics about this dataset are shown in Table 1. *ITA-SENS* consists of 15 144 Italian posts, of which 8 419 are labeled as sensitive and 6 725 as

---

[1] https://insegreto.com/it.
[2] https://github.com/MilaNLProc/feel-it.
[3] https://github.com/evalita2016/data.
[4] https://www.evalita.it/.

non-sensitive. We split it randomly by putting 55% of the data into the training set; 25% into the validation set and the remaining 20% into the test set[5].

Annotation. Exactly as was done in previous studies [22], for the annotation of our corpus we rely on the anonymity assumption, where the content is considered sensitive if the user has chosen to publish it anonymously, hiding their real identity or if they have made it visible to very few friends. If the content is visible to anyone or the author can be identified from it, then it is considered non-sensitive. After a careful reading and analysis of the collected posts, we have observed that those coming from Insegreto contain sensitive information that could harm the privacy of both the author and other identifiable people. Furthermore, they deal with sensitive topics and are published in a totally anonymous way. For these reasons, we label all Insegreto posts as *sensitive*. On the other hand, we consider all tweets in the corpus as *non-sensitive* because they come from public Twitter pages and profiles, following the anonymity assumption. Although it has been shown that this assumption is simplistic [12], we rely on it for this work, as the main goal is to study whether multilingual text analysis approaches can compete with monolingual ones for the specific task of content sensitivity analysis.

4.2   An Auxiliary English Corpus: SENS2+OMC

In our work, we also leverage an additional dataset of social media posts written in English to train multilanguage models able to solve the content sensitivity classification task by transferring the learned knowledge from English to Italian. To this purpose, we merge two corpora: *SENS2* [12] and CL-Aff #OffMyChest [31], hereinafter referred to as *OMC*.

SENS2 is a subset of the dataset introduced in [12]. It consists of 8 765 English posts from Facebook covering a wide range of topics. The posts have been manually annotated by a pool of experts according to some guidelines providing privacy-sensitive content definitions and examples. More in detail, *SENS2* contains posts that received the same "sensitive" or "non sensitive" tag by at least two annotators. Therefore, 3 336 posts are annotated as sensitive, the others 5 429 as non-sensitive.

OMC[6], instead, is a corpus of English conversations about family and intimate relationships, extracted from two subreddits in Reddit: *r/CasualConversations*, a subcommunity where users share their opinions about different topics; *r/OffmyChest*, a mutually supportive community where deep sentiments and emotions are shared. Each post is annotated depending on how much informational and emotional disclosure it contains. We exploit such annotations to assign a new label to each post: "sensitive" if post discloses informational or emotional data, "non sensitive" otherwise. Consequently, the dataset contains 17 860 posts, of which 10 793 are annotated as "sensitive" and 7 067 as "non sensitive".

---

[5] Our dataset is available online at https://github.com/federicopeiretti/ITA-SENS.
[6] https://github.com/kj2013/claff-offmychest.

Table 1. Details on the datasets used in our study.

Dataset	Language	#posts	#sens	#nosens
ITA-SENS	Italian	15 144	8 419	6 725
SENS2	English	8 765	3 336	5 429
OMC	English	17 860	10 793	7 067

4.3   Preprocessing

Before feeding posts to a language model, they need to be preprocessed. To this end, we use a Python library optimized for texts from social networks, called Ekphrasis [9] that allow us to perform tokenization, word normalization, word segmentation and spell correction. We also remove URLs, emoticons and emojis that are not that important for analyzing the sensitivity of the text and, additionally, may introduce biases in the machine learning processes. However, we keep hashtags (removing the # symbol) because they are often used as terms in a sentence. In addition, we sanitize the text by replacing e-mail addresses, dates, hours, currencies and phone numbers, with a generic placeholder using the format ⟨entity type⟩.

5   Monolingual and Cross-Lingual Content Classification

In this section, we introduce the classification strategies used to solve the content sensitivity analysis task for Italian posts. Our methodology is based on the findings reported by the authors of [8] and [12], that show how to solve the same task for English. The authors train and compare different classifiers based on several types of models, from the most traditional ones (e.g. k-NN, SVM, Random Forest) to more sophisticated deep neural network models (e.g. CNN, LSTM, Google BERT). They observe that the former are not suitable because they fail to capture the manifold of privacy-sensitivity with sufficient accuracy. Instead, the latter perform better due to the ability of deep learning models to take into account the context of words and sentences in their training processes. In conclusion they find that BERT, the only model based on Transformers considered in their study, outperforms all other models.

Hence, following these results, we focus on the most recent and accurate Language Models (LMs) based on the Transformer architecture in order to classify Italian posts according to their sensitivity and compare them. We also examine two recent alternative approaches: LASER [3], performing multilingual sentence embedding for over 93 languages in a shared space, and MultiFiT [26], a fine-tuning technique that is much cheaper to pre-train but more efficient than Transformers in terms of space-time complexity.

In the following, we firstly illustrate the two experimental settings. Then, we describe the language models we use and how we fine-tune them.

5.1   Experimental Settings

In our study, two different experimental settings are considered. The first is the most traditional one and consists in fine-tuning the language models using the training and validation sets of *ITA-SENS*. Then we test the learnt models on the test set and report the results. In the second experiment, we exploit the zero-shot transfer capabilities of multilingual models in order to perform zero-shot cross-lingual transfer learning [19,52]. It consists in the transfer of the knowledge learned using the data available for a reference language (English in our case) to solve the task in another target language (Italian in our application). This is useful when the former language is a high-resource one and latter is a lower-resource one. To this end, we first fine-tune the model on the English corpus (*SENS2+OMC*), then, we transfer the learned model on Italian, performing the inference on the test set of *ITA-SENS*.

All the experiments have been implemented in Python with the support of some libraries, especially PyTorch, Scikit-learn and Keras, and have been executed on a server with 32 Intel Xeon Skylake cores running at 2.1 GHz, 256 GB RAM, and one NVIDIA Tesla T4 GPU. In the remainder of the section, we provide the details about the different language models used in our study.

5.2   Language Models

In this section, we present the language models (LMs) used in our comparative analysis and, for each of them, we provide the details on parameter fine-tuning.

Transformer-Based LMs. As first category of methods, we consider several language models with a Transformer architecture, based on attention mechanisms [58]. These models are pre-trained on large text corpora (e.g. Wikipedia, CommonCrawl, Europarl, Books) on one or more typical NLP tasks (e.g. Next Sentence Prediction, Masked Language Modeling). Pre-training is useful to learn general language patterns and features, and avoids training the models from scratch. Consequently, it reduces the computation costs. More in detail, we take into account the most popular multilingual Transformers: mBERT [24] and XLM-RoBERTa [20]. We also consider monolingual versions specifically trained for Italian: AlBERTo [49] based on BERT, GilBERTo [50] and UmBERTo[7] [44] based on RoBERTa. We employ their respective versions for sequence classification made available in *HuggingFace*[8] by means of *Transformers APIs*, as they have already a linear layer for sequence classification on top of the pooled output. We use AdamW optimizer [38] with linear scheduler, with $\epsilon = 10^{-8}$ as default value, and the Binary Cross Entropy as loss function.

---

[7] We consider two versions of UmBERTo: *wikipedia-uncased*, uncased version trained on Wikipedia; *commoncrawl-cased*, cased version trained on CommonCrawl.

[8] https://huggingface.co/.

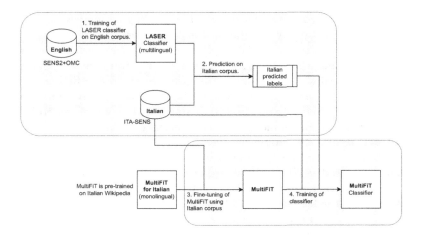

Fig. 1. Bootstrapping method adopted to perform zero-shot transfer with MultiFiT using LASER classifier as cross-lingual teacher.

LASER. As first alternative multilingual model, we consider LASER, a new architecture to learn joint multilingual sentence embeddings for over 93 languages, proposed by Meta [3]. More specifically, LASER uses a single Bidirectional LSTM (long short-term memory) encoder with a shared BPE (Byte Paired Encoding) vocabulary for all languages, which, in its turn, is coupled with an auxiliary decoder and pre-trained on parallel corpora. We refer the reader to the original paper for further details. In our experiments, we use the pre-trained model downloaded from the official GitHub repository[9] as follows: first, we encode all input texts into LASER embeddings. Then, we create a sequential neural network that works as a decoder for classification and consisting in: (i) an input layer taking a LASER embedding with fixed size of 1024 input neurons; (ii) 4 hidden dense layers with 512, 128, 32, 8 neurons, respectively, LeakyReLU as activation function, dropout rate of 0.25 and batch normalization; (iii) a dense output layer with one neuron, which produces the predicted class, using the sigmoid as activation function. For the learning process, we use the AdamW optimizer with default value of $\epsilon = 10^{-8}$ and Binary Cross Entropy as loss function.

MultiFiT. As second alternative multilingual model, we use MultiFiT, an alternative approach for fine-tuning monolingual models proposed by Eisenschlos *et al.* [26]. MultiFiT is an extended version of ULMFiT [29], designed to enhance its efficiency and applicability to NLP tasks in languages other than English. Its architecture includes subword tokenization and a Quasi-Recurrent Neural Network (QRNN) [15]. Instead of fine-tuning the classifier directly, MultiFiT first fine-tune the pre-trained model on the input corpus and then use that as the

---

[9] https://github.com/facebookresearch/LASER.

base for the classifier. To this purpose, several monolingual models, including for Italian, are pre-trained on Wikipedia on the Next Word Prediction task. Additionally, the authors recommend to apply one-cycle policy with cosine annealing [55] and label smoothing techniques: the former is to make the training and convergence of complex models faster, the latter to avoid overfitting and overconfidence. We use the pre-trained model for Italian downloaded from the official GitHub repository[10] and rely on the *fast.ai* Python library in order to fine-tune and train both the language model and the classifier.

It is worth briefly describing the bootstrapping method we adopt to perform zero-shot cross lingual transfer learning, proposed by the authors of the paper and illustrated in Fig. 1. First, we exploit a LASER classifier previously trained on the English corpus (*SENS3+OMC*) as cross-lingual teacher and we make inference on the Italian corpus (*ITA-SENS*) obtaining the predicted labels. Then, we perform zero-shot transfer with MultiFiT for Italian pre-trained on Wikipedia: we fine-tune MultiFiT on *ITA-SENS* and train the classifier on top using the pseudo-labels predicted by LASER.

5.3   Hyperparameter Selection

For each language model, with the exception of MultiFiT, we tune the hyperparameters by applying a grid search over a set of pre-defined values for the learning rate and for the batch size. To avoid overfitting, we use the early stopping criterion on the validation loss, initializing the epoch number to 100. The selected hyperparameter values of each language model in both the categories considered here are listed in Table 2. It is worth noting that all multilinguage models (mBERT, XML-RoBERTa, LASER and MultiFiT) have been configured for both experiments types: in the first one they are trained with *ITA-SENS*, as for the other monolanguage models, in the second one they are trained on *SENS2+OMC* and tested on *ITA-SENS*.

6   Results

In this section, we show and discuss the classification results of two experiments. In the first one, all language models are trained directly on *ITA-SENS*. In the second experiment, the models capable of performing cross-language transfer are trained on the English corpus and transferred to the Italian one. In both experiments, the results are reported for the test set of *ITA-SENS*.

We compare the different language models by computing the following evaluation metrics: accuracy, precision, recall, macro F1-score and Matthews correlation coefficient (MCC) [17]. Although accuracy and F1-score are the most popular metrics for evaluating binary classifiers, they can show overoptimistic inflated results, especially on unbalanced datasets. MCC is more reliable and yields a high score only if the outcome of the prediction is such that the values

---

[10] https://github.com/n-waves/multifit.

Table 2. Best hyperparameter values for each language model considered in this study.

Experimental setting	Language Model	Batch size	Learning rate	# Epochs
Traditional ITA → ITA	mBERT	32	$5 \cdot 10^{-7}$	4
	XLM-RoBERTa	32	$1 \cdot 10^{-6}$	9
	AlBERTo	32	$5 \cdot 10^{-7}$	5
	GilBERTo	16	$5 \cdot 10^{-7}$	4
	UmBERTo-wiki	32	$5 \cdot 10^{-6}$	3
	UmBERTo-commoncrawl	32	$2 \cdot 10^{-6}$	3
	LASER	32	$2 \cdot 10^{-5}$	28
	MultiFiT	20	$1 \cdot 10^{-3}$	8
Zero-shot ENG → ITA	mBERT	32	$1 \cdot 10^{-6}$	3
	XLM-RoBERTa	32	$5 \cdot 10^{-6}$	2
	LASER	32	$2 \cdot 10^{-5}$	28
	MultiFiT	20	$1 \cdot 10^{-3}$	7

of the four confusion matrix categories (true positives, true negatives, false positive and false negatives) are all high, proportionally to the number of positive and negative samples in the dataset. In fact it is defined as

$$MCC = \frac{TP \cdot TN - FP \cdot FN}{\sqrt{(TP + FP)(TP + FN)(TN + FP)(TN + FN)}}$$

where TP, TN, FP, FN represent the entries of the confusion matrix. The greater their correlations, the more accurate the model.

6.1 Experiment 1: Language Models Trained on ITA-SENS

Table 3 reports the results obtained by the language models trained on *ITA-SENS* directly. We indicate the metrics on the columns and the methods on the rows. The language models are grouped by type: Transformer-based multilingual ones, Transformer-based monolingual ones, LASER and MultiFiT.

The language models with the highest accuracy are MultiFiT (0.9366), AlBERTo (0.9260) and UmBERTo-wikipedia-uncased (0.9260). It is worth noting that, since accuracy is sensitive to class unbalance, the models cannot be compared based on this metric only. For our task, it is important to analyze the recall on the positive class as well, as we want the model to capture all posts which are really sensitive. The model with the highest recall is UmBERTo-wikipedia-uncased (0.9458), followed by XLM-RoBERTa (0.9387) that, however, has a lower accuracy (0.9181). Other models with almost the same recall as XML-RoBERTa are AlBERTo and MultiFiT, both with a value equal to 0.9352. As regards the precision, MultiFiT is the model that predicts the highest percentage (95%) of posts truly belonging to the positive class as sensitive. It is followed

Table 3. Results of the model trained on *ITA-SENS*, reported for the test set.

Model	Accuracy	Precision	Recall	F1-score	MCC
mBERT	0.8752	0.8691	0.9151	0.8722	0.746
XLM-RoBERTa	0.9181	0.9171	0.9387	0.9166	**0.927**
AlBERTo (it)	0.9260	0.9330	0.9352	0.9249	0.855
GilBERTo (it)	0.9098	0.9228	0.9157	0.9086	0.817
UmBERTo-wiki-U (it)	0.9260	0.9240	**0.9458**	0.9246	0.850
UmBERTo-CC-C (it)	0.9187	0.9347	0.9193	0.9177	0.836
LASER	0.9125	0.9168	0.9281	0.9110	0.822
MultiFiT (it)	**0.9366**	**0.9508**	0.9352	**0.9358**	0.872

by UmBERTo commoncrawl-cased (0.9347). Unlike MultiFiT, its precision is much higher than its recall. The only Transformer-based model exhibiting the highest precision and the highest recall at the same time is AlBERTo. On the other hand, precision does not gives us any information on the number of posts of the positive class that are not labeled correctly. Therefore, to capture the balance between precision and recall, we compare all language models according to the macro F1-score. Among the Transformer models, AlBERTo (0.9249) and UmBERTo wikipedia (0.9246) have the highest value. Despite that, MultiFiT continues to outperform all models also in terms of macro F1-score: its value (0.9358), indeed, is the highest one. Finally, as precision, recall and macro F1-score ignore the true negatives, we also analyze the Matthews correlation coefficient (MCC). In this case, the best model (XLM-RoBERTa with a MCC of 0.927) has also a lower accuracy, precision and F1-score than the other models discussed above. Interestingly, XLM-RoBERTa is followed by MultiFiT with MCC equal to 0.872, thus confirming the predominance of this latter model in this experiment.

Summing up, monolingual models (AlBERTo, UmBERTo-wikipedia and MultiFiT) achieve the highest performances in our first experiment. More specifically, MultiFiT, the only model based on Quasi-Recurrent Neural Networks, always ranks first or second for all metrics considered in our study, outperforming all Transformer-bases models in the content sensitivity analysis task.

6.2   Experiment 2: Zero-Shot Cross-Lingual Transfer Learning

Table 4 shows the classification results obtained when multilanguage models, trained on the English corpus, transfer the acquired knowledge on Italian.

The models achieving the highest accuracy are MultiFiT (0.7487) and LASER (0.7411). Both models also correctly classify the highest percentage of true positives, as their recall is, respectively, 0.7550 and 0.7544. They also have the highest macro F1-scores (0.7463 and 0.7383, respectively). When the precision on the positive class is considered, XLM-RoBERTa predicts the highest percentage (about 88%) of posts belonging to the positive class as sensitive, but

Table 4. Results of zero-shot cross-lingual transfer from English to Italian.

Model	Accuracy	Precision	Recall	F1-score	MCC
mBERT	0.7002	0.8458	0.5689	0.6990	0.447
XLM-RoBERTa	0.7306	**0.8814**	0.6001	0.7297	**0.508**
LASER	0.7411	0.7773	0.7544	0.7383	0.477
MultiFiT	**0.7487**	0.7879	**0.7550**	**0.7463**	0.494

this model also has a relatively low recall. Consequently, the macro F1-score of XLM-RoBERTa (0.7297) is similar to that of LASER and MultiFiT which, however, have a more balanced precision and recall values. The same applies to mBERT, which has an even lower macro F1-score (0.6990). Finally, it can be observed that XLM-RoBERTa has the highest MCC (0.508), which means that this model exhibits a high correlation between real and predicted labels despite having a much lower accuracy and recall than LASER and MultiFiT, whose MCC is not far from the one of XLM-RoBERTa (0.494).

In conclusion, despite being trained on noisy pseudo-labels predicted by the LASER classifier, even in the zero-shot learning scenario, MultiFiT turns out to be the most accurate language model and seems to be the best choice for solving a content sensitivity analysis task.

6.3   Discussion and Limitations

As seen in the previous sections, many language models achieve either high accuracy and F1-score or high values of the MCC, despite the task being generally known as difficult. One may argue that this is due to the fact that the language models are not learning to discriminate between sensitive and non sensitive posts; rather, they are learning to distinguish the sources of the posts (Insegreto or Twitter). In fact this could be a possible bias in our study and we think that, in part, this could explain the very good results obtained in the previous experiments. To try to dispel any doubt, we set up an additional experiment using the best classification models trained on *ITA-SENS* as predictors and, as test set, a further annotated single-source Italian corpus. As our goal is to study how *ITA-SENS* is adapted to the specific goal of content sensitivity analysis, we do not use the transfer learning models trained on *SENS2+OMC* (the English corpus) here. However, since we do not have an additional unbiased and annotated corpus of Italian posts (which will be part of our future work), we use a collection of posts taken from the *OMC* dataset and translated into Italian using DeepL[11], a famous and accurate automatic translator based on transformers. To limit the number of mistranslated posts, we include in this set only those posts with at least 20 words, as it is known that neural machine translation struggle with short texts [61]. The final dataset consists of 4 380 posts (3 182 sensitive

---

[11] https://www.deepl.com/it/translator.

Table 5. Results on the translated version of OMC using (some of) the language models trained on ITA-SENS compared with the majority class classifier as baseline.

Language Model	Accuracy	Precision	Recall	F1-score	MCC
Baseline	0.7264	0.7264	1.0	0.4207	0.0
mBERT	**0.7312**	0.7519	0.9402	0.5497	0.180
XLM-RoBERTa	0.7184	0.7392	**0.9462**	0.5053	0.104
AlBERTo	0.6212	0.7999	0.6382	0.5820	0.193
GilBERTo	0.6863	0.7880	0.7771	**0.6097**	**0.220**
UmBERTo-wiki-U	0.6214	0.7741	0.6763	0.5646	0.141
UmBERTo-CC-C	0.7166	0.7380	0.9456	0.5011	0.095
LASER	0.6687	0.7857	0.7479	0.5985	0.199
MultiFiT	0.6262	**0.8103**	0.6338	0.5906	0.216

and 1 198 non sensitive posts) annotated as described in Sect. 4.2. The results are reported in Table 5. As expected, the results are lower than those obtained when we apply the models to the test set of *ITA-SENS*. However, they are in general way better than a baseline consisting of a classifier assigning all posts to the majority class (the sensitive one in this case). In this experiments, the most accurate models according to the different performance indicators are mBERT (for the accuracy), MultiFiT (for the precision), XLM-RoBERTa (for the recall, if we exclude the baseline that, as expected, achieve 100% recall on the sensitive class) and GiLBERTo (for the macro F1-score and the MCC). More interestingly, the results are in line with (and even better than) those reported in [12] for the same dataset, where, however, the models where trained and tested on English only. According to these results, even if we can not totally exclude the source bias, we can safely confirm the conclusion drawn at the end of our experiments.

7   Conclusion

In this paper, we have proposed a new corpus specifically annotated for the content sensitivity analysis task. We use it to feed several state-of-the-art language models based on transformers and attention mechanisms to detect privacy-sensitive content in social media posts. We also show the performances of different multilingual models, including two alternative architectures based on bidirectional long short-term memory and quasi-recurrent neural networks. We have set up two different experiments, also including zero-shot cross-lingual transfer methods where the model is trained with an English corpus and tested on Italian posts. Despite some promising results, the models trained directly with the Italian corpus are still the best performing ones. Some limitations will be addressed in future works. First, our corpus is annotated following the anonymity assumption, which consists in labeling as sensitive every content item posted anonymously, and as non sensitive contents posted publicly with identifiable profiles.

However, as shown by some recent work, this assumption does not hold in many cases, hence we plan to launch a manual annotation campaign involving several domain experts. Second, in this work we only rely on text posts, but it is well-known that the most successful social media platforms are now fostering the sharing of audio-visual content, such as images and short videos. As future work we will investigate on sensitive content in such modalities and, more specifically, on multimodal content sensitivity analsyis, to exploit the manifold of the information provided by different representations of the same posted message.

Acknowledgements. The work presented in this paper is supported by Fondazione CRT (Grant No. 2022-0720).

References

1. Ahmad, Z., Jindal, R., Ekbal, A., Bhattachharyya, P.: Borrow from rich cousin: transfer learning for emotion detection using cross lingual embedding. Expert Syst. Appl. **139**, 112851 (2020)
2. Alemany, J., del Val Noguera, E., Alberola, J.M., García-Fornes, A.: Metrics for privacy assessment when sharing information in online social networks. IEEE Access **7**, 143631–143645 (2019)
3. Artetxe, M., Schwenk, H.: Massively multilingual sentence embeddings for zero-shot cross-lingual transfer and beyond. Trans. Assoc. Comput. Linguist. **7**, 597–610 (2019)
4. Baiocco, R., Laghi, F., Di Pomponio, I., Nigito, C.S.: Self-disclosure to the best friend: friendship quality and internalized sexual stigma in Italian lesbian and gay adolescents. J. Adolesc. **35**(2), 381–387 (2012)
5. Barak, A., Gluck-Ofri, O.: Degree and reciprocity of self-disclosure in online forums. Cyberpsychol. Behav. Soc. Netw. **10**(3), 407–417 (2007)
6. Barbieri, F., Basile, V., Croce, D., Nissim, M., Novielli, N., Patti, V.: Overview of the evalita 2016 sentiment polarity classification task. In: Proceedings of CLiC-it 2016 & EVALITA 2016. CEUR-WS.org (2016)
7. Barth, S., de Jong, M.D.T.: The privacy paradox - investigating discrepancies between expressed privacy concerns and actual online behavior - a systematic literature review. Telemat. Inform. **34**(7), 1038–1058 (2017)
8. Battaglia, E., Bioglio, L., Pensa, R.G.: Towards content sensitivity analysis. In: Berthold, M.R., Feelders, A., Krempl, G. (eds.) IDA 2020. LNCS, vol. 12080, pp. 67–79. Springer, Cham (2020). https://doi.org/10.1007/978-3-030-44584-3_6
9. Baziotis, C., Pelekis, N., Doulkeridis, C.: DataStories at SemEval-2017 task 4: deep LSTM with attention for message-level and topic-based sentiment analysis. In: Proceedings of SemEval-2017, pp. 747–754. ACL (2017)
10. Bianchi, F., Nozza, D., Hovy, D.: FEEL-IT: emotion and sentiment classification for the Italian language. In: Proceedings of WASSA@EACL 2021, pp. 76–83. ACL (2021)
11. Biega, J.A., Gummadi, K.P., Mele, I., Milchevski, D., Tryfonopoulos, C., Weikum, G.: R-susceptibility: an IR-centric approach to assessing privacy risks for users in online communities. In: Proceedings of ACM SIGIR 2016, pp. 365–374 (2016)
12. Bioglio, L., Pensa, R.G.: Analysis and classification of privacy-sensitive content in social media posts. EPJ Data Sci. **11**(1), 12 (2022)

13. Blanco-Herrero, D., Rodríguez-Contreras, L.: The risks of new technologies in black mirror: a content analysis of the depiction of our current socio-technological reality in a TV series. In: González, M.Á.C., Rodríguez-Sedano, F.J., Llamas, C.F., García-Peñalvo, F.J. (eds.) Proceedings of the Seventh International Conference on Technological Ecosystems for Enhancing Multiculturality, TEEM 2019, León Spain, October 2019, pp. 899–905. ACM (2019)

14. Bosco, C., Patti, V., Frenda, S., Cignarella, A.T., Paciello, M., D'Errico, F.: Detecting racial stereotypes: an Italian social media corpus where psychology meets NLP. Inf. Process. Manag. **60**(1), 103118 (2023)

15. Bradbury, J., Merity, S., Xiong, C., Socher, R.: Quasi-recurrent neural networks. In: Proceedings of ICLR 2017. OpenReview.net (2017)

16. Celli, F., Pianesi, F., Stillwell, D., Kosinski, M.: Workshop on computational personality recognition: shared task. In: Proceedings of ICWSM 2013 (2013)

17. Chicco, D., Jurman, G.: The advantages of the Matthews correlation coefficient (MCC) over F1 score and accuracy in binary classification evaluation. BMC Genomics **21**, 1–13 (2020)

18. Choi, H., Park, J., Jung, Y.: The role of privacy fatigue in online privacy behavior. Comput. Hum. Behav. **81**, 42–51 (2018)

19. Choi, H., Kim, J., Joe, S., Min, S., Gwon, Y.: Analyzing zero-shot cross-lingual transfer in supervised NLP tasks. In: 2020 25th International Conference on Pattern Recognition (ICPR), pp. 9608–9613. IEEE (2021)

20. Conneau, A., et al.: Unsupervised cross-lingual representation learning at scale. arXiv preprint arXiv:1911.02116 (2019)

21. Conneau, A., Lample, G.: Cross-lingual language model pretraining. In: Advances in Neural Information Processing Systems 32: Annual Conference on Neural Information Processing Systems 2019, NeurIPS 2019, 8–14 December 2019, Vancouver, BC, Canada, pp. 7057–7067 (2019)

22. Correa, D., Silva, L.A., Mondal, M., Benevenuto, F., Gummadi, K.P.: The many shades of anonymity: characterizing anonymous social media content. In: Proceedings of ICWSM 2015, pp. 71–80 (2015)

23. Danet, M., Miljkovitch, R., Deborde, A.S.: Online self-disclosure: validation study of the French version of the real me on the net questionnaire. Curr. Psychol. **39**, 2366–2370 (2018)

24. Devlin, J., Chang, M.W., Lee, K., Toutanova, K.: Bert: pre-training of deep bidirectional transformers for language understanding. arXiv preprint arXiv:1810.04805 (2018)

25. Dong, X., de Melo, G.: Cross-lingual propagation for deep sentiment analysis. In: McIlraith, S.A., Weinberger, K.Q. (eds.) Proceedings of the Thirty-Second AAAI Conference on Artificial Intelligence, (AAAI-18), the 30th innovative Applications of Artificial Intelligence (IAAI-18), and the 8th AAAI Symposium on Educational Advances in Artificial Intelligence (EAAI-18), New Orleans, Louisiana, USA, 2–7 February 2018, pp. 5771–5778. AAAI Press (2018)

26. Eisenschlos, J., Ruder, S., Czapla, P., Kardas, M., Gugger, S., Howard, J.: MultiFiT: efficient multi-lingual language model fine-tuning. In: Proceedings of EMNLP-IJCNLP 2019, pp. 5701–5706. ACL (2019)

27. El Ouirdi, M., Segers, J., El Ouirdi, A., Pais, I.: Predictors of job seekers' self-disclosure on social media. Comput. Hum. Behav. **53**, 1–12 (2015)

28. Gill, A.J., Vasalou, A., Papoutsi, C., Joinson, A.N.: Privacy dictionary: a linguistic taxonomy of privacy for content analysis. In: Proceedings of ACM CHI 2011, pp. 3227–3236 (2011)

29. Howard, J., Ruder, S.: Universal language model fine-tuning for text classification. In: Proceedings of ACL 2018, pp. 328–339. ACL (2018)
30. Jaidka, K., Guntuku, S., Ungar, L.: Facebook versus twitter: differences in self-disclosure and trait prediction. In: Proceedings of ICWSM 2018, pp. 141–150. AAAI Press (2018)
31. Jaidka, K., Singh, I., Liu, J., Chhaya, N., Ungar, L.: A report of the CL-Aff OffMyChest shared task: modeling supportiveness and disclosure. In: Proceedings of AffCon@AAAI 2020, pp. 118–129. CEUR-WS.org (2020)
32. Jourard, S.M.: Self-Disclosure: An Experimental Analysis of the Transparent Self. Wiley, Hoboken (1971)
33. Kosinski, M., Stillwell, D., Graepel, T.: Private traits and attributes are predictable from digital records of human behavior. PNAS **110**(15), 5802–5805 (2013)
34. Lewis, M., et al.: BART: denoising sequence-to-sequence pre-training for natural language generation, translation, and comprehension. In: Proceedings of ACL 2020, pp. 7871–7880. ACL (2020)
35. Liu, D., Brown, B.B.: Self-disclosure on social networking sites, positive feedback, and social capital among Chinese college students. Comput. Hum. Behav. **38**, 213–219 (2014)
36. Liu, K., Terzi, E.: A framework for computing the privacy scores of users in online social networks. TKDD **5**(1), 6:1–6:30 (2010)
37. Liu, Y., et al.: Multilingual denoising pre-training for neural machine translation. Trans. Assoc. Comput. Linguist. **8**, 726–742 (2020)
38. Loshchilov, I., Hutter, F.: Decoupled weight decay regularization. In: Proceedings of ICLR 2019. OpenReview.net (2019)
39. Ma, X., Hancock, J.T., Naaman, M.: Anonymity, intimacy and self-disclosure in social media. In: Proceedings of the 2016 CHI Conference on Human Factors in Computing Systems, San Jose, CA, USA, 7–12 May 2016, pp. 3857–3869. ACM (2016)
40. Mondal, M., Correa, D., Benevenuto, F.: Anonymity effects: a large-scale dataset from an anonymous social media platform. In: Gadiraju, U. (ed.) Proceedings of ACM HT 2020, Virtual Event, USA, 13–15 July 2020, pp. 69–74. ACM (2020)
41. Oukemeni, S., Rifà-Pous, H., i Puig, J.M.M.: IPAM: information privacy assessment metric in microblogging online social networks. IEEE Access **7**, 114817–114836 (2019)
42. Oukemeni, S., Rifà-Pous, H., i Puig, J.M.M.: Privacy analysis on microblogging online social networks: a survey. ACM Comput. Surv. **52**(3), 60:1–60:36 (2019)
43. Pan, X., Wang, M., Wu, L., Li, L.: Contrastive learning for many-to-many multilingual neural machine translation. In: Proceedings of ACL/IJCNLP 2021, pp. 244–258. ACL (2021)
44. Parisi, L., Francia, S., Magnani, P.: Umberto: an Italian language model trained with whole word masking (2020). https://github.com/musixmatchresearch/umberto
45. Peddinti, S.T., Korolova, A., Bursztein, E., Sampemane, G.: Cloak and swagger: understanding data sensitivity through the lens of user anonymity. In: Proceedings of IEEE SP 2014, pp. 493–508 (2014)
46. Peddinti, S.T., Ross, K.W., Cappos, J.: User anonymity on Twitter. IEEE Secur. Priv. **15**(3), 84–87 (2017)
47. Pensa, R.G., Di Blasi, G.: A privacy self-assessment framework for online social networks. Expert Syst. Appl. **86**, 18–31 (2017)
48. Pensa, R.G., Di Blasi, G., Bioglio, L.: Network-aware privacy risk estimation in online social networks. Social Netw. Analys. Mining **9**(1), 15:1–15:15 (2019)

49. Polignano, M., Basile, P., De Gemmis, M., Semeraro, G., Basile, V., et al.: Alberto: Italian BERT language understanding model for NLP challenging tasks based on tweets. In: CEUR Workshop Proceedings, vol. 2481, pp. 1–6. CEUR (2019)
50. Ravasio, G., Di Perna, L.: Gilberto: an Italian pretrained language model based on Roberta (2020). https://github.com/idb-ita/GilBERTo
51. Ren, S., Wu, Y., Liu, S., Zhou, M., Ma, S.: Explicit cross-lingual pre-training for unsupervised machine translation. In: Proceedings of EMNLP-IJCNLP 2019, pp. 770–779. ACL (2019)
52. Ruder, S.: Neural transfer learning for natural language processing. Ph.D. thesis, NUI Galway (2019)
53. Sanguinetti, M., Poletto, F., Bosco, C., Patti, V., Stranisci, M.: An Italian twitter corpus of hate speech against immigrants. In: Proceedings of LREC 2018. ELRA (2018)
54. Schroepfer, M.: An update on our plans to restrict data access on Facebook (2018). https://about.fb.com/news/2018/04/restricting-data-access/
55. Smith, L.N.: A disciplined approach to neural network hyper-parameters: part 1 - learning rate, batch size, momentum, and weight decay. CoRR abs/1803.09820 (2018). http://arxiv.org/abs/1803.09820
56. Tang, D., Chou, T., Drucker, N., Robertson, A., Smith, W.C., Hancock, J.T.: A tale of two languages: strategic self-disclosure via language selection on Facebook. In: Proceedings of ACM CSCW 2011, pp. 387–390. ACM (2011)
57. Vasalou, A., Gill, A.J., Mazanderani, F., Papoutsi, C., Joinson, A.N.: Privacy dictionary: a new resource for the automated content analysis of privacy. JASIST 62(11), 2095–2105 (2011)
58. Vaswani, A., et al.: Attention is all you need. In: Advances in Neural Information Processing Systems, vol. 30 (2017)
59. Vulic, I., Moens, M.: Monolingual and cross-lingual information retrieval models based on (bilingual) word embeddings. In: Proceedings of ACM SIGIR 2015, pp. 363–372. ACM (2015)
60. Wagner, I., Eckhoff, D.: Technical privacy metrics: a systematic survey. ACM Comput. Surv. 51(3), 57:1–57:38 (2018)
61. Wan, Y., et al.: Challenges of neural machine translation for short texts. Comput. Linguist. 48(2), 321–342 (2022)
62. Wang, D., Chen, J., Zhou, H., Qiu, X., Li, L.: Contrastive aligned joint learning for multilingual summarization. In: Proceedings of ACL/IJCNLP 2021, pp. 2739–2750. ACL (2021)
63. Wang, Y., Burke, M., Kraut, R.E.: Modeling self-disclosure in social networking sites. In: Proceedings of ACM CSCW 2016, pp. 74–85. ACM (2016)
64. Xue, L., et al.: mT5: a massively multilingual pre-trained text-to-text transformer. In: Proceedings of NAACL-HLT 2021, pp. 483–498. ACL (2021)
65. Yang, D., Yao, Z., Kraut, R.E.: Self-disclosure and channel difference in online health support groups. In: Proceedings of the Eleventh International Conference on Web and Social Media, ICWSM 2017, Montréal, Québec, Canada, 15–18 May 2017, pp. 704–707. AAAI Press (2017)
66. Yu, J., Kuang, Z., Zhang, B., Zhang, W., Lin, D., Fan, J.: Leveraging content sensitiveness and user trustworthiness to recommend fine-grained privacy settings for social image sharing. IEEE Trans. Inf. Forensics Secur. 13(5), 1317–1332 (2018)

67. Yu, J., Zhang, B., Kuang, Z., Lin, D., Fan, J.: iPrivacy: image privacy protection by identifying sensitive objects via deep multi-task learning. IEEE Trans. Inf. Forensics Secur. **12**(5), 1005–1016 (2017)
68. Zlatolas, L.N., Welzer, T., Hericko, M., Hölbl, M.: Privacy antecedents for SNS self-disclosure: the case of Facebook. Comput. Hum. Behav. **45**, 158–167 (2015)

Edge Local Differential Privacy
for Dynamic Graphs

Sudipta Paul[1]($\boxtimes$), Julián Salas[2], and Vicenç Torra[1]

[1] Department of Computing Science, Umeå Universitet, Umea, Sweden
{spaul,vtorra}@cs.umu.se
[2] Internet Interdisciplinary Institute, Universitat Oberta de Catalunya,
Barcelona, Spain
jsalaspi@uoc.edu

Abstract. Huge amounts of data are generated and shared in social networks and other network topologies. This raises privacy concerns when such data is not protected from leaking sensitive or personal information. Network topologies are commonly modeled through static graphs. Nevertheless, dynamic graphs better capture the temporal evolution and properties of such networks. Several differentially private mechanisms have been proposed for static graph data mining, but at the moment there are no such algorithms for dynamic data protection and mining. So, we propose two locally ϵ-differentially private methods for dynamic graph protection based on edge addition and deletion through the application of the noise-graph mechanism. We apply these methods to real-life datasets and show promising results preserving graph statistics for applications in community detection in time-varying networks.

The main contributions of this work are: extending the definition of local differential privacy for edges to the dynamic graph domain, and showing that the community structure of the protected graphs is well preserved for suitable privacy parameters.

1 Introduction and Related Work

A huge amount of data is generated every day in networked systems such as social networks [4,5], biological networks, internet peer-to-peer networks [13], and other technological networks [3]. These data can be modelled using graph theory in which, the nodes represent the users or objects and the edges represent the relationship between two nodes in such networks. All networks undergo changes, with nodes or edges arriving or going away as the system develops. Therefore, static graph networks are not adequate to model these kinds of network structures.

It is known that naif anonymization of a graph can lead to disclosure because the adversaries can use information that they posses to infer private information from the structure of the graph. Several types of such attacks have been developed. See e.g., de-anonymization attack [18], degree attacks [14], 1-neighborhood

B. Arief et al. (Eds.): SocialSec 2023, LNCS 14097, pp. 224–238, 2023.
https://doi.org/10.1007/978-981-99-5177-2_13

attacks [23], and sub-graph attacks [11]. Proper privacy models have been developed for static graphs. These models can be broadly classified into those following k-anonymity and those following differential privacy. We focus here in the differential privacy model [8].

The definition of "adjacent graphs" is the key to extending differential privacy to social networks [12]. So far different definitions have been provided: node privacy [10], edge privacy [19], out-link privacy, and partition privacy [19,20]. The most commonly used are node and edge differential privacy. Node privacy, provides desirable privacy protection but is impractical to deliver high utility (precise network analysis). Edge privacy shields users from attackers trying to learn about precise relationships between them, and it has been more widely adopted since it offers effective privacy protection in many practical applications.

Data on dynamic networks can take many different forms, but the most popular form and the one we consider in this paper is a collection of successively obtained, typically (but not necessarily) equally spaced snapshots of the network topology [22]. We restrict ourselves to networks based on a constant set of nodes. That is, nodes do not change but only edges do. This is not a limitation, because as we consider a finite set of snapshots all known a priori, the set of nodes appearing in at least one snapshot is known beforehand.

Keeping all of these in mind, here we propose dynamic graph privacy models and two novel edge-differentially private mechanisms for dynamic graphs. The closest related work, are the differentially private algorithms for counting-based problems in [9]. However, their algorithms are based on sensitivity and hence the edge randomization cannot be carried out locally, as in the present work.

1.1 Contributions and Paper Structure

In this work, our contributions are:

- the extension of the definition of local differential privacy for edges to dynamic graphs;
- the privacy mechanisms for providing graphs compliant with edge-local differential privacy for dynamic graphs. This is achieved by applying the noise-graph mechanism;
- an empirical analysis of such privacy mechanisms. We show that the community structure in dynamic graphs can be preserved while still protecting the edges with local differential privacy.

The remainder of the paper is arranged in the following manner. We conclude this section presenting basic definitions related to graph protection (Subsect. 1.2). In Sect. 2 we propose two differentially private algorithms for dynamic graph protection. In Sect. 3 we implement the algorithms and describe how they work on real datasets. Lastly, we draw a conclusion and give a sketch of the future work on the basis of all these discussions. This is in Sect. 4.

1.2   Basic Definitions

For graph randomization, we consider adding noise-graphs as in [16], that is, a simplification from the original definition in [21], assuming that the original graph and the noise graph have the same sets of nodes.

We denote by $G(V, E)$ the graph with the set of nodes V and set of edges E.

Definition 1. *Let $G_1(V, E_1)$ and $G_2(V, E_2)$ be two graphs with the same nodes V; then the addition of G_1 and G_2 is the graph $G = (V, E)$ where:*

$$E = (E_1 \setminus E_2) \cup (E_2 \setminus E_1).$$

We denote G as

$$G = G_1 \oplus G_2.$$

We will add noise using the *Gilbert model*, which is denoted by $\mathcal{G}(n, p)$. That is, there are n nodes and each edge is chosen with probability p. The Gilbert and the Erdös-Rényi random graph models are the most common and general in the literature. It has been proved that they are asymptotically equivalent in [1]. So, to add noise to a graph G, we will draw a random graph G' from the Gilbert model (i.e., $G' \in \mathcal{G}(n, p)$) and add it to G, to obtain $\tilde{G} = G \oplus G'$.

Now, we can define the general noise-graph mechanism [15] that we will use.

Definition 2 (Noise-graph mechanism). *For any graph G with n nodes, and two probabilities p_0 and p_1, we define the following noise-graph mechanism:*

$$\mathcal{A}_{p_0,p_1}(G) = G \oplus G_0 \oplus G_1, \tag{1}$$

where G_0 and G_1 are such that:

$$G_0 = G' \setminus G \text{ for } G' \in \mathcal{G}(n, 1 - p_0)$$
$$G_1 = G'' \cap G \text{ for } G'' \in \mathcal{G}(n, 1 - p_1).$$

Definition 3 (Stochastic matrix associated to the noise graph). *The probabilities of randomization of an edge or a non-edge in a graph G after applying the noise-graph mechanism $\mathcal{A}_{p_0,p_1}$ are represented by the following stochastic matrix:*

$$P = P(\mathcal{A}_{p_0,p_1}) = \begin{pmatrix} p_0 & 1 - p_0 \\ 1 - p_1 & p_1 \end{pmatrix} \tag{2}$$

2   Dynamic Graphs

Considering that the relations in a dynamic network may remain or disappear over time, a basic model that accounts for the ratios of appearence or disappearance of edges in a graph over a period of time was proposed in [22].

Formally, the network is observed at an initial state G_0 at time $t = 0$, and for every snapshot G_t each node pair not connected by an edge at the previous snapshot gains an edge with probability α, or not with probability $1-\alpha$. Similarly each existing edge disappears with probability β or not with probability $1 - \beta$, from one snapshot to the next.

We denote the set of all dynamic graphs with n nodes V and T timestamps as $\mathcal{G} = \{(G_0, G_1 \ldots G_T) : G_t = G_t(V, E_t) \text{ for } t = 0, \ldots T\}$.

Thus, we can formally define a dynamic network graph model G iteratively by considering the initial state G_0 and applying the noise-graph mechanism $\mathcal{A}_{p_0, p_1}$ to G_{i-1} to obtain G_i, where $p_0 = 1 - \alpha$ and $p_1 = 1 - \beta$, for $i = 1, \ldots T$.

Definition 4 (Dynamic-network-graph-model). *The dynamic network graph model consists of an initial state G_0 and states G_t, for $t = 1, \ldots T$, defined by:*

$$G_t = \mathcal{A}_{1-\alpha, 1-\beta}(G_{t-1})$$

We will denote it as: $G(G_0, T, \alpha, \beta)$.

In the other way around, if we have a series of snapshots $G_0, G_1, \ldots, G_T$ of a graph that evolves with time, and we know that it follows the basic model of dynamic graphs, then, we can estimate α and β from these snapshots. The expressions to compute the parameters from the adjacency matrices are given in [22].

2.1 Differential Privacy for Dynamic Graphs

We adapt the definition of local differential privacy from [6] to be applied specifically to edges in a graph. Edge differential privacy is about the presence or absence of any edge, and local differential privacy is related to local randomization of each of the outputs. We combine both definitions for dynamic graphs to consider the edges in any of the graphs (snapshots) of the dynamic graph.

Definition 5 (Local differential privacy). *[6] A randomized algorithm π, satisfies ε-local differential privacy if for all inputs x, x' and all outputs $y \in Range(\pi)$:*

$$P(\pi(x) = y) \leq e^{\varepsilon} P(\pi(x') = y) \tag{3}$$

We denote by $\mathbb{1}_{uv(t)}$ the indicator function of edge uv in G_t, that is $\mathbb{1}_{uv(t)} = 1$ if $uv \in E_t$, and $\mathbb{1}_{uv(t)} = 0$ otherwise. Similarly, $\mathbb{1}_{\mathcal{A}(uv(t))}$ is the indicator function of edge uv in $\mathcal{A}(G_t)$, the randomized graph.

Definition 6 (Edge-local differential privacy for dynamic graphs). *An edge randomization algorithm $\mathcal{A} : \mathcal{G} \to \mathcal{G}$, satisfies ε-edge local differential privacy if for every pair of nodes $u, v \in V$, any timestamp $t \in \{1, \ldots T\}$ and $x, x', y \in \{0, 1\}$:*

$$P(\mathbb{1}_{\mathcal{A}(uv(t))} = y \mid \mathbb{1}_{uv(t)} = x) \leq e^{\varepsilon} P(\mathbb{1}_{\mathcal{A}(uv(t))} = y \mid \mathbb{1}_{uv(t)} = x'), \tag{4}$$

we say that $\mathcal{A}$ is ε-edge locally differentially private (ε-eLDP).

Observe that when we consider local differential privacy at edge level, it implies the same probability of presence or absence of every edge in the protected graph independently of whether the edge was present or not in the original graph.

Thus, Definition 6 can be obtained from Definition 5, considering that the inputs x, x' represent whether any edge uv is present in the snapshot-graph G_t or not, and output y is the presence or absence of the same edge in the randomized graph.

2.2   Protection Mechanisms for Dynamic Graphs

Considering that a dynamic graph can be modelled with the dynamic-network-graph-model from Definition 4, it is natural to use it as a first approach to protect dynamic graphs. Thus, we show that the dynamic random graph model $G(G_0, T, p_0, p_1)$ is edge-differentially private for specific parameters p_0 and p_1.

Additionally, we define the parallel protection mechanism that adds noise to each snapshot of the dynamic graph, and therefore it may have a better utility.

Definition 7 (Dynamic-network-mechanism). *Let $G = (G_0, G_1 \ldots G_T)$ be a dynamic graph. We define the protected dynamic graph $G' = (G'_0, G'_1 \ldots G'_T)$ by letting:*

$$G'_0 = \mathcal{A}_{p_0,p_1}(G_0) \text{ and } G_i = \mathcal{A}^{i+1}_{p_0,p_1}(G_0).$$

That is, the dynamic-network-mechanism is:

$$\mathcal{D}_{p_0,p_1}(G) = G(G'_0, T, 1 - p_0, 1 - p_1),$$

Remark 1 (Randomization probabilities matrix). The probabilities of randomization for the dynamic network mechanism $\mathcal{D}_{p_0,p_1}(G)$ are calculated by the $(t = 1, \ldots, T+1)$ powers of the stochastic matrix P in (2), we denote them as as:

$$P^t = \begin{pmatrix} p_0 & 1 - p_0 \\ 1 - p_1 & p_1 \end{pmatrix}^t = \begin{pmatrix} p_{00}[t] & p_{01}[t] \\ p_{10}[t] & p_{11}[t] \end{pmatrix} \tag{5}$$

Note that $p_{xy}[t]$ corresponds to: $P(\mathbb{1}_{\mathcal{A}(uv(t))} = y \mid \mathbb{1}_{uv(t)} = x)$, with $x, y \in \{0,1\}$.

Theorem 1. *The mechanism $\mathcal{D}_{p_0,p_1}$ is ε-eLDP if*

$$e^\varepsilon \geq \max_{t=1,\ldots T+1} \left\{ \frac{p_{10}[t]}{p_{00}[t]}, \frac{p_{11}[t]}{p_{01}[t]}, \frac{p_{00}[t]}{p_{10}[t]}, \frac{p_{01}[t]}{p_{11}[t]} \right\} \tag{6}$$

See proof on page 13.

Lemma 1. *Assume that the following inequality holds:*

$$e^\varepsilon \geq \max \left\{ \frac{p_{10}}{p_{00}}, \frac{p_{11}}{p_{01}}, \frac{p_{00}}{p_{10}}, \frac{p_{01}}{p_{11}} \right\} \tag{7}$$

Then (6) holds, that is:

$$e^\varepsilon \geq \max_{t=1,\ldots T+1} \left\{ \frac{p_{10}[t]}{p_{00}[t]}, \frac{p_{11}[t]}{p_{01}[t]}, \frac{p_{00}[t]}{p_{10}[t]}, \frac{p_{01}[t]}{p_{11}[t]} \right\}$$

See proof on page 14.

Corollary 1. *The mechanism $\mathcal{D}_{p_0,p_1}$ is ε-eLDP if*

$$e^{\varepsilon} \geq \max\left\{\frac{p_{10}}{p_{00}}, \frac{p_{11}}{p_{01}}, \frac{p_{00}}{p_{10}}, \frac{p_{01}}{p_{11}}\right\} \tag{8}$$

Theorem 1 from [17] provides a complete characterization of the values for the probabilities (p_{00}, p_{11}) for which this equation holds, hence (p_{00}, p_{11}) can be parameterized depending on the ε required for protection.

Let us now consider an alternative protection mechanism. We call it the parallel protection of a dynamic graph. We define it as follows.

Definition 8 (Parallel protection mechanism). *Let $G = G_0, G_1, \ldots, G_T$ be a dynamic graph. Let $\mathcal{A}_{p_0,p_1}$ denote the noise-graph mechanism. Then, we define the parallel protection of the dynamic graph with parameters p_0 and p_1 as the protection process that provides $\tilde{G} = \tilde{G}_0, \tilde{G}_1, \ldots, \tilde{G}_T$ with $\tilde{G}_i = \mathcal{A}_{p_0,p_1}(G_i)$ for $i = 0, \ldots, T$.*

We denote the parallel protection of a dynamic graph G with parameters p_0 and p_1 as $\mathcal{A}^{||}_{p_0,p_1}(G)$.

Equivalently to Corollary 1, the following can be proven.

Proposition 1. *The parallel protection mechanism $\mathcal{A}^{||}_{p_0,p_1}$ satisfies ε-local differential privacy when*

$$e^{\varepsilon} \geq \max\left\{\frac{p_{10}}{p_{00}}, \frac{p_{11}}{p_{01}}, \frac{p_{00}}{p_{10}}, \frac{p_{01}}{p_{11}}\right\}$$

See proof on page 15.

3   Application to Community Detection Algorithms

This section consists of an experimental analysis of previous theoretical claims for an application of the proposed privacy algorithms. We base our utility analysis on *community detection algorithms* through *normalised mutual information*.

3.1   Experiment Description

We used two real-life datasets to evaluate the application of the proposed privacy protection algorithms. They are: CAIDA-AS relationship and DBLP datasets. We provide their basic statistics in Table 1.

One dataset is the *CAIDA-AS relationship dataset* [2] – Autonomous Systems (AS), which roughly corresponds to Internet Service Providers (ISP) and their relationships. We consider the p2p links, that are those that connect two ISPs who have agreed to exchange traffic on a quid pro quo basis. From this data we took the 1-month snapshot graphs for each of the 12 months in 2015.

The computer science bibliography *DBLP* provides its whole dataset of bibliographical entries in XML format, under the terms of the Open Data Commons Attribution License (ODC-BY 1.0). We use the coauthorship graph from [7], which has 1,482,029 unique authors and 10,615,809 timestamped co-authorship edges between authors. We preprocess the DBLP dataset, considering only the authors that published a paper each of the years between 2005 and 2013.

Table 1. Preprocessed datasets statistics

Dataset	No. of nodes	No. of Edges	Avg. Snapshot Density
CAIDA-AS	5,715	403,761	0.0010
DBLP	25,439	450,878	0.00007

The experiments are divided into five parts, that we summarize as follows:

1. We divide the data into snapshots such that the same vertices appear in every snapshot. In the case of DBLP this is the set of authors that have published at least a paper each year of the period from 2005 to 2013.
2. We fix the value of p_0, p_1 as in Table 2. We choose the smaller values of p_1 for smaller ε, otherwise the data will have a huge amount of edges. For larger ε values we may choose larger p_1 which also yields better utility. Note that the same ε can be obtained from several pair of values p_0, p_1, cf. [17].
3. We protect the data with our two proposed protection algorithms: the dynamic-network and the parallel mechanisms. We apply them five times each to obtain the average and confidence intervals of the utility measures.
4. We detect the community structure on each of the snapshot graphs, and compare it to the original community structure without privacy protection, we report the average and 95% confidence intervals on the figures.
5. We measure the density of each snapshot graph and compare them.

Table 2. Values of p_0 and p_1 to obtain the ε in the experiments.

ε	2	4	6	8	10	12	14	16	18	20
p_0	0.986602	0.998187	0.999755	0.999967	0.999955	0.999994	0.999999			
p_1	0.099				0.999					

Utility Measures: We use *Community Detection Algorithms*, to assess the partitioning or clustering of nodes as well as their propensity to stick together or disintegrate. Communities make it possible to map a network at a wide scale because they operate as meta-nodes in the network, that are used to facilitate analysis. The prediction of missing connections and the detection of fake links in the network are the two most significant applications of community detection in network research.

NMI, or *Normalised Mutual Information*, is a metric used to assess how well community discovery methods execute network partitioning. Due to its broad meaning and ability to compare two partitions even when there are different numbers of clusters, it is frequently taken into consideration.

Finally, the *Graph Density* is defined to be the ratio of the number of edges with respect to the maximum possible edges.

3.2   CAIDA Dataset

In this section, we compare the effects of the dynamic-network and the parallel mechanisms for small and large ε values on the NMI and density measures of the CAIDA-AS dataset in Figs. 1 and 2.

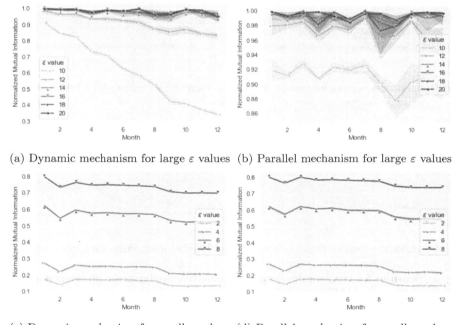

(a) Dynamic mechanism for large ε values   (b) Parallel mechanism for large ε values

(c) Dynamic mechanism for small ε values   (d) Parallel mechanism for small ε values

Fig. 1. Normalized mutual information between the communities detected on the CAIDA-AS data and the data protected with the dynamic and parallel mechanisms for several ε values.

In Fig. 1, we notice that for $\varepsilon = 20$ the NMI of both algorithms is almost 1, which means that the communities discovered over the protected data are almost the same as the original ones. Additionally, the NMI in the dynamic mechanism tends to decrease as the timestamp increases, whereas the parallel does not has this effect. For smaller values of ε, as the protection is stronger, the difference between the NMI values in both mechanisms is small. This may be explained with the larger densities obtained for small ε values in Fig. 2 (a) and (b). In contrast, in Fig. 2 (c) and (d), we note that for large ε values, the densities for each protected snapshot graphs are similar to the original density, and tend to it as the ε value increases.

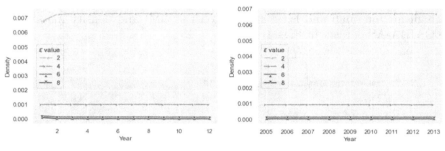

(a) Dynamic mechanism for small ε values (b) Parallel mechanism for small ε values

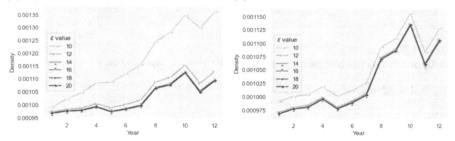

(c) Dynamic mechanism for large ε values (d) Parallel mechanism for large ε values

Fig. 2. Densities for the snapshot-graphs obtained by applying the dynamic and parallel mechanisms to CAIDA-AS.

3.3   DBLP Dataset

We compare the effects of the dynamic-network and the parallel mechanisms for small and large ε values on the NMI and density measures of the DBLP dataset in Figs. 3 and 4. In Fig. 3, it is shown that for larger ε, the communities detected on the protected graph are similar to the original communities, since the NMI is around 0.9. Also, it can be noted that the parallel mechanism has better NMI than the dynamic-network mechanism for large ε values. Additionally, the dynamic-network mechanism's NMI decreases in time, whereas the parallel does not. For smaller ε values the performance of both mechanisms is similar.

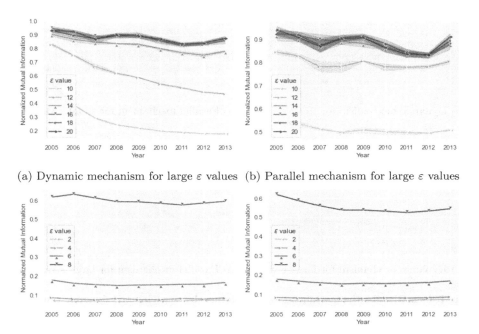

(a) Dynamic mechanism for large ε values (b) Parallel mechanism for large ε values

(c) Dynamic mechanism for small ε values (d) Parallel mechanism for small ε values

Fig. 3. Normalized mutual information between the communities detected on the DBLP data and the data protected with the dynamic and parallel mechanisms for several ε values.

In Fig. 4 (a) and (b), we show the effect of both mechanisms on the densities of the graph for small ε values. We notice that for $\varepsilon = 2$ the density of the protected snapshots is near to 0.007 which means that they have around 4,529,999 of edges, which is 100 times the original average snapshot density of 0.00007. In Fig. 4 (c) and (d), we show the effect of both mechanisms on the densities of the graph for large ε values. An increase in the density means that there have been created more noise-edges than there have been erased real-edges. Again, the parallel mechanism incurs a lower increase in density than the dynamic. Moreover, the increase in density for $\varepsilon = 10$ is more steep for the dynamic than for the rest of ε values.

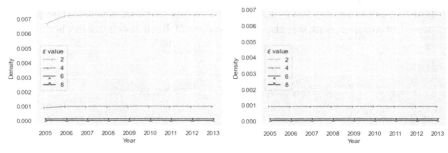

(a) Dynamic mechanism for small ε values (b) Parallel mechanism for small ε values

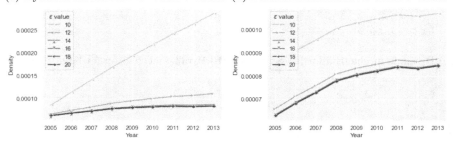

(c) Dynamic mechanism for large ε values (d) Parallel mechanism for large ε values

Fig. 4. Densities for the snapshot-graphs obtained by applying the dynamic and parallel mechanisms to DBLP.

4   Conclusions and Future Scope

We proposed two protection methods for dynamic graphs: the dynamic-network and the parallel protection mechanisms. We extended the definition of local differential privacy for edges in dynamic graphs. We showed that both our proposed methods are ε-edge locally differentially private for specific values of randomization probabilities in the noise-graph mechanism p_0 and p_1. We performed an empirical analysis of such algorithms, to show that they keep the community structure of the dynamic graphs while protecting their edges with local differential privacy.

In this work, we only focus on edge privacy with fixed nodes which extend the ε-edge local differential privacy notion. But, there is still room to look over changing nodes and change of edges and nodes simultaneously. We also would like to extend this notion of privacy in the path of graph neural networks and federated learning. We plan to extend the empirical analysis to other graph utility metrics and other definitions of dynamic graphs.

Acknowledgements. This research was partly supported by the Spanish Ministry of Science and Innovation under project PID2021-125962OB-C31 "SECURING" and the Wallenberg AI, Autonomous Systems and Software Program (WASP) funded by the Knut and Alice Wallenberg Foundation.

A   Proofs

Proof (Proof of Theorem 1). Let $G = G_0, G_1, \ldots G_T$ be a dynamic graph. Recall that $\mathcal{D}_{p_0,p_1}(G) = G(g_0, T, 1 - p_0, 1 - p_1)$, which outputs the initial state $g_0 = \mathcal{A}_{p_0,p_1}(G_0)$, and the further snapshots $g_1, \ldots, g_T$ such that $g_i = \mathcal{A}_{p_0,p_1}^{i+1}(G_0)$.

To prove that mechanism $\mathcal{D}_{p_0,p_1}$ is ε-eLDP we must show that:

$$\frac{P(\mathbb{1}_{\mathcal{A}(uv(t))} = y \mid \mathbb{1}_{uv(t)} = x)}{P(\mathbb{1}_{\mathcal{A}(uv(t))} = y \mid \mathbb{1}_{uv(t)} = x')} \le e^\varepsilon$$

We assume that $x \ne x'$, otherwise the inequality holds.

Now, suppose that $x = 1$ and $x' = 0$, and that (6) holds.

Therefore, we must prove that, for $y = 0, 1$ and $t \ge 1$:

$$\frac{P(\mathbb{1}_{\mathcal{A}(uv(t))} = y \mid \mathbb{1}_{uv(t)} = 1)}{P(\mathbb{1}_{\mathcal{A}(uv(t))} = y \mid \mathbb{1}_{uv(t)} = 0)} \le e^\varepsilon \tag{9}$$

Note that, these probabilities can be calculated using the stochastic matrix P^t in (5), and by Remark 1 they are the following for $y = 0$:

$$P(\mathbb{1}_{\mathcal{A}(uv(t))} = 0 \mid \mathbb{1}_{uv(t)} = 1) = p_{10}[t]$$

$$P(\mathbb{1}_{\mathcal{A}(uv(t))} = 0 \mid \mathbb{1}_{uv(t)} = 0) = p_{00}[t]$$

and the following for $y = 1$:

$$P(\mathbb{1}_{\mathcal{A}(uv(t))} = 1 \mid \mathbb{1}_{uv(t)} = 1) = p_{11}[t]$$

$$P(\mathbb{1}_{\mathcal{A}(uv(t))} = 1 \mid \mathbb{1}_{uv(t)} = 0) = p_{01}[t]$$

Thus, for $y = 0, 1$, the Eq. (9) becomes:

$$\frac{p_{10}[t]}{p_{00}[t]} \le e^\varepsilon \text{ and } \frac{p_{11}[t]}{p_{01}[t]} \le e^\varepsilon$$

The argument is similar when $x = 0$ and $x' = 1$. As all these probabilities are bounded by e^ε by (6), we finish the proof.

Proof (Proof of Lemma 1). Assume that (7) holds. We first show that (6) is true for $t = 2$. Note that:

$$\frac{p_{00}[2]}{p_{10}[2]} = \frac{p_{00}p_{00} + p_{01}p_{10}}{p_{10}p_{00} + p_{11}p_{10}}$$

Divide all by p_{10} and, by (7), to obtain:

$$\frac{(\frac{p_{00}}{p_{10}})p_{00} + p_{01}}{p_{00} + p_{11}} \le \frac{e^\varepsilon p_{00} + p_{01}}{p_{00} + p_{11}}.$$

And,

$$\frac{e^\varepsilon p_{00} + p_{01}}{p_{00} + p_{11}} \le e^\varepsilon \iff \frac{p_{01}}{p_{11}} \le e^\varepsilon.$$

Which is true from (7).

Note that:

$$\frac{p_{10}[2]}{p_{00}[2]} = \frac{p_{10}p_{00} + p_{11}p_{10}}{p_{00}p_{00} + p_{01}p_{10}}$$

Again, divide all by p_{10} and, by (7), obtain:

$$\frac{p_{00} + p_{11}}{(\frac{p_{00}}{p_{10}})p_{00} + p_{01}} \leq \frac{p_{00} + p_{11}}{(\frac{1}{e^\varepsilon})p_{00} + p_{01}}.$$

Moreover,

$$\frac{p_{00} + p_{11}}{(\frac{1}{e^\varepsilon})p_{00} + p_{01}} \leq e^\varepsilon \iff \frac{(\frac{1}{e^\varepsilon})p_{00} + p_{01}}{p_{00} + p_{11}} \geq \frac{1}{e^\varepsilon} \iff \frac{p_{01}}{p_{11}} \geq \frac{1}{e^\varepsilon} \iff \frac{p_{11}}{p_{01}} \leq e^\varepsilon,$$

which is true from (7). The proof is similar for $\frac{p_{11}[2]}{p_{01}[2]}$ and $\frac{p_{01}[2]}{p_{11}[2]}$. Finally, since (6) is true for $t = 2$, considering that it is true for $t = 1$, the proof for all t follows by iteratively letting the corresponding $p_{ij}[2] = p_{ij}$, and all the rest is the same.

Proof (Proof of Proposition 1). We need to consider two cases. In the first case, the edge uv is in $\mathcal{A}^{\|}_{p_0,p_1}(G)$ and also in $\mathcal{A}^{\|}_{p_0,p_1}(G')$. We consider that we have a graph G with an edge uv and the graph G' does not have this edge. Then, the protection mechanism will produce graphs $\tilde{G}_1$ and $\tilde{G}'$. With probability p_1 we have that the edge uv is still in $\tilde{G}_1$ and with probability $1 - p_0$ the edge uv has appeared in $\tilde{G}'$. In order that the condition for differential privacy holds we need

$$p_1/(1 - p_0) \leq e^\varepsilon.$$

Similarly, if the edge uv is in G' but not in G, we will have

$$(1 - p_0)/(p_1) \leq e^\varepsilon.$$

The second case is when we have that the edge uv is neither in $\mathcal{A}^{\|}_{p_0,p_1}(G)$ not in $\mathcal{A}^{\|}_{p_0,p_1}(G')$. Let us consider that the graph G does not have the edge uv but the graph G' has this edge. Then, the protection mechanism will add the edge uv to G with probability $1 - p_0$, and the edge uv will be kept in G' with probability p_1. So, we need that

$$(1 - p_0)/p_1 \leq e^\varepsilon.$$

Similarly, if the edge uv is in G but not in G', then

$$p_0/(1 - p_1) \leq e^\varepsilon.$$

References

1. Aiello, W., Chung, F., Lu, L.: A random graph model for power law graphs. Exp. Math. **10**(1), 53–66 (2001)

2. As rank. https://catalog.caida.org/dataset/as_rank. Accessed 25 Jan 2023
3. Asharov, G., et al.: Privacy-preserving interdomain routing at internet scale. Cryptology ePrint Archive (2017)
4. Backstrom, L., Huttenlocher, D., Kleinberg, J., Lan, X.: Group formation in large social networks: membership, growth, and evolution. In: Proceedings of the 12th ACM SIGKDD International Conference on Knowledge Discovery and Data Mining, pp. 44–54 (2006)
5. Bergami, G., Bertini, F., Montesi, D.: On approximate nesting of multiple social network graphs: a preliminary study. In: Proceedings of the 23rd International Database Applications & Engineering Symposium, pp. 1–5 (2019)
6. Cormode, G., Jha, S., Kulkarni, T., Li, N., Srivastava, D., Wang, T.: Privacy at scale: local differential privacy in practice. In: Proceedings of the 2018 International Conference on Management of Data, SIGMOD 2018, pp. 1655–1658. Association for Computing Machinery, New York (2018)
7. Demaine, E., HajiaGhayi, M.T.: BigDND: big dynamic network data. https://projects.csail.mit.edu/dnd/DBLP/
8. Dwork, C.: Differential privacy: a survey of results. In: Agrawal, M., Du, D., Duan, Z., Li, A. (eds.) TAMC 2008. LNCS, vol. 4978, pp. 1–19. Springer, Heidelberg (2008). https://doi.org/10.1007/978-3-540-79228-4_1
9. Fichtenberger, H., Henzinger, M., Ost, W.: Differentially private algorithms for graphs under continual observation. In: 29th Annual European Symposium on Algorithms (ESA 2021). Schloss Dagstuhl-Leibniz-Zentrum für Informatik (2021)
10. Hay, M., Li, C., Miklau, G., Jensen, D.: Accurate estimation of the degree distribution of private networks. In: 2009 Ninth IEEE International Conference on Data Mining, pp. 169–178. IEEE (2009)
11. Hay, M., Miklau, G., Jensen, D., Towsley, D., Weis, P.: Resisting structural re-identification in anonymized social networks. Proc. VLDB Endow. $1(1)$, 102–114 (2008)
12. Jiang, H., Pei, J., Yu, D., Yu, J., Gong, B., Cheng, X.: Applications of differential privacy in social network analysis: a survey. IEEE Trans. Knowl. Data Eng. $35(1)$, 108–127 (2021)
13. Lakshmanan, L.V., Ng, R.T., Ramesh, G.: To do or not to do: the dilemma of disclosing anonymized data. In: Proceedings of the 2005 ACM SIGMOD International Conference on Management of Data, pp. 61–72 (2005)
14. Pedarsani, P., Grossglauser, M.: On the privacy of anonymized networks. In: Proceedings of the 17th ACM SIGKDD International Conference on Knowledge Discovery and Data Mining, pp. 1235–1243 (2011)
15. Salas, J., González-Zelaya, V., Torra, V., Megías, D.: Differentially private graph publishing through noise-graph addition. In: Modeling Decisions for Artificial Intelligence: 20th International Conference, MDAI 2023, Umeå, Sweden, 19–22 June 2023, Proceedings, pp. 253–264 (2023)
16. Salas, J., Torra, V.: Differentially private graph publishing and randomized response for collaborative filtering. In: Proceedings of the 17th International Joint Conference on e-Business and Telecommunications, ICETE 2020 - Volume 2: SECRYPT, Lieusaint, Paris, France, 8–10 July 2020, pp. 415–422. ScitePress (2020)
17. Salas, J., Torra, V., Megías, D.: Towards measuring fairness for local differential privacy. In: Garcia-Alfaro, J., Navarro-Arribas, G., Dragoni, N. (eds.) DPM CBT 2022. LNCS, vol. 13619, pp. 19–34. Springer, Cham (2023). https://doi.org/10.1007/978-3-031-25734-6_2

18. Takbiri, N., Shao, X., Gao, L., Pishro-Nik, H.: Improving privacy in graphs through node addition. In: 2019 57th Annual Allerton Conference on Communication, Control, and Computing (Allerton), pp. 487–494. IEEE (2019)
19. Task, C., Clifton, C.: A guide to differential privacy theory in social network analysis. In: 2012 IEEE/ACM International Conference on Advances in Social Networks Analysis and Mining, pp. 411–417. IEEE (2012)
20. Task, C., Clifton, C.: What should we protect? Defining differential privacy for social network analysis. In: Can, F., Özyer, T., Polat, F. (eds.) State of the Art Applications of Social Network Analysis. LNSN, pp. 139–161. Springer, Cham (2014). https://doi.org/10.1007/978-3-319-05912-9_7
21. Torra, V., Salas, J.: Graph perturbation as noise graph addition: a new perspective for graph anonymization. In: Pérez-Solà, C., Navarro-Arribas, G., Biryukov, A., Garcia-Alfaro, J. (eds.) DPM/CBT -2019. LNCS, vol. 11737, pp. 121–137. Springer, Cham (2019). https://doi.org/10.1007/978-3-030-31500-9_8
22. Zhang, X., Moore, C., Newman, M.E.: Random graph models for dynamic networks. Eur. Phys. J. B **90**(10), 1–14 (2017)
23. Zhou, B., Pei, J.: Preserving privacy in social networks against neighborhood attacks. In: 2008 IEEE 24th International Conference on Data Engineering, pp. 506–515. IEEE (2008)

Temporal Analysis of Privacy Enhancing Technology Traffic Using Deep Learning

Monika Kumari[1], Mohona Ghosh[2] (ID), and Niyati Baliyan[3(✉)] (ID)

[1] Goldman Sachs, Bengaluru, India
monika.kumari@gs.com
[2] Indira Gandhi Delhi Technical University for Women, Delhi, India
mohonaghosh@igdtuw.ac.in
[3] National Institute of Technology, Kurukshetra, India
niyatibaliyan@nitkkr.ac.in

Abstract. Tor is an open-source communications software program that enables anonymity on the Internet. Tor's ability to hide its users' identity means it is incredibly popular with criminals, who use it to keep their online activities secret from law enforcement authorities. Tor uses layers of encryption to hide its users' data on the Web. However, most encryption techniques implemented till date do not provide full anonymity. We can use classification algorithms based on machine learning and deep learning to extract information about the users from network traffic. In this paper, we show that by performing a temporal analysis of Tor network traffic flowing between the user node and guard node, one can classify the Tor network traffic into various application types such as browsing, chat, email, P2P, FTP, audio, video, VoIP, and file-transfer. We apply many standard and popular machine learning and deep learning algorithms to categorize traffic by application and achieved an accuracy of 95.75% for Random Forest which outperforms the best work done till date on the ISCXTor2016 dataset.

Keywords: Deep Learning · Traffic-classification · Tor · Machine Learning · PET

1 Introduction

The continuously increasing usage of the Internet has led to the development of sophisticated attacks. Attackers are coming up with innovative ideas to exploit the vulnerabilities in technologies which are developed to ease the user's life. Identity disclosure, linkage of network traffic with user identity, location disclosure, and data disclosure during data transfer are examples of privacy threats. Privacy Enhancing Technology (PET) is a collective term for technologies that aim to increase the levels of privacy. PET creates an encrypted tunnel to hide the information related to URL visits; from external/passive adversaries or attack vectors as shown in Fig. 1. These adversaries can capture the outgoing traffic from the client's workstation and execute a traffic fingerprinting attack [1].

© The Author(s), under exclusive license to Springer Nature Singapore Pte Ltd. 2023
B. Arief et al. (Eds.): SocialSec 2023, LNCS 14097, pp. 239–251, 2023.
https://doi.org/10.1007/978-981-99-5177-2_14

Traffic classification into different applications holds significant importance for a variety of reasons. Firstly, it provides network administrators with valuable insights into application usage, enabling them to efficiently manage the network by optimizing resources and prioritizing traffic based on application types. Secondly, it plays a vital role in enhancing security measures as it allows for the identification and prevention of unauthorized or malicious activities. Thirdly, traffic classification aids in optimizing network performance by tailoring resource allocation and implementing traffic-shaping techniques to meet the specific requirements of different applications. Furthermore, it assists in capacity planning by facilitating efficient resource allocation and preventing congestion. In summary, traffic classification is essential for effective network management, security enforcement, performance optimization, capacity planning, and compliance adherence.

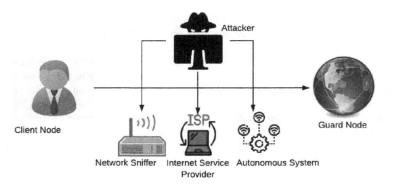

Fig. 1. Types of attack vectors sniffing traffic between the client node and guard node in Tor

Our research experiment focuses on the passive traffic classification attack as shown in Fig. 2 on Tor, one of the most popular PET. To launch this attack, the attacker captures the traffic coming from the user node to the guard node. This traffic dump captured will then be sent to the trained machine learning model to identify the application name. To train the machine learning model, an attacker already has a huge size of the database that maps the traffic pcap to the application name.

Tor [2] is one of the most interesting and controversial web developments of the 21st century. It is a piece of software that comes bundled with a stand-alone browser that can help users remain anonymous when online. The attack scenario assumed by us for our research study is discussed in Sect. 2. The classification of Tor network traffic can downgrade the users' privacy by revealing their activity within Tor. In our paper, we show that by analysing only the time statistics of Tor network traffic flows between the client node and the guard node, one can classify traffic into different applications- browsing, chat, audio-streaming, video-streaming, file-transfer, email, VoIP and P2P. We also evaluate the effectiveness of multilayer perceptron autoencoder models for traffic classification.

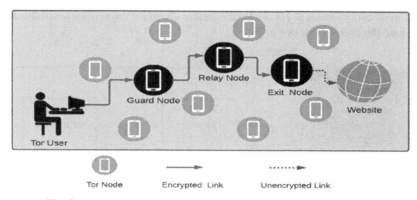

Fig. 2. Tor user connecting to a website through three proxy servers

Improving the accuracy of traffic classification into different application types can be considered innovative work for several reasons. Firstly, it involves the development of new techniques, algorithms, or models to enhance classification accuracy. This requires exploring novel approaches to extract meaningful features from network traffic data, improving classification algorithms, and utilizing advanced machine learning or deep learning methods. Secondly, novel work in this area focuses on addressing the challenges posed by emerging technologies. This includes adapting existing classification techniques or developing new ones specifically tailored to the unique characteristics of these technologies. Examples include classifying traffic from streaming platforms, virtual reality applications, IoT devices, or encrypted traffic. Encryption poses another challenge, and innovative approaches are required to accurately classify encrypted traffic by analyzing characteristics like packet size, timing, or statistical features. Finally, considering multiple data sources, such as flow-level information, payload content, or contextual data, can improve classification accuracy. Novel work involves integrating these data modalities and developing hybrid models or fusion techniques to leverage their complementary information.

Overall, advancing the accuracy of traffic classification into different application types requires innovative approaches to tackle new challenges, emerging technologies, evolving traffic patterns, encrypted traffic, and multi-modal data. In further sections, we will show how our proposed model outperformed the models in prior research work by 0.15% in terms of accuracy using the same dataset.

2   Background

Tor does not provide enough protection against traffic classification attacks [3]. Adversary aims to identify the source and destination of communication over Tor. At present, the design of Tor ignores the fact that adversaries can monitor both entry and exit guards in the Tor communication network. Based on this, attackers can enable the traffic classification attack. The focus of this type of attack is to develop an efficient algorithm to accurately identify the users' activities within Tor. Our research focuses on the passive traffic classification attack in Tor. The configuration used for the generation of the dataset to facilitate the attack is shown in Fig. 3.

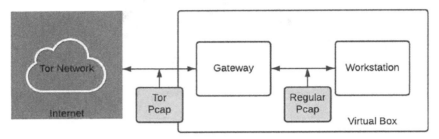

Fig. 3. Traffic fingerprinting attack on Tor

Whonix operating system is configured to route the traffic through Tor. Whonix is composed of two VMsgateway and a workstation. Adversary (Network Sniffer, ISP, Autonomous System) captures the outflowing traffic at the workstation and the gateway at the same time. The collection consists of a set of pairs of regular and Tor traffic pcap files. The regular pcap file is the one collected at the workstation and Tor traffic pcap file is the one collected at the gateway. Once the pcap files are collected, it is labelled simultaneously as traffic generated by application X. Then, using ISCXFlowMeter [4], pcap files are converted into csv files of selected features. Since the attackers are operating the attack in a controlled environment where they are executing the application one at a time, they know which Tor flows belong to which application [5].

2.1 Related Work

Most of the research on Tor focuses on either compromising the anonymity of Tor or improving its performance. For our research study, we went with the former. We studied the previous work focused on traffic classification attacks on Tor network traffic, and identified a few gaps which are as follows:

- Except for Research Work [6], none of the previous researches balanced the dataset before training the model for traffic classification. The problem with an imbalanced dataset is that most machine learning algorithms ignore the minority class or give poor performance for the minority class although typically it is the performance of the minority class that is most important.
- Most of the research directly applied ML classifiers without selecting the features using feature selection algorithms. Feature selection is the process of reducing the number of features or selecting the relevant features from the total available in the dataset to build an efficient machine-learning model.
- Choice of metrics is important to depict the result of the attack. The wrong choice of metric can understate the effectiveness of the attack. For asymmetric class distribution like our dataset, accuracy is not as useful a parameter as it is for symmetric class distribution, here, F1-score is a more useful metric than accuracy. F1- score

is a weighted average of Precision and Recall and therefore, it considers both false positives and false negatives.

- Lastly there was no mention of hyperparameter optimization in most of the research papers. Hyperparameter optimization has a significant impact on the performance of the trained model.

Hence, in our research work, we have addressed these gaps and improved the model's performance. Since our research work is specifically focused on Tor traffic classification into different application types, i.e., passive traffic classification attacks, we have tabulated the characteristics of research closest to our study in Table 1, which depicts the limitations of each research work.

Table 1. Related work

Citation	Feature Selection	Class Balancing	Hyperparameter Tuning	Accuracy	F-1 Score
[1]	✓	X	X	X	X
[19]	X	X	X	X	X
[20]	✓	X	✓	✓	✓
Our Work	✓	✓	✓	✓	✓

The maximum accuracy and macro-averaged F1-Score achieved for a similar problem to date is 95.60% and 95%, respectively using the same dataset ISCXTor2016 [1]. Hence, our goal is to improve these metrics' value with a better classification model.

2.2 Contributions

Our work focuses on the classification of Tor network traffic into different application types using time-related features only. This classification can reveal the users' activities thereby downgrading their security. We also compare the efficiency of various machine learning and deep learning algorithms in detecting the application's type in the ISCX-Tor2016 [1] dataset. The results are presented in the form of accuracy, precision, recall and macro-averaged F1-score of the proposed model. We conducted six experiments with a cross-combination of feature selection algorithms and classification algorithms. Our SMOTE-based experiment performed better than all the other experiments. We also checked the efficiency of the autoencoders in feature extraction for traffic type classification.

2.3 Paper Organization

The structure of the rest of the paper is as follows. Section 3 discusses the dataset, and methodology adopted to solve the Tor traffic classification problem accurately. In Sect. 4, we analyse the result from different experiments and compare them with that of related works. Finally, Sect. 5 provides the conclusion and future scope of work.

3 Methodology

This section outlines the methodology adopted for the classification of traffic. We address the dataset collection, methods of feature selection, algorithms of classification, and metrics for measurement. The experimental model is shown in Fig. 4.

We first divide the dataset into training and test sets into 70:30 ratios. Then the training data is pre-processed as discussed in Sect. 3.2. Then, we apply different feature selection algorithms and note down the important features obtained as discussed in Sect. 3.3. We also tried class balancing before feeding the dataset for training as discussed in Sect. 3.4. Then using the selected features, we apply ML-based classification algorithms and train the model. We then test the performance of trained model on test data and note the accuracy, precision, recall and macro-averaged F1-score obtained.

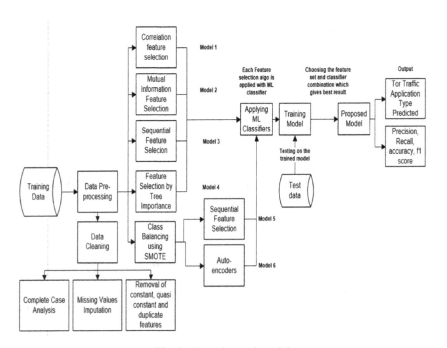

Fig. 4. Experimental model

3.1 Dataset Description

We constructed our machine-learning models for use on the ISCXTor2016 dataset [1], generated using the attack model discussed in Sect. 2. It consists of Tor network traffic captured using Wireshark [7] and Tcpdump [8]. The total size of the raw dataset is 22GB in pcap format. Using ISCXFlowMeter [4], we get csv files with 23 features.

Features extracted from Tor traffic flow

- Forward Inter Arrival Time(fiat): Time between two packets sent forward.
- Backward Inter Arrival Time(biat): Time between two packets sent backward.
- Flow Inter Arrival Time(flowiat): Time between two packets sent in either direction.
- Active Time(active): It is the amount of time a flow was active before idle.
- Idle Time(idle): It is the amount of time a flow was idle before becoming active.
- Flow Bytes per second(flowBytesPerSecond): Number of bytes flown per second.
- Flow packets per second(flowPacketsPerSecond): No. of packets flown per second.
- Duration of flow(duration): It is the total time duration of the flow.

We take the minimum, maximum, standard deviation, and mean values of fiat, biat, flowiat, active and idle as the features.

Traffic Categories

- Browsing: Firefox and Chrome
- Email: POP3, SMTP and IMAP
- Chat: Facebook, Hangout, Skype, IAM and ICQ
- Audio-Streaming: Spotify
- Video-Streaming: YouTube, Vimeo
- File Transfer: File transfer over Skype, SSH and SSL
- VoIP: Voice-calls using Facebook, Hangouts, and Skype.
- P2P: BitTorrent, uTorrent

3.2 Feature Engineering

In our work, we utilized the complete case analysis (CCA) [9] for missing data imputation. CCA discards the observations where any of the features are missing. Hence, we only analyse observations where all features are present. CCA is simple to use, does not require the manipulation of data and preserves the distribution of features. We also removed any constant or quasi-constant features [10].

3.3 Feature Selection

It is the process of reducing the number of features or selecting the relevant features from the total available in the dataset to build an efficient machine-learning model [11]. Various types of feature selection methods are:

Filter Methods. They select features based on their correlation with the target variable. They do not involve ML algorithms at the time of screening the features. That means, these methods are model agnostic. We used the Mutual Information (MI) Method and Correlation Feature Selection (CFS) Method of Feature Selection.

Mutual Information. It is the measure of the mutual dependence of two random features. It quantifies the amount of information that we gain about one variable by observing the values of the other variable [12]. We plot the Mutual Information plot that ranks the features in descending order as shown in Table 2. Using this plot, we select the top 10 features out of all features. These features are: min_biat, max_fiat, max_biat, mean_fiat, mean_biat, flowPktsPerSecond, flowBytesPerSecond, max_flowiat, mean_flowiat, std_flowiat.

Correlation Feature Selection. Correlation is the measure of the association of two or more features. Highly correlated features are those which show more than 0.7 correlation coefficient values. We took the threshold value of 0.8 for eliminating correlated features. Using CFS, we get seven features: total_biat, flowBytesPerSecond, min_biat, min_ flowiat, std_active, max_idle, std_idle.

Table 2. MI values of features

Feature	MI Value
Duration	0.315
total_fiat	0.330
total_biat	0.325
min_fiat	0.527
min_biat	0.610
max_fiat	0.652
max_biat	0.629
mean_fiat	0.733
mean_biat	0.744
flowPktsPerSecond	0.747
flowBytesPerSecond	0.800
min_flowiat	0.466
max_flowiat	0.632
mean_flowiat	0.753
std_flowiat	0.602
min_active	0.307
mean_active	0.292
max_active	0.282
std_active	0.133
min_idle	0.270
mean_idle	0.283
max_idle	0.278
std_idle	0.142

Wrapper Method. They build an ML algorithm for each evaluated feature subset. Then, they select the subset of features that give the highest performance. Step Forward Feature Selection (SFS) is the most popular wrapper method for feature selection

[13]. We used SFS with Random Forest (RF), XGBoost, AdaBoost, Decision Tree, K-nearest neighbor, Logistic Regression and SVM. However, RF achieved the highest accuracy. Features selected for RF using SFS: min_fiat, min_biat, mean_fiat, mean_biat, flowBytesPerSecond, min_flowiat, std_flowiat, std_active, max_idle, std_idle.

Embedded Method. They complete the feature selection process along with the ML model construction process as its part. They are also far less computationally expensive than wrapper methods [5]. Features selected using this method: min_fiat, min_biat, max_fiat, max_biat, mean_fiat, mean_biat, flowPktsPerSecond, flowBytesPerSecond, max_flowiat, mean_ flowiat, std_flowiat.

Autoencoders for Feature Selection. Autoencoder [14] is a neural network that can learn from a compressed form of raw data. First, the encoder compresses the input data with 23 features into data with 12 features and then the decoder tries to recreate the original input from the compressed representation of data as in Fig. 5.

After training, the encoder is saved and the decoder is discarded. Then, we apply the machine learning algorithms to the encoder model to perform the classification. We define the encoder model with three hidden layers, the first with all 23 features, the second with more than the double number of features, i.e., 56 and the third with 12 features. Decoder is defined similarly as an encoder just reversed. The output layer will have the same number of nodes as the number of original features. The flow of data through the model can be seen through layers of our multilayer perceptron autoencoder model as shown in Fig. 5. We use batch normalization [15] and the leakyReLu activation function [16] to make sure the model learns well. We also tuned the hyperparameters of the autoencoder using grid search [17].

3.4 SMOTE for Imbalanced Classification

Since our dataset has a severe imbalance as shown in Fig. 6, we used SMOTE [18] for class balancing. The problem with an imbalanced dataset is that most machine learning algorithms ignore the minority class or give poor performance for the minority class although typically it is the performance of the minority class that is most important. In SMOTE, we oversample the minority class. It involves duplication of examples in minority classes, although it does not add any information to the model. Here, new data is created from the available dataset. SMOTE improved the performance of our machine-learning models significantly.

3.5 Applying Machine Learning Classifiers

We applied various ML algorithms like K-Nearest Neighbour (KNN), Logistic Regression, Decision Tree, RF, XGBoost, AdaBoost and SVM. However, RF performed better than the rest of the algorithms. Hence, we further worked with RF and tried increasing its accuracy by hyperparameter tuning via grid search [17].

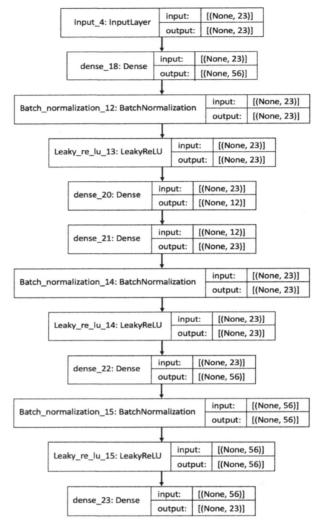

Fig. 5. Autoencoder model

4 Experimental Results

In this section, we discuss the results obtained from our experiments and show the effectiveness of our proposed model. All experiments were performed with Windows 10 operating system, Intel core i7 processor with 16 GB RAM. Based on the traffic dataset collected, we evaluate the performance of the classification model to label traffic into a specific category (i.e., browsing, email, chat, audio, video, file transfer, P2P, VoIP).

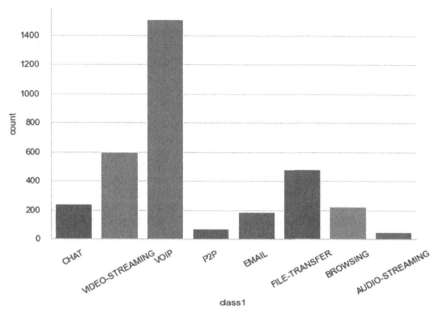

Fig. 6. Application-Traffic frequency in the dataset

The goal is to identify the type of traffic flow existing within an encrypted Tor session. The comparative analysis of our best-performing model (SMOTE + SFS) with the performances of models in prior research using the same dataset is in Table 3.

Table 3. Comparative Evaluation

Works→ Metrics↓	[19]	[20]	[1]	Our best model
Precision	0.87	unavailable	0.84	0.96
Recall	unavailable	unavailable	0.85	0.95
F1-score	unavailable	0.95	unavailable	0.95
Accuracy	unavailable	0.956	unavailable	0.9575

5   Conclusion and Future Work

In this paper we analysed that by using time characteristics alone we can classify Tor traffic into different applications like Chat, VoIP, File-Transfer, Video Streaming, Audio-Streaming, Email, Browsing and P2P. We saw that class balancing by SMOTE signifi-cantly improved the accuracy by 7.46% outperforming the models in prior research work by 0.15% in terms of accuracy using the same dataset [1]. Additionally, we applied multi-layer perceptron autoencoders for traffic classification and inferred that they are not very effective in classifying Tor traffic accurately. In future work, we may apply variants of autoencoders and deep learning methods to further improve accuracy.

References

1. Lashkari, A.H., Draper-Gil, G., Mamun, M.S.I., Ghorbani, A.A.: Characterization of tor traffic using time-based features. In: ICISSP, pp. 253–262 (2004)
2. Dingledine, R., Mathewson, N., Syverson, P.: Tor: the second-generation onion router. Technical report, Naval Research Lab Washington DC (2002)
3. Back, A., Möller, U., Stiglic, A.: Traffic analysis attacks and trade-offs in anonymity providing systems. In: International Workshop on Information Hiding, pp. 245–257 (2002)
4. Draper-Gil, G., Lashkari, A.H., Mamun, M.S.I., Ghorbani, A.A.: Characterization of encrypted and VPN traffic using time-related. In: Proceedings of the 2nd International Conference on Information Systems Security and Privacy (ICISSP), pp. 407–414 (2016)
5. Lal, T.N., Chapelle, O., Weston, J., Elisseeff, A.: Embedded methods. In: Guyon, I., Nikravesh, M., Gunn, S., Zadeh, L.A. (eds.) Feature Extraction, pp. 137–165. Springer, Heidelberg (2006). https://doi.org/10.1007/978-3-540-35488-8_6
6. Gurunarayanan, A., Agrawal, A., Bhatia, A., Vishwakarma, D.K.: Improving the performance of machine learning algorithms for tor detection. In: 2021 International Conference on Information Networking (ICOIN), pp. 439–444 (2021)
7. Lamping, U., Warnicke, E.: Wireshark user's guide. Interface 4(6), 1 (2004)
8. Klevinsky, T.J., Laliberte, S., Gupta, A.: Hack IT: Security Through Penetration Testing. Addison Wesley Professional, Boston (2002)
9. Fischetti T.: Data Analysis with R. Packt Publishing Ltd. (2015)
10. Duch, W.: Filter methods. In: Guyon, I., Nikravesh, M., Gunn, S., Zadeh, L.A. (eds.) Feature Extraction, pp. 89–117. Springer, Heidelberg (2006). https://doi.org/10.1007/978-3-540-354 88-8_4
11. Guyon, I., Elisseeff, A.: An introduction to variable and feature selection. J. Mach. Learn. Res. 3(Mar), 1157–1182 (2003)
12. Yang, J.B., Ong, C.J.: An effective feature selection method via mutual information estimation. IEEE Trans. Syst. Man Cybern. Part B (Cybern.) 42(6), 1550–1559 (2012)
13. Maldonado, S., Weber, R.: A wrapper method for feature selection using support vector machines. Inf. Sci. 179(13), 2208–2217 (2009)
14. Goodfelow, I., Bengio, Y., Courville, A.: Deep Learning. MIT Press, Cambridge (2016)
15. Bjorck, J., Gomes, C., Selman, B., Weinberger, K.Q.: Understanding batch normalization. arXiv preprint arXiv:180602375 (2018)
16. Dubey, A.K., Jain, V.: Comparative study of convolution neural network's relu and leaky-relu activation functions. In: Mishra, S., Sood, Y.R., Tomar, A. (eds.) Applications of Computing, Automation and Wireless Systems in Electrical Engineering. LNEE, vol. 553, pp. 873–880. Springer, Singapore (2019). https://doi.org/10.1007/978-981-13-6772-4_76
17. How to grid search hyperparameters for deep learning models in python with Keras. https://machinelearningmastery.com/grid-search-hyperparameters-deep-learning-models-python-keras. Accessed 10 Oct 2022
18. Chawla, N.V., Bowyer, K.W., Hall, L.O., Kegelmeyer, W.P.: Smote: synthetic minority oversampling technique. J. Artif. Intell. Res. 1, 321–357 (2002)
19. Xu, J., Wang, J., Qi, Q., Sun, H., He, B.: Deep neural networks for application awareness in sdnbased network. In: 28th International Workshop on Machine Learning for Signal Processing (MLSP), pp. 1–6. IEEE (2018)

20. Sarkar, D., Vinod, P., Yerima, S.Y.: Detection of tor traffic using deep learning. In: IEEE/ACS 17th International Conference on Computer Systems and Applications (AICCSA), pp. 1–8. IEEE (2020)

Author Index

A

Arief, Budi   149

B

Baliyan, Niyati   239
Bianchi, Giuseppe   109
Borrion, Hervé   149
Brant, Christopher   3
Buchegger, Sonja   93

C

Ceschin, Fabrício   3
Chen, Shi   187
Connolly, Lena   149
Conti, Mauro   38
Cosuti, Luca   38

D

De Faveri, Francesco Luigi   38

F

Feng, Hao   187
Fernandes, Juliana   3

G

Ghosh, Mohona   239
Gilda, Shlok   3
Giovanini, Luiz   3
Grégio, André   3

I

Iordanou, Costas   58
Ishimaru, Takayuki   23

J

Jensen, Michael J.   58

K

Kaddoura, Sanaa   149
Khan, Md Sakib Nizam   93
Kourtellis, Nicolas   167
Kumari, Monika   239
Kwatra, Saloni   79

L

Li, Shujun   129
Liang, Ting   187
Liao, Rongtao   187

M

Mahaini, Mohamad Imad   129
Mimura, Mamoru   23

O

Oliveira, Daniela   3

P

Paphitis, Aristodemos   167
Paul, Sudipta   224
Peiretti, Federico   203
Pensa, Ruggero G.   203

R

Roscoe, Sophia   149

S

Salamanos, Nikos   58
Salas, Julián   224
Shrestha, Prakash   3
Silva, Catia S.   3
Silva, Mirela   3
Sirivianos, Michael   58, 167

B. Arief et al. (Eds.): SocialSec 2023, LNCS 14097, pp. 253–254, 2023.
https://doi.org/10.1007/978-981-99-5177-2

T
Torra, Vicenç   79, 224
Tricomi, Pier Paolo   38

V
Valeriani, Lorenzo   109

W
Wang, Jingjing   187
Wang, Yichao   149

Y
Yu, Zheng   187

Printed in the United States
by Baker & Taylor Publisher Services